Praise for *Devil Dancer*

"Kentucky thrives on vice," says a character in *Devil Dancer*, and in this dark neo-noir it's true of both sides of Lexington. How do you beat a crooked house? William Heath pits his Chandleresque shamus against the America of Manson and Vietnam, and the only winner is the reader.

—Stewart O'Nan, author of *Songs for the Missing*

A novel of intrigue, decadence, and complex human relations, William Heath's *Devil Dancer* stands with the best of those that find their way through place and its implications. What Raymond Chandler does for California, Heath does for Kentucky. One can live in this novel, but the living is not easy.

—Toby Olson, author of *Seaview*

With prose that is both muscular and lyrical, William Heath takes us on a journey through the swanky horse farms and seedy back streets of Lexington, Kentucky, in the early 70s in pursuit of the killer of a majestic thoroughbred. Mingling wry humor and tough guy dialogue that Elmore Leonard would be proud of, *Devil Dancer* is brimming over with haunting characters who are never exactly who they first appear. This is a first-rate novel of suspense that also accomplishes all the things we expect from our best works of literature.

—James W. Hall, author of *The Hit List* and *Mean High Tide*

Devil Dancer is an edgy un-put-downable novel. Heath is both original and elegant; he is, in fact, an engagingly entertaining writer. *Devil Dancer* reminds us all that love and life can be fragile and dangerous, and this comes vibrantly alive because of the author's sleek and graceful style. This is eloquent writing and compelling story telling by someone who knows his craft.

—Bob Leuci, author of *All the Centurians*, a memoir of his life as the real "Prince of the City."

Praise for William Heath's previous books

The Walking Man: William Heath is one of the most brilliantly accomplished and gifted young poets and critics to appear in the United States in quite some time. I am especially moved by the delicacy and precision of the language, which indicates a distinguished intelligence, and by the purity and depth of feeling in all of his poems.

—James Wright

William Heath is a gifted and mature writer and his work merits a wide public audience.

—Philip Levine

The Walking Man is the work of a poet who knows how to tell a story.

—Richard Wilbur

The Children Bob Moses Led: The blend of fact and fiction is so brilliantly written, the reader is completely absorbed into the unfolding drama. In a masterfully told manner, William Heath brings alive a disturbing piece of our history.

—*Small Press*

Engaging and suspenseful, this is contemporary fiction at its best.

—*Dayton Daily News*

A fascinating story that needed to be told. The book is a fine achievement that vividly brings to life the issues and personalities of the time.

—Robert Stone

An important and timely book. I am grateful that *The Children Bob Moses Led* provided me with this re-introduction to an important part of my history.

—James A. McPherson

Blacksnake's Path: The True Adventures of William Wells: Heath ably combines the craft of the novelist with the deep research of the historian to make *Blacksnake's Path* as informative as it is enjoyable.

—Andrew Cayton

Blacksnake's Path is one of the best books, perhaps *the* best book that describes the earliest, wild and bloody days of the American Midwest.

—Jerry Crimmins

Any good piece of historical fiction introduces us into the strangeness and particularity of earlier worlds and this is what William Heath does in *Blacksnake's Path*. Heath recreates those worlds and what was at stake when they clashed.

—Richard White

Blacksnake's Path tells the remarkable story of William Wells, an Indian captive turned Indian fighter-scout-spy-translator-agent, in a way that alters our sense of American Indian history.

—Frank Bergon

DEVIL DANCER

To my best friend and tennis partner
for fifty years

Marshall Dunn

We make trifles of terrors,
Ensconcing ourselves into seeming knowledge,
When we should submit to an unknown fear.

— Shakespeare

DEVIL DANCER

William Heath

SOMONDOCO
PRESS

P.O. Box 3602 | Shepherdstown, WV 25443

Excerpts from this novel were previously published in
Hudson River Anthology and *Inertia Magazine*

For information address Somondoco Press,
P.O. Box 1014, Shepherdstown, WV 25443.
www.somondocopress.com

Printed in the Unites States of America.

ISBN 978-0-9853898-4-0

Cover design and author photo by Josep Caminals.
Cover image, "Unbridled Folly" (detail) by Francisco de Goya,
by permission of Carnegie Musuem of Art, Pittsburgh, Pennsylvania

PART ONE

1

After his wife left, Wendell had trouble sleeping. Night after night he lay awake, a sharp tingling ache running up and down his arms, and waited for the heart attack. He would take the cautious shallow breaths of a man with broken ribs and try to relax, but his jaw clenched, his chest constricted, and his legs twitched. Sleeping pills didn't help, although some mornings he caught a short nap before noon. He began drinking a bottle of wine every evening in exchange for a dazed immobility that passed for sleep. Before dawn his full bladder would wake him up to the test pattern on the television, and he would stagger from the couch and go stare at the bleary-eyed stranger in the bathroom mirror.

The apartment came down about him, dishes filled the sink and dust gathered in corners, whispering behind his back. The internal difference between presence and absence seemed to unbalance the air because only one person was breathing it; when he looked across the table at her empty chair, the food went dry in his mouth; even the silence was the wrong kind of silence because only one person was hearing it. He could feel desolation settling into his body, making itself at home in his bones and in his blood, so that whatever the old friends or new faces, there would still be the same familiar pain.

He lay in bed and thought of Laura. He had grown to love that everyday intimacy, eating the food she cooked and talking about the little things. He could picture the way she turned her head at an attentive angle as she sat at her dresser and rhythmically brushed her glorious hair. His heart tightened as he remembered how once years ago they had wrapped up in a quilt on the throw rug in front of the fireplace and reached for each other. Laura's life was in her lips, and in time he believed that he tasted less in her kisses. When he began to watch her for signs she asked, "Why are you always looking at me like that?" and he retorted, "Like what?"

She frowned when he said that and left the room. Later she told him, "Wendell, you can't keep love. You can only give it, receive it, or kill it." "Is that what you're doing," he had demanded, "giving it away?"

They had a terrible fight that night and afterwards everything began to drift downstream. She stayed out late, he drank heavily, they made love less and less. The last time she kept a T-shirt on. When he came home from work the next day, all her clothes were gone and there was a note on the bathroom mirror:

> *Dear Wendell*
> *I wish I could love you more than I can. Try to remember*
> *the good times.*
>
> *Laura*

He searched everywhere for her. Finally a friend told him that she had moved in with the manager of the branch bank where she once worked as a teller. A god-damned paper pusher in a three-piece suit, an Italian, a languid-eyed ladies' man who wore pointy-toed shoes, lived in one of the new pseudo-Tudor condominiums next to the golf course, and kept a power boat on the Kentucky River. Wendell had stood in the dark and looked up at the man's windows. He bought a gun and thought of honor. At last he went to see Laura to ask her to come back. She had a new hairdo, a polite smile, and a reluctance to look him in the eye. He had rehearsed making his case so often that he made it badly, mixing down-to-earth offers to cook, clean, and talk more with ambitious plans to change his life and occupation. She said what he knew she would say: it was too late, she didn't care about those things any more, she was happy now. "You still don't understand me, Wendell," she said. "You never will."

He dreaded having to begin all over again, of going from bar to bar in an unlikely quest for love, feeling as awkward as an acne-faced kid on his first date and fearing that women would see the urgency in his eyes and instinctively pull away. He felt more forlorn in crowds than at home, so he began to concentrate on getting through first this day, then that one, telling himself that if he could go on living he would start forgetting, and that if he went on hurting one day the pain would stop. He rejected the idea of suicide because he assumed that there was a valid reason to live. In time, it would occur to him what it was.

Two months after Laura left he decided on a whim to quit his job as a house painter and become a detective. He had few qualifications for the work other than his Marine training and an inborn sense of curiosity and fair play. Even though he had botched up his own life, he thought he might be able to help straighten out the lives of others. Because he was a local boy and knew the right people, it wasn't hard to get licensed. He listed his name in the Yellow Pages, ran a few ads in the paper, and started operating out of his own place at Idle Hour Apartments. His fee was the cheapest in town—one hundred dollars a day and expenses.

What that usually got him was the lowest job around: jealous husband, "Follow that bitch!" jealous wife, "Follow that bastard!" Assignments like that didn't give him much of an opportunity to right the world's wrongs, but at least they provided a good excuse to step outside and cruise the streets, or go door to door talking to people and looking for the meaning of things. It certainly took his mind off his own troubles by giving him some daily motivation, and it brought in grocery money and paid the rent. Actually, he found that he liked the work and was re-energized by it. He stopped moping around his apartment and began looking forward to the challenges of the new day. He enjoyed following someone without being noticed; his innate curiosity and analytical mind were very useful in putting together the pieces of a puzzle; and, when he wasn't feeling sorry for himself, he could be very personable. People responded favorably to his sincere manner and his country charm. Because he seemed genuinely interested in what they had to say, they opened up to him and talked freely. Also, he had to admit, he got a vicarious satisfaction out of catching cheaters. It wouldn't always be divorce suits and custody cases, or exposing phony whiplash claims, or taking statements from potential witnesses to petty thefts. One day he would have a chance to move up to the better cases.

Lately he had been sleeping better and thinking about Laura less. This morning he was deep into his favorite daydream, the Naked Hitchhiker: she was waiting for him around some sudden curve in the road with her thumb slung up from her out-thrust hips and making the round offer of her breasts. Once in the car she reached for his crotch and her tongue turned in his ear like a melting key until his head was ringing, ringing.

Impulsively he flung his arm out at the nightstand. Something fell to the floor with a dull metallic clunk and a heart-stopping crack of thunder. He swallowed once to calm himself, stifled the alarm clock, and turned on the radio. He tried to clear his head while Mick Jagger whined about how he couldn't get any satisfaction. After Laura left, lyrics seemed to hold hidden meanings. He listened closely to the next song:

> *Don't let it bring you down*
> *It's only castles burning*
> *Just find someone who's turning*
> *And you will come around*

He didn't know what to make of that. The lines were elusive and haunting, suggesting that if he really concentrated they would reveal their secrets, but it was too early to worry about riddles.

After the song came the morning news and the lead item was a shocker: Devil Dancer, the prize stallion of Bradford Davis's Sycamore Springs Farm, had been found shot to death in a field shortly after sunrise. Wendell sat up in bewilderment, staring at the cracks in the ceiling. Why would anyone want to shoot Devil Dancer? They'd have to be crazy. And in Lexington, Kentucky, to boot, the goddamn heart of the Bluegrass.

Wendell had vivid memories of watching Devil Dancer make a thrilling come-from-behind stretch run to win the Blue Grass Stakes at Keeneland. He was stunned by the horse's death and felt drained of strength. An acrid odor of burnt powder hung in the air and a faint haze of blue smoke hovered near the window. He felt like the sea must feel after a long day of beating its brains out on the rocks. As he swung his feet to the floor his toes touched chilly metal. He bent over slowly, feeling dizzy, picked up his gun, and put it back on the nightstand. Using the bed for support he achieved an upright position and shuffled on unsteady legs toward the bathroom. He swiped the back of his wrist across his tongue, filled the sink with cold water, dipped his face in quickly, pulled it out sputtering, and turned around, reaching blindly for a towel to dry his eyes. He bent over, lifted the lid, and sat down on the toilet, picturing to himself a big dead horse in a wide field of verdant grass whose blue was in the eye of the beholder.

He took a quick shower and dried off with a thick white motel towel. For a man in his late forties, he noted proudly, his body wasn't in such bad shape. His legs were still strong, though his midriff was a little flabby. Back at the mirror he made a slip with his Gillette, taking a nick out of the center of his chin. He dabbed at the thin red line sliding toward his throat with a piece of toilet paper and returned to the bedroom to get dressed.

A bottle of Deep Ruby Fruity Native and a crumpled Kleenex lay on the floor beside the bed. He had spent last night stretched out in his skivvies watching the late show—Ann Margaret in *Made in Paris*. It was a stupid movie about Ann Margaret as an apprentice clothes buyer in Paris. The high point was one scene in a nightclub when she danced for a handsome fashion designer, played by Louis Jourdan, who had given her the cold shoulder. She did a showy sex-laden walk out to the middle of the floor. Very slowly at first, she began to undulate her body and thrust her breasts; then she sped it up, and with hips a-wiggle and breasts a-bob she won him over, and Wendell too, for that matter.

He sat down on a high stool by the counter, poured dark brown beans in a small wooden coffee grinder, and turned the handle furiously until it spun without resistance. He often thought of Kathy, his first wife, when he did this; the coffee grinder had been a wedding present, which for some reason was not on her side of the divorce settlement. By now grinding his own coffee beans had become a morning ritual he looked forward to. He pulled out the miniature drawer that caught the grounds and scooped them into the coffee maker. When the kettle on the stove began shrieking, he put on a padded glove the size old-time outfielders once wore, poured in the boiling water, and listened to it drip. He filled a tan earthenware mug with coffee before the dripping stopped, took a swig, and singed his tongue.

"God damn it to hell," he hissed.

Not until then did he admit how hurt he was that Brad Davis hadn't called him about the horse shooting. After all, hadn't he worked for him last spring? And didn't Davis thank him, even if he hadn't found what was expected?

Although his racing days were long over, Devil Dancer was famous enough to attract the media and involve the police, but what could a homicide squad know about a horse slaying? Nothing like this had ever happened before. Why not drive out to Sycamore Springs Farm and offer his services? Maybe this was the break he had been waiting for. That wasn't just any horse.

Resolved on a plan, Wendell waited for his coffee to cool and tried to clear his head. He went to the front door to get the *Lexington Herald*, which the paperboy had failed for the umpteenth time to throw accurately onto the landing. He found the paper, dark with dew, under a hedge. He picked it up carefully, so the news wouldn't fall apart, and brought it in. As he spread the paper out on the rug to dry he glanced at the headlines:

NIXON RULES OUT HALT IN BOMBING
KIDNAPPED MAID IS SLAIN
McGOVERN REVISES WELFARE PROGRAM AGAIN
U. K. DRAMA PROF DIES IN FALL
FLORIDA JAILS INNOVATOR OF "DARE TO BE GREAT"
KENTUCKY SLAUGHTER DUE TODAY—
CHOLERA FEARS SPREAD

Wendell didn't know the murdered maid or the unfortunate professor, but he did know several farmers who would be spending the day killing their hogs. Tomorrow the front page would belong to Devil Dancer.

When Wendell looked up from the paper he saw his cat on the back balcony with a mouse in its mouth. Moving closer, he sat down in a deck chair, sipped his coffee, and watched, strangely fascinated by what he saw. The cat bean-bagged the mouse across the floor and around the legs of Wendell's chair until it fell on its side and the tiny pink feet hung limp. Then the cat gnawed at the back of its neck until the skin broke and blood spurted down the fur. The face came off in a single decisive bite. The skull took chewing, but the front feet and chest went down with ease. The guts were licked out delicately and placed to one side. The cat paused then, as if puzzled by the small green intestinal coil, before gobbling the hindquarters—the tail dangling out from the mouth for a moment before sliding, quite suddenly, in. Finally the cat sniffed the entire area, wondering where his beanbag had gone. Only some entrails, twisted like a question mark, were left uneaten.

Wendell returned to the bedroom and picked up his .38 Beretta from the nightstand. Ever since he was a kid and his father had taught him how to hunt, he had always experienced an eerie thrill when he fingered cold metal and a well-oiled trigger. Had he left the hammer cocked? He jacked a round into the chamber. How could he have been so careless? A vague whiff of burnt powder lingered in the room, yet for the life of him he couldn't see where the bullet went.

Twenty years ago he had come home from Korea vowing that he was through with guns. He had seen so much of mud and blood and good men dead that he had actually done what many Marines swore they would: he had buried his service revolver in the backyard of his house and told the sonofabitch to rust. He thought he had left all that war horror behind. He simply wanted to settle down and live an ordinary life. But now he found himself liking the heft of a compact weapon in his hand again. He pointed the gun at the gold-framed picture of Laura he still kept beside his bed, seeing his own grim reflection in the glass. Although he had once known all-too-well what it felt like to kill, a tremendous gap now separated his middle-aged self from that audacious leatherneck who had fought foot by foot for the stinking volcanic ash and rock of Iwo Jima and that stoic two-time loser who had been called back seven years later to slog through impossible snows on the retreat to Hungnam. Since that time he had never raised his hand in anger against anyone and had tried his best to forget the terrible scenes he had witnessed.

Strapping on his shoulder holster he suddenly flashed what it must have felt like to lie in hiding and draw a steady bead on a stallion grazing in an open field. Once on Saipan he had shot a goat he saw gnawing on a dead Marine's boot. He lifted his hands to his face. He didn't want to remember all that.

The last time he had thought about Saipan was the 4th of July. He had drunk a bottle of wine and images of bulldozers pushing bodies into a ditch had started filling his mind. Sitting on his bed and listening to the firecrackers, he had realized with merciless clarity that those ghosts would never go away. Then he had picked up his gun and touched the barrel to his ear. But that was the Jap way out. Instead he had stepped onto the balcony, the gun dangling in his hand, and impulsively fired a quick potshot at his neighbor's birdfeeder, spewing broken glass and birdseed across the courtyard. The next morning the manager knocked on his door to ask if he had heard or seen anything suspicious the previous night. Wendell replied that he'd been out on a case and promised to keep his eyes and ears open. The manager said he felt more secure knowing that a detective was living there.

Now, nearly two months later, he smiled half-embarrassed and half-amused as he thought of the earnest look on the manager's face. Wendell picked up his car keys from the ashtray and stepped outside, taking a dazzling direct hit in the eyes from the sun. He turned his back on the glare until the spots cleared and descended the steps with caution. It was going to be one of those hot humid days when pasty hair sticks to the scalp, sweat stings the corners of the eyes, and everybody feels lackadaisical. Wendell walked across the drive, unlocked his black Cougar, and lowered himself into the sweltering bucket seat; but when he turned the key he got "clunk," not "roar". Funny, the battery was dead.

He released the hood, checking the water level in the radiator and the battery and testing the fan belt for tautness. Then he noticed that his "peek-a-boo" headlights were up. He must have left them on last night when he came home. He pulled the key out of the ignition and went around and opened the trunk, searching for his jumper cables beneath a pair of binoculars, an old raincoat, a small aluminum ladder, a camera with a zoom lens, and a theatrical assortment of hats. Then he remembered that he had lent his cables to Joel Bradley a week ago.

He scanned the parking lot to see if anyone was up and about. He glanced nervously at his watch and cursed under his breath. By the time he arrived at Sycamore Springs, Devil Dancer would already be buried. He was about to start ringing doorbells when a woman came out of an apartment and walked across the drive toward a green VW station-wagon. Wendell recognized her immediately. Her appearance at the Idle Hour pool in the briefest of bikinis had made his day on several occasions, and he had hoped for an opportunity to talk to her. He hurried over to her car and tapped on the window. She rolled it down without hesitation.

"Sorry to bother you," he said calmly, "but my battery is dead. Do you by any chance have some jumper cables?"

"Sure," she answered, giving him a quick look-over, "you're welcome to them."

Wendell pointed to his car and she parked beside it. Then she retrieved the cables. Holding a loop in each hand like a pair of slim snakes, she walked toward him smiling as if she knew a secret. There was something exotic about the way she wore her hair—a cluster of short curls over her forehead and dark ringlets down to her shoulders, with one particularly long strand dangling in front of each ear. She had large dark eyes, a thin aristocratic nose, a wide sensuous mouth, and an arresting angularity to her high cheek bones and precise chin. Wendell noted her breasts pressed against her tie-dyed T-shirt and how her tight jeans made a faint whistling sound as her thighs brushed lightly together when she walked.

Wendell took the cables and clamped them on the two batteries, while she stood beside him and watched. Then they both got back in their cars and turned the keys; the Cougar whined for a moment and growled to life. Wendell unclamped the cables and put them back in her car.

"Thank you. That was a big help. I'm in a rush today."

"What's your hurry?"

"Did you hear that a horse named Devil Dancer was shot this morning?"

"Brad Davis's horse? Was he killed?"

"I'm afraid so," Wendell said, wondering how she knew who Brad Davis was.

"That's awful! I hate it when things die. I feel all droopy when my plants die. I talk to them, I sing them songs, I water them; still, sometimes they die."

Her face assumed such a look of concern as she spoke that Wendell was sure she was referring to the demise of specific pampered plants.

"This could ruin Davis," Wendell mused.

"Devil Dancer, wow! Who could do such a thing? That was some horse."

"He was terrific; no telling what he could've done if he hadn't pulled up lame in the Derby. His stud fees alone must pay most of the bills at Sycamore Springs Farm. Do you know much about horse farms?"

"I'm learning."

"I guess you're not from around here."

"No."

"But you know Brad Davis?" Wendell instantly regretted that he was being so direct.

"What are you, a cop?"

"No. I'm private. A detective."

"Are you putting me on?" A hint of an ironic smile flitted at the corners of her mouth.

"It's true. I'm in the habit of asking questions."

"I guess so."

Wendell rubbed the palms of his hands together and looked at her with undisguised earnestness. Although he had intended to be tactful, the woman's beauty put him in an expansive mood.

"How do you know him?"

"I've worked at Sycamore Springs."

"So you knew Devil Dancer."

"Of course; he was hard to miss. He was magnificent."

"What did you do at the farm?"

"This and that, whatever Brad asked me to do."

"Are you a hot walker?" Wendell blurted out, the words sounding unintentionally suggestive.

She gave him a wicked twitter with her dark eyes, suppressed a smile, and said, "Sometimes. I ride them around the track in the mornings."

"So you're an exercise girl?"

"Yes. I love it."

"Isn't it dangerous?"

"Not if you know what you're doing. Horses sense who you really are inside. If you don't like yourself, or if you're afraid of them, they can turn on you. They can even kill you. But I'm not afraid, and I know who I am, so there's no problem."

"Sounds simple. Is that all you do?"

"I go to school, too. I'm pre-vet. You *are* curious, aren't you?"

"Sorry. I didn't mean to be pushy. I've seen you at the pool, and I wanted to talk to you."

"What about?"

"Nothing in particular. You know, just talk."

"Well, now we're talking."

"Only, damn it, I've got to go. I'm on my way out to Sycamore Springs to see if I can help out with this Devil Dancer killing."

"You didn't say that with much conviction," she said, surprising Wendell with her insight.

"I may get there too late to do anything." Wendell was reluctant to admit that unless Brad hired him there wasn't much he *could* do. "Devil Dancer was a hell of a horse and I'd sure like to find out who shot him."

"I think you can do anything you want to," she stated in a voice that implied more than vocational goals. "People have more power than they realize."

"I hope you're right."

"Of course I'm right." She was smiling at him brazenly now.

"Maybe I could come by and see you after I get back."

"What for?"

"Tell you what happened."

"Maybe."

"Is that a 'Yes maybe'?"

"You're pretty persistent."

"I'd like to see you again. Show my thanks."

"For what?"

"The jump."

"Oh, that," she said, laughing. "I really don't know what I'm doing tonight. I'm waiting to hear from somebody."

"Could I drop by to see if you're in?"

"Sure. I guess so. Why not?"

"Great!"

"Don't count on anything, OK?"

Wendell detected a note of pleading in her voice and there was an elsewhere look on her face as if she were trying to remember something.

"OK."

She was sitting in her car with the same preoccupied expression when he pulled out onto Richmond Road. Wendell was already in downtown Lexington before he realized that he hadn't even asked her name.

2

As Wendell drove through Lexington the weirdness of the Devil Dancer killing preyed on him. He felt it first in his body, in his clenched hands, hunched shoulders, and queasy stomach. He had seen horses put down before, and it was never a pleasant sight, no matter how badly the horse was hurt. There was something about hearing that shot, seeing that puff of smoke, and watching the noblest of animals drop to the ground, that tore into his guts, as if he were the one being killed. Lethal injection was no better, simply more scientific. To murder a beautiful stallion for no apparent reason was outrageous. A crime like that defied understanding.

Wendell had known Brad Davis—Bradford Ashton Davis III to the Social Register—when they were growing up together in Lexington. Although Wendell's parents actually lived in nearby Athens, Kentucky, he and Brad had attended Lafayette High School and played football together. It was a very good team, state-ranked their senior year, but Wendell's one vivid memory of that season was of dropping a Brad Davis pass in the end zone which had cost them a victory over Bryan Station. Wendell had made a lot of clutch catches during that season, but the one he dropped was the one he remembered. It was stupid, really, he had it right in his hands.

Wendell met Brad once during the war, when he landed his Grumman F6F Hellcat at Aslito Field on Saipan. Brad had started out as a Seabee, but he was such an eager beaver that he had gone to flight school and become a fighter pilot. They sat in the remnants of a Japanese garden, a cast-iron Buddha on a pedestal at one end and a bamboo crucifix at the other, sharing cold K rations and swapping stories. Brad had shot down a Betsy during The Great Marianas Turkey Shoot; his hands dipped and pivoted in the air as he described how the plane had burst into flame, winged over, and splashed into the sea. "Let's get together stateside," Brad suggested. "We'll throw a whizdinger."

After the war Brad went to Yale, married Elizabeth Todd Hamilton, and became owner and manager of her family farm Sycamore Springs, which once had been among the biggest in the Bluegrass. During the Depression the family had split the farm into three parts and sold two of them, supposedly to pay off Colonel Hamilton's medical bills, but everyone knew it was really to settle his gambling debts. What remained was a thousand acres of the best grazing land in the Bluegrass and a few excellent thoroughbreds to base a business on. Brad had made some shrewd buys at the Keeneland Select Sales, and by the late fifties the Sycamore Springs colors of shamrock green and midnight blue were beginning to show up in the winner's circle at the top tracks again. Best of all had been Devil Dancer (a son of the great Native Dancer) who had excited the racing world as a two-year-old. Anticipation had been high that he'd win the triple crown the following year.

Wendell would never forget the day he saw him race in the Blue Grass Stakes at Keeneland. Devil Dancer broke late from the gate and seemed content to coast along with the rest of the pack. Eddie Arcaro was sitting pretty, waiting for the field to sort itself out and for Devil Dancer to stop sulking. On the backstretch he was twenty lengths behind the leader. Wendell's heart dropped as he refused to make his move. Then on the far turn Arcaro asked the question, Devil Dancer answered with an awesome burst of speed, and it was "So long, Charley." Even though he was on the outside, the horse's ground-devouring stride was so strong and smooth it made the competition look awkward. As Devil Dancer came swooping around the final turn into the homestretch, it was clear that the two horses in front of him were doomed. Once he had flashed past and left them eating his dust, Devil Dancer, in spite of Arcaro's urgings, eased up, pricked his ears, glanced over at the ecstatic crowd shouting his name, and with head held high he pranced triumphantly under the wire. Devil Dancer's phenomenal display of speed that day was the stuff of legend. Wendell had seen many a horse race, but he had never felt such exhilaration. For that reason, he took the horse's death personally.

A few weeks later, Devil Dancer injured his coffin bone in the Derby. Miraculously, he recovered and was retired to stud; his fees had been the cornerstone of Sycamore Springs's renewed success. Since then Brad Davis hadn't come up with any horse of the same category, yet over the past few years Wendell had read about the purchase of promising yearlings sired by Devil Dancer.

As far as Wendell knew, Davis didn't have any enemies; although a person as ambitious for success as he was in the highly competitive world of big-time horse racing was bound to stomp on more than a few toes. Brad had always been a man to speak his mind. Since Elizabeth died in 1964 he had acquired a reputation as a bad-tempered drinker with a nasty mouth who ogled other men's wives and provoked fights. Nevertheless, people tended to be forgiving with him. Some guests can fidget with their forks and never get invited back to dinner, while Brad might fondle the hostess, break a treasured vase, spill his drink on the host, and still be considered the life of the party. Sober, he could be charming; and he was rich and good-looking enough to be forgiven almost anything. Besides, everyone was sympathetic about Liz.

When Brad married Charlene Prentice in 1967 the Society section of the paper played up the wedding as *the* event of the season. Charlene wasn't from one of the established families, but she was a striking beauty who had been to finishing school. She was considered the perfect match for Brad. Then last year Lily, Elizabeth's daughter, had captivated everyone at the Lexington Ball. Over the years the newspaper had run articles about Sycamore Springs Farm and printed photos of Brad, Charlene, and Lily at various events. What Wendell had gathered was that Brad's life wasn't as successful as it appeared to be. Davis talked as if Sycamore Springs had surpassed its former glory even though the farm's fortunes hinged on the potency of Devil Dancer and there hadn't been a major stakes winner since his marriage to Charlene.

A few months after Wendell traded in his Dodge Dart for a Mercury Cougar and spread the word that he was now a detective, Davis had called and asked him to come out to the house. When Wendell arrived Brad was ranting and raving about how he couldn't trust Charlene and wanted her followed. He had no creditable evidence to support his doubts, yet he was convinced that she was keeping things from him. Wendell, who couldn't help seeing his own fits of jealousy reflected in Davis's face, agreed to take the case.

Wendell kept Charlene under surveillance for a few weeks, never observing enough to confirm Davis's notions. She certainly was beautiful—there was no shortage of men making overtures; and she could turn on her Kentucky charm, so that a man didn't always know where courtesy ended and come-on began; but as far as he could see, she wasn't having an affair. Wendell spent hours trying to alleviate Brad's suspicions. In the end he seemed satisfied; he paid Wendell two thousand dollars—his biggest fee to date—and thanked him for his troubles. Wendell hadn't spoken with him since.

To get out of Lexington, Wendell turned left off Main onto Tucker and then right down the ramp onto Manchester, an ugly out-of-the-way street the city fathers would prefer visitors didn't see. Stowed away between two warehouses he caught a glimpse of Hunley's Danceland, notorious for its late night brawls. The woman they called Fat Carla, who played the piano and sang bawdy songs, was out front putting up another neon beer sign. Further on loomed the cement-block shell of a four-story building where the firemen practiced extinguishing fires. Then came a rise, with the Armory on the right, and after that the bridge over New Circle Road.

Like most American cities, Lexington couldn't keep its shape, slopping over the beltways and gobbling up the surrounding farm land. Where Manchester Road became Old Frankfort Pike, however, a dramatic change from city to country took place. Now both sides of the pavement were lined with white board fences streaming past like bridal lace in hypnotic regularity. Wendell loved to watch for the stately mansions set back on their tree-shaded knolls in the middle of an intricate maze of board fences which segregated the mares from the stallions, the foals from the yearlings, and the stallions from each other.

When he noticed that the Thomas Equine Surgery truck was gone, Wendell sped up, leaving the huge King Ranch behind on his left while Darby Dan and Danada farms blurred by on the right. A hand-lettered sign announced the Headley Museum. No doubt old man Headley would be lounging out on the veranda in one of his velvet smoking jackets while his wife fussed with her glut of bibelots. After that came some long black tobacco barns with reddish rust-streaked tin roofs where bunches of tobacco leaves hung upside down in solid tiers to dry.

As the road rose and dipped to the contour of the land, Wendell registered the images: a contented cow haunch-high in a scum-covered pond, an orange backboard and hoop rigged over a brown barn door, an old plow left in the furrow, a black cat curled up for its last rest, a striped mattress tossed in a ditch, a row of unpainted shacks, each with a washing machine on the porch, and a pink house that had SEE ROCK CITY painted on the roof. Mostly what he saw were the world's finest horses grazing in a lustrous sea of the greenest of bluegrass.

Sycamore Springs Farm was several miles out on a lovely stretch of road lined with old dry stack stone fences slaves had built. A row of rugged trees, whose branches arched and intertwined overhead to form a tunnel, edged the road; the sun slanted down through the leaves and dappled the pavement with shifting patterns of sunlight and shadow. Unlike most other horse farms, the houses and barns of Sycamore Springs were all made of the locally quarried limestone called Kentucky marble. The main house, known as the Old Hamilton Place, was nestled in a grove of towering oaks and elms, and the cared-for ground beneath them was carpeted with yellow and white jonquils every spring. The trees that gave the farm its name lined a tributary of Elkhorn Creek that meandered through the pastures.

As Wendell pulled in at the gate house a large black Doberman pinscher bounded out from behind a clump of shrubs, barking. He put his big paws on the window and bared his fangs at Wendell through the glass. A short red-faced man with a double-barrel shotgun appeared, yelling at the dog to shut up. He grabbed the beast's collar and pulled him away from the car.

"He won't hurt you," the man said. "He's just a pup. Who are you, another cop?"

Wendell asserted that he was a special investigator and an old friend of Brad Davis. The guard took his word for it and swung open the serrated jaw of the gate to let him in. Wendell drove through the stone pylons and up the long curving drive which branched off into others that led to the various horse barns. A bird's eye view of all those looping, labyrinthine ways would present an amazing design, contrasting sharply with the more linear grid of the neighboring horse farms. The road snaked through a woods, over a quaint stone bridge, and into a final circular drive, with a fountain in the center, that fronted the imposing Greek Revival edifice Brad Davis called home. He was standing at that moment on the porch steps and gesturing forcibly at a policeman. Wendell parked behind the white cruiser and walked toward the two men.

"We'll be working full time on this, Mr. Davis. There'll be cars checking the farm every hour." The policeman's voice was laden with apology. Although he was as tall as Davis, and almost as heavy, he seemed to take up only half as much space. The man stood slightly off balance and touched his nose as he talked. Brad Davis was nobody to put an edgy man at ease; now in his righteous rage he was firing off a salvo of words.

"You guys sat on your thumbs back when Mary Cawein was murdered and I don't expect any better from you this time. You've even got the shells from the rifle. I'd think that ought to be enough to run the sonofabitch down. If you don't lose them in the lab."

"Now I know you're upset," the policeman said, staring at his shoes. "I'm sure sorry this happened. I really am. I've seen horses killed in barn burnings, but never anything like this. I'll run those shells into the lab and let you know when I get the report."

"No offense, Doug," Davis mumbled without enthusiasm. "Let me know what you find."

"I heard what happened on the news this morning, Brad," Wendell said, stepping forward to shake hands. "I'd like to help."

"I guess you would." Brad smiled strangely to himself then waved half-heartedly as the cruiser disappeared into the trees.

"Doug Anderson is a wimp," Davis said, still looking down the now empty drive. "If you spit in his face he'd tell you it was raining. I hear his wife beats up on him. What use is a man like that to me?"

Brad Davis was a true Kentucky hard-boot, a blood-proud man of vehement opinions. Now, his face twisted with grief, he looked angry enough to throw down the pillars that flanked him on the portico. He had a blunt belligerent jaw, a tight determined mouth, and shrewd black predatory eyes countersunk beneath bushy close-set eyebrows. An unruly shock of thick black hair, streaked with silver, hung over his broad forehead. He had the rough granite good looks that Hollywood might have found a use for, although an exacting director might have been put off by the puffy pouches under his eyes, the farmer's squint, a certain slackness in the jowls, the crimson tinges of high blood pressure, and a general expression of chiseled disdain that failed to mask the spoiled child Brad Davis could so easily be. In *his* version of existence, the killing of Devil Dancer should never have happened.

"I know the police are working full time on this," Wendell said, "but they've got that maid's murder to think about already. Besides, a horse killing is a little out of their line. If you hired me, I could give the case my complete attention."

"Maybe so. But what do *you* know about horse killings?"

"Not a thing, Brad, to be honest. But I grew up in this town, and I know a lot of people. Besides, I knew Devil Dancer; I saw him race and you showed him to me last spring, remember? I'm sure I could be of more use to you than Doug Anderson, I'll say that."

"Anybody would be better than Doug Anderson. He's pathetic."

"Look at it this way. I'm not a guy to sit behind a desk. I'll hit the streets for you on this one. I'll break down the motives and follow up the leads and talk to anyone who needs talking to. I give you my word, I'll leave no stone unturned. Not one. What do you say? I really do need the work. Devil Dancer was a once-in-a-lifetime horse."

"Don't you think I know that?" Brad eyed Wendell for a suspended moment, as if he were pondering a *Racing Form.* "I suppose you expect a retainer," he added, reaching in his pocket for his money clip and pulling off several bills.

"Five hundred will do just fine," Wendell said.

The two men walked through the porte cochere on the left side of the house and down the drive to a four-car garage in the back; from there a path led to a large paddock with diamond-mesh fencing that bordered Old Frankfort Pike. Doctor Thomas's truck was parked in the middle of the field where two veterinarians in white medical coats were crouched over the dead horse. Three cops were wandering around among the shrubs by the road like duffers lost in the rough. Wendell noted that the crime scene hadn't even been roped off. They were out there stumbling in circles without any system to their search.

"They found a shell over by the fence," Brad said, pointing at the cops kicking the undergrowth.

"What caliber?"

"A .243."

"That's a lot of gun."

Between the piled stones along the road and the white fences with dark green gates that defined the pastures of Sycamore Springs Farm, there was a narrow strip of land lined with trees and packed with shrubbery. Someone could have crouched down in that area to hide both from workers on the farm and any cars passing by on the road.

"Here's where," Brad said, indicating the spot. "Watch your step after you climb over the fence. There's a pile of dog shit right in front of you."

"Looks fresh." Wendell stepped carefully. "What kind of person would bring his dog along with him to shoot a horse?"

"Probably just some mongrel. Stray dogs are a problem—they can cause a lot of damage if they start chasing the foals. I doubt if there's any connection. The shell is all they found."

"Since the cops have stomped around here, I can't tell who made what depressions."

"There's a spot by the fence where the grass is mashed down. That's where he waited."

"Yeah. I see the place. That's how it looks. He could have rested his rifle right here on the bottom board of the fence. Do you usually turn Devil Dancer out at night?"

"Hell yes. He *liked* to be out. He's a horse, he needs open ground and good grass, especially on nights when it's hot as a bitch and there's no breeze blowing. I'm not raising orchids here, I'm raising athletes. I don't believe in pampering my animals."

"You always put Devil Dancer in the same paddock?"

"Of course. This one is his."

"So somebody who knew a little bit about your farm would know where Devil Dancer might be on a hot summer night."

"That's right."

"Who found the body?"

"One of the horseboys, Jimmy Picket, found him about seven o'clock this morning."

"Anybody hear a shot?"

"Not a soul. At least nobody admits they heard anything."

"What do you mean by that?"

"You know how the colored are. They can be all eyes and ears when they want to be, but other times they're fast asleep by ten o'clock."

"Think somebody's trying to hide something?"

"How the hell do I know? Sure, I think it's funny no shot was heard. But for that matter I didn't hear anything either."

"I guess he was probably shot around dawn."

"Could be. The vets are trying to figure out how long he's been dead."

Wendell decided to take a closer look at the immediate area. He didn't know what he was searching for; the cops had broken down most of the surrounding bushes and crushed all the grass, so it wasn't likely that he'd find any clues—no dropped glasses, shoe prints, laundry labels, or cigarette butts. Before long, he was turning in circles like the rest of them.

Brad flashed Wendell a look of no confidence. The vets were bending like white vultures over the body of Devil Dancer. The dead horse's mouth was half-open as if in mute appeal. Wendell noted the identification number tattooed on the inside of his upper lip, a white blaze on his forehead, prominent veins running along his fine-boned, aristocratic face. The tip of his thick tongue lolled out over vaguely yellowish teeth, touching the grass. A line of elated ants had already started marching up that pink ramp into another world, while one large luminous eye faded beneath a milky film. Ants were also swarming around a sticky-looking substance on the horse's lower belly. The rippling musculature from his shoulders to his rump was remarkably defined; in his prime he was a perfect blend of strength and delicacy, a half ton of pure power propelled by stiletto legs and four fragile ankles as slim as a girl's wrist. On closer inspection he saw that his hide was a mix of light and dark hairs which gave a granite cast to his coat reminiscent of his father, who was known as the Grey Ghost. Wendell stepped back and stared at the stallion's hooves, clipped to the quick to make them tender. Now there was no more danger that a rambunctious Devil Dancer would crack through fences.

"Can't you keep the goddamn flies off of him?" Davis grimaced with revulsion.

They were everywhere—distinct black dots on the jackets of the vets, dark clusters on the horse's face and sleek flank, barely visible shadows on his nostrils.

Suddenly, as if shot off at the legs, Davis dropped to the ground and started vomiting into the grass. Wendell bent over and put one hand on his shoulder to steady him against the convulsions shaking his big frame. After he stopped vomiting, he stayed on his knees for a minute, breathing deeply and exhaling curses.

"I'm all right." He wiped his lips on his shirt front, brushed off Wendell's assistance, and rose slowly to his feet

"When did it happen?" Wendell asked one of the vets.

"I'd say before sunrise, somewhere between three and six this morning. Can't be sure until we run tests back in the lab."

"How many times was he shot?"

"Once." The vet pointed at a small hole in the neck.

"He didn't bleed much."

"No. The slug severed the spinal cord."

Wendell looked back at the fence, estimating the distance. It wasn't an especially long shot, about fifty yards at the most. No need for a scope. Anyone with hunting experience and a steady hand could have done the shooting—that narrowed it down to half the male population of Kentucky. But how many owned a high-powered rifle that fired .243 caliber bullets?

Brad and Wendell left the vets to their work and returned along the path to the main house. They entered a spacious oak-beamed room, which looked solid enough to withstand an earth tremor, and walked down a long carpeted hallway lined with oil paintings of ancestors. Once in the den they settled into some deep-cushioned leather easy chairs in front of a huge stone fireplace. A Remington bronze of rearing stallions was displayed on a pedestal and an oil painting of Devil Dancer hung over the mantel. On the walls were winner circle photos of smiling owners and jockeys flanking a sweating horse.

They sat in silence while a pretty black maid in a light blue cap, dark blue skirt and blouse, and a white apron brought them Maker's Mark on the rocks. Both men gulped their drinks greedily.

It reminded Wendell of mornings he had known when it took a couple of swigs of bourbon and branch water to steady his hands enough to tie his shoes.

"If I'm going to be any good to you, you'll have to help me all you can," Wendell said, looking solemnly at Brad. "You've got to be as straight with me as possible."

"Yes. Yes. I know that." Davis fussed with his drink and avoided Wendell's eyes.

"Do you have any idea who might want to do a thing like this? Does any little detail come to mind that might suggest somebody had it in for you?"

"You know this business, Wendell. You breed the best to the best and hope for the best. Then one day, if you're very lucky, a great horse comes along who can race a hole in the wind. Devil Dancer was that horse for me. He was a true champion. He knew it, too. He had that gleam in the eye, that command presence. I tell you, he was a tenacious competitor with the will to win. Nobody kicked dirt in his face."

"It's tragic, both his racing career and his life as a stallion were cut short," Wendell remarked, brooding out loud on the unfairness of it all.

"Thoroughbreds are mortal. You live every day with the knowledge that they could suddenly die. A freak accident can kill them—a horse can catch its neck in a fence, even get struck by lightning—to say nothing of all the illness they're prone to. This whole hot-blood business is one huge gamble; it's not for the weak of heart. Of course if you've got a stakes winner, everybody's your friend." Davis made an expansive gesture that conjured up past glories, then he spoke in a more confiding tone. "Secretly they're all wishing your horse would break a leg or prove impotent."

"Wishing and doing are two different things."

"That's right. Why, I could name you lots of people who might want to see me ruined, but I can't believe any of them would deliberately set out to kill my best horse."

Davis winced as though he were still suffering from an unhealed wound.

"Name some names. I know you're not accusing anybody. Which of the big owners might have wanted to do you harm?"

After a little more prodding Davis proceeded to reel off the names of several of the most prominent horse families in the Bluegrass. When pressed to provide solid evidence, his suspicions sounded more like paranoia than proof: Jim Dryman of Domino Stud had not looked him in the eye recently; Bull Handcock shook his hand half-heartedly at Keeneland a week or so ago; the Maddens did not invite Charlene and him to a recent party; Leslie Combs at Spendthrift had not returned his last call. Nothing he said gave Wendell anything substantial to go on.

"What about your help? Have you had any trouble lately? Have you let anyone go?"

"What help?" Davis whined, making a gesture of futility. "I get my hands dirty just like everybody else on this farm, but I don't have any help. I'm always having to let somebody go. Or somebody quits. It's hard as hell to get good workers these days, and it's even harder to keep them. Money doesn't mean a damn thing to these bums. I could pay them eight-hundred dollars a month and they still wouldn't work. These damn drifters come in here, pitch a few bales, rub down a few horses, then disappear for a few days—off on a drunk. I fire them as soon as they come back. Lord knows, I can forgive a man for drinking, but I've got to have reliable men who show up on time. If I don't watch what's happening every minute of the day, some damn fool is liable to take pity on my teaser and turn him loose with the mares and there goes your horse farm. I fired one fella day before yesterday, Grady Shifflet. He's worked off and on for me before, but it never worked out."

"Where could I find him?"

"That's easy. He drinks down at the Mecca Bar."

"I'll check him out." Wendell made note of his name, which sounded vaguely familiar. "What about racial problems, have you had any of that?"

"No. No problems at all. I get along real good with my colored. Real good." Davis stopped and glared at Wendell a moment as if to assert his credibility. "You know how it is with nigrahs, Wendell; you've got to know how to handle them. I do. I stay on top of them all the time, so they don't get outa line, and I tell them real plain what I want done. They respect me for it. Why, Old Louie down at the stud barn has been with this farm forty years. I'm firm but I'm fair and I don't let anybody get pushy and start wanting what they can't have."

"Nothing serious?"

"Serious? No sir. Lately here I've had a few colored fellas that I didn't keep. I don't remember their names—Louie could tell you. A couple of cocky young bucks fresh out of the army where all they learned was how to ignore orders. They looked mean enough. But when I told them to get off my place, they left. I don't think it was them."

"Why not?"

"Even a nigrah isn't low enough to do a thing like that. No. It had to be some sick psycho-type person who did it for the sheer hell of it. He probably doesn't even know why."

"If that's true, he could be hard to catch."

"I know it."

"And he could try to kill again."

"I've thought of that."

Wendell took a slow sip from his drink and gazed meditatively into his glass for a moment before he started another line of interrogation. He was reluctant to ask his next question because he knew that it would set Brad off.

"What about Charlene or Lily—do you know of any reason why anyone might want to terrorize either of them?"

"By God," Davis snarled in a harsh whiskey bark, "nobody better try to frighten my wife and daughter. I'll kill any sonofabitch who threatens my family with my bare hands."

He paced the room like a famished panther.

"I hate to bring up the possibility, but have you had any worries about Charlene or Lily since I ran that check for you?"

"I don't know. I really don't." His voice sounded almost pleading. "Sometimes I wonder if I know my own mind. I could have sworn they both were acting strange, but you said I had nothing to fear. I see things every day that make me wonder—secret smiles, mysterious looks, both of them always on the phone talking to God knows who. I can't keep track of them. Charlene's off at Midway College working for Meals on Wheels or planning the next Lexington Ball, and Lily's going to Transylvania this fall. She's staying in town now at the Thomas January House. She comes out every weekend to ride, but I hardly ever see her except at Sunday dinner. Neither, as far as I can tell, has seemed frightened. If they were, they would have told me. Of course they were both upset when I told them about Devil Dancer. That was one beautiful stallion. We all loved him. As perfect a horse as you'll ever see."

Brad scowled at the painting over the mantle.

"Where are they now?"

"Upstairs. I called a few close friends to come over."

"I'd like..."

"No. I don't want you questioning them until I say so. Is that understood?"

Wendell resented Davis's overbearing manner. He assured him coldly that everything was perfectly understood. The time had come to change the subject.

"Was Devil Dancer syndicated?"

"No. I could have for a couple million dollars…there was certainly interest…I had offers, but he was mine. I owned all of him."

"What about insurance?"

"I pay an arm and a leg for the stuff, but it doesn't cover murder."

"Have you ever run up any big gambling debts? I mean really big debts—the kind a guy might ask another guy to collect for him."

"How would you know about that?"

"I didn't. It's just that you and Charlene go to Vegas a couple of times a year—that always makes the papers. You in the hole to somebody?"

"I'm not the Colonel, you know. This past summer at Caesar's Palace I stayed a little too long at the baccarat table with too much booze and not enough sense. I ran up quite a tab. But with Devil Dancer there was no sweat paying that off. I could make that up on his stud fees alone. If they wanted to get their money back, why shoot my best source of income?"

"Think about it. Maybe they didn't want to be paid back. It might be to their advantage to make it difficult for you to pay them back until the interest on your principal got so large you might have to do something drastic, like sell the farm, or hand over part ownership to them. Then they could milk you for life, or launder some of their dirty money here. Nothing looks classier than a big successful horse farm. It happens all the time, you know that."

"Not to *me* it doesn't. All I can say is that better not be it. I know some people too who know a guy who wouldn't like to hear about what you're suggesting, if you catch my drift."

"Keep your hat on, Brad. All we need now is to have a bunch of guys who know some other guys running around here trying to settle scores. For Christ's sake let's not get those people involved. This thing doesn't look to me like it was done on orders. It's too crazy."

Wendell knew that there was a distinct possibility that it *was* done on orders; but having suggested it himself, he now wanted to get off the subject. Although Davis might be bluffing about his underworld connections, he didn't want to take any chances. He wished he hadn't brought the idea up in the first place, because he was the one who would have to stick his neck out to investigate the notion.

"Whoever did it," Davis said, "I hope to hell he's done with his killing. Devil Dancer was in a class by himself, but I have some other fine animals out there."

"I hope so too. What kind of security do you have set up now?"

"We've got six trucks, all with two-way radio, at least one of them is going to be on patrol at any given time."

"Who was on duty?"

"Just Walter Boyd, the night man. He checked Devil Dancer's paddock at three a.m."

"Is he dependable?"

"I believe so. Yes."

"Could I talk to your trainer?"

"He's up in Saratoga for the sale."

"Where are your horses?"

"All the stallions are in their barns. There are still some brood-mares out in the back pastures with their foals, away from the road. I've got several men out watching them and every time the guard swings by the barns he punches the clocks, so I know where he's been."

"Plus the cops will be on patrol."

"Which doesn't mean diddly shit in my opinion."

"What's your beef against the cops?"

"Well. Let's just say I have my reasons." Brad's voice indicated the topic was closed.

The two men were silent until Wendell felt compelled to bring up the Davis family again.

"I hate to say this, but Lily and Charlene may be in danger. I'd keep everybody close to home if I were you."

"I hope that bastard tries to get in here." Davis reached in his jacket and pulled out a snub-nosed revolver. "I've got a license to carry this, you know."

Wendell looked sharply at the gun to see if the safety was on, took a last taste of his drink, and smiled sadly at Brad. The two men walked out to the portico and shook hands. Wendell promised to keep in touch.

He drove to the stud barn, which had columns copied after the main house. A man on a tractor with a backhoe was digging a deep pit on the grassy knoll where the horse cemetery was located. Another man was unloading sacks of lime from a pickup truck. Devil Dancer, a horse who always made the other horses eat *his* dust, was about to have dirt thrown on his face.

Wendell walked up to a lanky black boy in blue jeans and a baseball cap who was mucking out a large pine-paneled stall with Devil Dancer's name engraved in brass on the door. A lone goat wandered up and down the shed row, lamenting his dead companion. A peacock outside dragged its tail and uttered sudden unearthly shrieks.

The boy glared at him with cloudy resentful eyes and nodded slightly toward an open area at the end of the row of stalls. Wendell could feel the boy's eyes on his back as he approached an old black man in overalls who was propped against the wall in a wooden chair, using a saddle for a footrest. A straw hat tilted down over the top half of his face and a long strand of sweet grass jutted out from his lips. He looked like he was asleep. Stepping closer, Wendell saw one half-open eye watching him.

"Louie? Wendell Clay. Remember me? How are you today?"

"I feels all right." He spoke without enthusiasm, lifting up a large calloused hand which returned no pressure when Wendell squeezed it.

"Mr. Davis said I should talk to you about this horse shooting."

"He say talk to *me*? I don't know nothin' about it. I lives down the other side of that hill. We got a cabin in the valley by the creek. I didn't hear nothin'. What you wanta talk to me for?"

"Thought you might know something about a couple of boys he let go the other day."

"Boys? I don't know *nothin'* about no boys."

"My mistake. I take that back. Perhaps you could give me the names of two black men, veterans, he had to fire."

"Yeah. Yeah. I knows what you wants. But they didn't do it. Mr. Davis caught Russell and Julian hangin' around the lab. He tole them to stay away from that place. Next day them two fools be back an he caught 'em cold. So he thrown 'em off. They ain't no boys. They mens. They bin to Viet Nam."

It wasn't hard to imagine the situation. Every large horse farm had its own lab, usually as a part of the office complex, where a wide variety of drugs and medicines were stored. Probably they would have a supply of morphine on hand. Certainly there would be lots of hypodermic needles and syringes. Wendell wondered why Brad Davis hadn't been more specific about why he had fired Russell and Julian.

"Were Russell and Julian mad when they left?"

"Russell, he mad all the time. Julian don't show what he be feelin'. Both say they ain't stole nothin' an they ain't done nothin'. I feels they both takes it in stride. Ain't the first time, I reckon, for neither of 'em. Me, I bin here on this same place over forty year. I remembers the first time Miss Lily rode her pony down to the gate to meet her daddy. I remembers when her mother, Miss Lizzy, was a little girl on a pony."

Louie's voice became thick with mucus as he began to fish the ebbing tide of his memories. He stopped talking, pulled out a rumpled handkerchief from a breast pocket of his coveralls, and spat. He looked at the hanky a moment, then slowly folded it and put it back in his pocket. After that he sank into a heavy silence.

Wendell got out a pad and pen, asked for the two men's full names, and tried to keep Louie talking, but the words came with increasing reluctance. The old man became extra cautious when he saw Wendell taking notes. He wouldn't say anything about workers' complaints or the amount anyone was paid, vaguely alluding to the fact that he and Mr. Davis had their own arrangement. He did say that both Russell and Julian lived on Jefferson Street.

Two dozen men worked at Sycamore Springs Farm, including a crew of three who did nothing all year but put up new locust post and oak plank fences and paint the old ones; another only mowed the grass and whacked weeds. Wendell knew it would take weeks to get information on everyone, but since few of the men had much direct contact with Davis, and the petty day-to-day disputes of maintaining a horse farm were not the stuff to trigger a murderous rage, he decided to look for some unusual grievance. The crime was so bizarre, the killer's motive would have to be bizarre too. He took brief notes on the men who handled Devil Dancer in the breeding shed, asking about recent firings. One name in particular stood out, Clifford Hargis, a boyhood pal of Wendell's, whom Louie mentioned in passing as having resigned last year. Good Old Cliff, how long had it been?

After a while Louie gave Wendell a sad-eyed look and said, "Ain't no sense writin' none a this down, whitefolks, it's all bad news."

Wendell handed Louie a dollar and thanked him for his time.

Louie squinted at the bill a moment, then he folded it and said, "I preciate it, sir," and put it in his breast pocket.

Wendell took one last whiff of the pungent aroma of old leather, fresh oats, sodden straw, and warm dung, glanced uneasily at the flecked red and yellow of Louie's weary eyes, and walked away on a mumbled noted of departure. As he settled into his car and eased off down the circular drive through the trees, Wendell was acutely aware that he was now on the side of the fence where the grass *was* greener and always would be; yet on this farm that was simply too beautiful for something horrible to happen, it had.

3

It was getting on toward noon, the time when the winos start wandering back onto lower Broadway to see what was happening on the street. Those with a little cash on hand would be buying their first bottle at Pietro's, and those without would be trying to cadge some drinks outside the Mecca Bar, Weiner's Bar, and Bobby's Broadway Bar. In a few hours the battered white Lexington paddy wagon would make its first slow swing by—a warning to the men to stay inside. When evening came, they would begin the nightly round-up, hauling the drunks over to the Walnut Street jail for booking, another night in the bucket, and another morning in court. Out on the rim of the city, at the motel bars and cocktail lounges on New Circle Road, the solid citizens would be pawing waitresses and throwing chairs, but unless somebody climbed in his car and started taking shortcuts across lawns, the cops would stay clear.

Wendell parked on Short Street and walked over to the Mecca Bar. Three stories above, on the fire escape balcony of the Troy Hotel, someone had constructed a personal shrine: two draped American flags, a beach towel patterned like a dollar bill, and a wreath of wilted flowers around a portrait undistinguishable from the street. Outside the sun was going full blast. Inside the bar it was dark and muggy. The place reeked of stale beer, booze gas, cigarette smoke, and old urine. The feeble light from a few bubbling beer signs left the back part of the bar in obscurity. At the pool table by the front window a bald block-headed giant was stroking his walrus moustache and squeezing his cue back to sawdust. He was staring so hard at the remaining balls it was a wonder they didn't all go hide in their holes. Naturally enough, he was playing alone.

The Mecca Bar was considered a cut above the other joints on the street. What made it special was a magnificent oak bar, reputed to be the oldest in Lexington, with a wraparound brass rail and a set of leather-cushioned stools. The stacked glassware and shelved liquors, multiplied in tall mirrors, were flanked by curly maple columns. Clearly the bar had once known better days; now it looked incongruous across from the jerry-built booths of plywood that lined the opposite wall. Nevertheless, the Mecca Bar had character: it wasn't a dive, it had its regular customers, and you didn't have to pick a fight to meet somebody; yet it wasn't a place for strangers. Dipping in loops from the ceiling was a large fishing net fringed with orange cork floats. Apparently intended as an atmospheric gesture, in reality it was rigged to drop on the customers if trouble started. Maybe it was the fishing net and not the fancy woodwork that gave the place its reputation. In truth, the Mecca Bar always made Wendell feel edgy.

He walked up to a baggy-eyed bartender who glanced at him with bored hostility while absent-mindedly slicing a lemon. Wendell asked for a Bud on draft and the bartender smacked it down in front of him, sloshing foam.

"I'm looking for somebody," he said.

"Isn't everybody?"

"No. I mean a guy."

"So?"

Before Wendell could reply he felt a soft touch on his sleeve. He jerked his arm back in overreaction, poking his elbow into the stomach of the elderly man who had come up beside him.

"This joint is for bums and has-beens," the man said. "That ain't you, is it?"

Wendell turned; he was looking at a slightly built guy with an angry purple bruise where his left eye should have been and a black scab on the bridge of his bulbous nose. He was wearing a dirty blue misbuttoned shirt. At first Wendell didn't recognize him. It was hard to pull his eyes away from that terrific shiner in order to see his whole face. The moment recognition came, he stuck out his hand.

"I didn't know you were back in town, Conor. Last I heard you and Oakley were in the slammer. You didn't turn trusty and kiss ass to freedom?"

"Young man," Conor said with surprising solemnity, "that is not my style. I simply told the parole board I was packing it in. I been to the hole so often I got arthritis in my fingers. Look at my hands."

He lowered his head toward his withered hands, which were gripping glass and bottle as if in fear they might slide away.

"I showed those bent bastards to the board and they let me go. My dukes are shot. I can't hardly even hold a bottle. I'm not fit to bust a lush or help pappy on the bus. Hell, I'm a pappy myself. They don't call me Kid Whiz anymore, I can tell you that. They used to, you know, back in the days when me and Oakley and Sally was a working mob. We knocked up sometimes a grand a day at Keeneland. Not even counting what we made if our nags came in."

Conor Maguire was just getting started. He was an inexhaustible talker, full of shamrock malarkey, now warming to his story. His hands lifted up from the bar and began to punctuate his remarks with emphatic gestures. As he spoke his voice rose an octave with excitement.

"We'd watch that fifty-dollar window, waiting for the lucky suckers to turn in their tickets. Then Oakley would edge in to fan the mark, next Sally would sidle up and plant her keister where it counts, and right when this egg starts to wonder why this gorgeous babe is rubbing her butt against his balls, I'd move in and fork the leather. Let me tell you, I was fast, a real live wire. I was one lightning tool, no lie. I could snatch it right out of your eyes singlehanded. Left britch, right britch, left and right prat, wipe kick, coat pit, I could do them all. And I jostled nobody. They never felt a thing."

Conor tapped Wendell's jacket, marking the spot where his wallet covered his heart. He gave him one sidelong glance, smiled an enigmatic smile, and drained his glass with a tremulous hand. When he resumed speaking his voice took on a quieter, more intimate tone.

"I worked so close I could smell their underwear; I counted the hairs on the back of their necks; I knew their every move before they even thought of making them. I worked all the big cities—Chi, St. Loo, K.C.—and I never got nabbed when the fix was in."

Wendell liked to listen to Conor. He was one of the last of the old timers. Whenever he spoke he signed his name. Nobody would talk that way again. Wendell bought another round and steered Conor over to a booth.

Wendell first met Conor several years ago when he had gone on a spree and ended up spending a night in the drunk tank with him, so he already had vague memories of having heard his share of stories of what life in the whiz was like when, as Conor put it, "things was organized and the fix was in." He had worked Keeneland for years, until his face became so familiar, and the complaints about pickpockets so frequent, that he was sent to Eddyville as a habitual.

"I'm looking for Grady Shifflet." Wendell hoped to obtain some information before Conor got off on the whiz again. "He been in lately?"

"Grady's in here all the time. Seems like he's never *not* in here. But I don't see him now." He squinted toward the booths at the back of the room. "Come to think of it, I don't think he was in here yesterday. That's strange, you ask me, he's always in here."

Barney brought another round. When Conor resumed speaking, his voice had picked up a touch of an Irish lilt.

"What would you be wanting with Grady? You wouldn't be looking to score, now would you Wendell? You know old Grady's idea of a holiday is one red bird on top of two Christmas trees with maybe some angel dust sprinkled on for trimmings, if you know what I mean. If he ever packs it in he could open his own Bagleys and sell his surplus right over the counter. I'm not telling you nothing you don't already know, right?"

Actually, he was. Wendell had assumed that Grady was a straight-out boozer—the drug angle added a new dimension. Maybe Russell and Julian weren't the only ones interested in the contents of Brad Davis's lab.

"Is Grady a heavy user?"

"He dabbles. Strictly a hit-and-miss habit. These goof ball artists are all pitiful."

Conor looked down sadly into his already empty glass.

"I got it," Wendell hurried to offer. "It's on me."

"Young man, I was hoping you'd say that."

When Wendell came back he told Conor about the shooting of Devil Dancer.

"That's one for the books!" Conor was fascinated by such an unusual crime. "I remember many years ago somebody cut the ear off a horse over in Mercer County and let it bleed to death, part of a revenge feud I believe, but that horse was no thoroughbred. You don't think Grady had anything to do with it, do you? I hear he used to be a pretty fair shot, but he's so dopey-eyed these days nobody will play darts with him. Damn near killed some waitress at Freddy's, what I hear, threw a dart that changed the part in her hair. Yes sir, when he's high he's crazy enough to do a thing like that, but I don't think his eyes would focus.

"You know, that reminds me of the story they tell about the old Capone mob. Nails Morton, see, got thrown by a horse and accidentally trampled to death. That happened, if I'm not mistaken, over in Lincoln Park. Well, the boys were very upset, didn't know what to do. Finally that night some of them broke into the riding stable, nabbed the horse, took him over to the park, and plugged him. It was a real gangland-style execution. Then they called the guy who owned the horse and told him they just taught his horse a lesson and if he wanted his bridle back he could pick it up in Lincoln Park. Can you beat that? Well, hell, maybe you can. Nobody, to my knowledge, has ever shot a famous thoroughbred before. Now horses dying accidentally on purpose as part of an insurance scam, that's different. Why try to pin it on Grady?"

"Davis fired Grady recently. He'd been doing some odd jobs for him, helping out around the stalls. I'm checking out the grudge angle, that's all, trying to see if any of the hired help might feel bitter about getting sacked."

"If Grady can't take getting sacked, it would have come out long before this. All his life he's been getting the sack. If it's the grudge angle you're after, maybe you ought to talk to me first. I've got an old score to settle with that fella."

Wendell was surprised by the enmity in Conor's voice.

"That rat bastard took Sally away from me, years ago. Back in the fifties. Sally, Oakley, and me used to work the whiz during the day. In the evenings she was an exotic dancer at Comers. She used to come out dressed like a Southern belle and when she got done with her act she wasn't wearing stitch one. That, my friend, was a sight. Davis used to come to see the show. People thought he was so broken up when his first wife died. Hell, he cheated on her all the time. He was always hanging around Comers trying to dick the dancers. One night he was sitting up front with his buddies when Sally was on stage and he started moaning, 'That one. Get her. She's showing, she's in heat. Get a whiff of her.' Those were his words. I picked up a bottle by the neck and I was all set to dust his skull when the bouncer caught me by the arm and hauled me outside. He'd been watching me, see. He talked to me, tried to calm me down, told me to stay away from the club. So I went off on a three-day drunk."

"That must have been what, at least fifteen years ago? Why not forgive and forget?"

"I know, I know, that story has a beard, but you know the definition of a senile Irishman, don't you—a guy who's forgotten everything except the grudge."

"How old were you then?"

"Hell, I don't know, early fifties I guess. I wasn't no spring chicken, that's for damn sure, and I didn't have no horse farm to flash around. And Sally wasn't even my woman, she played the field. But let me ask you something," Conor said, leaning forward and tugging Wendell's sleeve. "Who do you think the ladies went for?"

"You tell me."

"Me. That's who. I still feel like a thirty-five-year-old stud in a seventy-year-old body. I need my nookie like everybody else. See that fat woman over there in the booth? That's Margaret. She does it for a bottle of beer. Now isn't *that* a hell of a situation?"

Wendell glanced over at a booth where Margaret was talking to a crippled man who had piled his crutches under the table. Rolls of fat covered her elbows and it was hard to tell where her breasts ended and her belly began. She was talking very excitedly, and her laughter rumbled through the whole room. Wendell wondered if she got her beer before or after.

"You know what all these winos want?" Conor added. "A better piece of ass, that's what they want. Only these guys know they can't get it: they're too old, too ugly, too mean. They got no social graces, or they can't take the threat of rejection, so they drink instead."

Wendell acknowledged the truth in Conor's theory, but he wasn't sure what point he was trying to make. For a moment he pictured the girl he met that morning, how her body moved as she brought him the jumper cables in her uplifted arms. Now *there* was a workout.

"Sally was the best whiz moll I've ever seen; she had a keister on her that could hypnotize a mark from twenty feet. She didn't even have to plant it; a mark would take one look at her and I could have stolen his shoes and he'd never know it. But she was tired of the life, so she quit the mob and let that bastard Davis set her up in a suite at the Phoenix Hotel. That was when Oakley and I started getting the bulls at our throats.

"Back in the days when the fix was in, the fuzz knew me on sight, but those right coppers always gave me the pass up. They didn't dare lay a finger on me, because they knew the score, so I was sitting pretty and working in the shade. Then Sally came along—and let me tell you a good stall is hard to find—and for several years there the money rolled in like popcorn. Any sucker with pockets, he was mine. Never had to reef a britch, it was all so easy. For a prat poke I'd just top it up, pinch it, and let the mark walk away from it. Presto I pass the leather to Oakley and I'm clean. But after Sally left, me and Oakley were on our own, reduced to dribs and drabs, strictly nickel and dime stuff. And with the heat on at the tracks, the fix was out of reach, so we had to work on the sneak and naturally we got nabbed."

Conor paused and looked up expectantly. Wendell was tempted to ask how he got caught if he was so slick, but then realized that what Conor was waiting for was a refill, so he went for another round. Conor half-emptied his glass with one swallow and smiled his appreciation.

"I know alcohol is an addiction," he said, "but it is a *wonderful* addiction." Then he lowered his voice and half-whispered, "The problem is, young man, that the thirst of the heart can never be assuaged by drink."

He gave Wendell a moment to ponder that before he went on with his story.

"The fix, you understand, is never off. The price fluctuates, that's all. It used to be that you could show the cops a few patriotic pictures and you'd be home free, but now they know some presidents I never seen before, so I couldn't make the nut. Ended up in the joint with the hopheads and deadbeats. Time I get out, Sally is long gone. Davis kept her around for a month or so, then he dumps her. For him, she's a side dish, a piece of strange to put some flavor in his life, but for me...." Conor's voice cracked under the weight of his emotions. He emptied his glass, calmed himself, and said simply, "She was stuff."

Wendell felt sorry for Conor; he felt sorry for himself; he felt sorry for Margaret and the cripple and everybody in the Mecca Bar. Beer will do that to you—after a few bottles it starts leaking out your eyes.

"Where did you get the shiner, did you run into a doorknob?" Wendell felt guilty that he hadn't inquired about his injury sooner.

"A doorknob!" Conor snapped resentfully. "Yeah, that's about how smart the fuzz is around here. I'm out on the street the other night. It's late, must be four o'clock. I usually stay off the streets that late; as many times as I've been there, I still hate the bucket. But it's one of those sweaty humid nights, you know, when you lie in bed feeling like an armpit and can't sleep. So I figure I'll walk over to Gratz Park and cool off under the trees. But these two town clowns spot me and pull over by the curb to arrest me for drunk."

"What did they say?"

"Get in."

"Did you tell them you weren't drunk?"

"Hell, with me every day's a double-header. I'm never not drunk. And they hate back talk. You try to buck the bulls and they'll hand you your head. Half the drunks they pick up never get to the bucket. They'll pile some tramps and dingbats in the back of the wagon, drive them out into the country, and rough them up."

"Can't they complain about that?"

"None of it ever gets to court. Drunks can't accuse, if they can't remember. Who's the judge gonna believe anyway, a rumdum or one of Lexington's finest?"

"Is that what happened to you—a nice nighttime tour of the horse farms?"

"Naw. These guys were in a car. They didn't have the wagon with the no-look-in windows in back. You beat somebody up in a car, there's always the chance some irate citizen will witness it. What happened to me was the guy on the passenger side got out, opened the back door, and made like he was gonna help me in. The second I stopped watching him he slugged me in the face and pushed me into the back seat. Gave me a hell of a bloody nose. Then the other guy, the one driving, turns around and looks at me and starts yelling, 'If you get one drop of blood on my upholstery I'll blow your fucking head off.' That's what he tells me. They worked me over some more in the elevator on the way up to book me. All body punches, so nothing would show. When we get out of the elevator they give me a hard shove in the back and I go crashing face-first into the booking window. That's how I got my eye."

"Did you do anything to set them off?"

"That I did. You know me, Wendell. All the time this is going on, I'm commenting."

"I can imagine."

"That was Saturday night. So I'm in the bucket doing dead time until Monday morning, waiting to go before the judge. Lucky for me I had some fall dough stashed in my shoe. If you haven't got any scratch, you are dead on the water. I knew a trusty in there; he found me a razor and a pocket flask. This judge, he makes all the drunks line up in front of him and hold out their hands. If your hands are shaking, it's sixty days. If you can keep them still, you might be able to talk your way out. Tell him your ambition is to find work in another state. That'll tickle his pecker. He said he hadn't seen me for a while, so I told him I'd been on the wagon. Just had a temporary set-back, you know. He give me thirty days probated, like I was a first offender."

Conor paused while Wendell bought another round. He had a difficult time navigating his way over to the bar and back; all the beers on top of the bourbons with Brad Davis were having their effect. After this one he'd better call it quits.

"The old whiz mobs are gone now," Conor said, waxing even more nostalgic. "Nobody has any finesse, no style. Now it's all rawjaw: clout and lam, rip and tear, snatch and grab. There were real pros in the old days, now it's nothing but ball-busting amateurs. Not like the whiz, where you need the gentle touch. These young colored guys, they become muggers. Nobody learns the whiz, everybody relies on the arm. I used to know some fine shine cannons in the old days, guys who had learned the soft touch, the delicate timing. All moll mobs too, they had that perfect clockwork teamwork. It was a joy to watch, how smooth it could be! Who knows, the whiz could come back. The play is still there. You just need a little nerve and the grift sense to score. Hell, every time I see a moving crowd and start smelling all that scratch, let me tell you I get the itch."

"You've packed it in," Wendell reminded him. "If I were you, I'd stay straight if I could. Eddyville isn't my idea of a retirement home. What about Oakley, is he still around?"

"Oakley's dead. Got killed in prison. We were in different cell blocks so I never saw it. Somebody stuck a shiv in his back and left him to die. I don't know what for. Hell, I've seen throats get cut for a box of butts. You tell me what for. When I heard the news, I went on a crying jag, lasted all day. I hadn't cried like that since Sally... Shit, I don't want to talk about it. But you come around again, Wendell. I do love to punch whiz. I'll tell you about some of the eggs I've broken, you know what I mean. You listen. I'll punch guff with you anytime. You know what I'm talking about. Hell, some guys have never done nothing."

Wendell slid out of the booth and looked toward the front of the bar. The giant was still there playing pool alone. "Who's the moose?"

"That, my friend, is trouble. His name is Ed 'Bull' Fuller. He'd just as soon kill you as look at you. He could get himself voted sonofabitch by acclamation. I'm waiting for the day he misses an easy shot and throws the pool table through the front window."

"I'm sure he could do it. Is there a back door?" Wendell asked, only half joking.

"Oh, he's harmless. Just don't breathe on him when you go by."

"Right. You take it easy. And if Grady shows, I'd appreciate it if you'd give me a call."

Wendell handed Conor his card and smiled at him with real affection. Who knew, one day that might be him. He'd be the one with the broken nose and the red whiskey webs on his cheeks, and maybe the black eye too.

"Taking it easy," Conor said reflectively, "that's what I used to be good at. I wish I could still take it easy. You wouldn't happen to have any small change on you would you, Wendell? Just in case I see Grady and need to make that call?"

"Sure thing, Conor," he said, pulling out his wallet and putting a five dollar bill down on the table. "You drink it slow now."

4

After leaving the Mecca Bar, Wendell walked down to Main Street, entered McGee's Bakery, which smelled of cinnamon rolls, sat down at a booth in the back, and ordered coffee and a Reuben. While waiting for his food he used a phone up front to make a few calls, finally obtaining Grady Shifflet's last known address on North Limestone.

A half hour later he was driving slowly up Limestone past the bars, restaurants, antique stores, and used bookshops. One of the antique stores had recently sold out to a massage parlor—the kind that starts out Oriental and ends up French. The display window, covered over with purple paint, had the body of a nude woman etched on in white. A new bus station across the street already looked a hundred years old. Among the hungry-eyed men milling around out front lurked probably at least one chicken-hawk, jingling the quarters in his pocket and watching for runaways. Take the kid to the pinball arcade, treat him to a few games, invite him back to your place for a joint, and then make your move.

Beyond the bus station and a bottling plant, twenty motorcycles were parked in the drive of a white-columned mansion turned funeral parlor. Further along came second-hand furniture stores, dollar-a-night flophouses, and ramshackle rooming houses spaced between vacant lots where weeds almost covered the For Sale signs.

Occasionally, among these run-down buildings Wendell noticed a classic home of an earlier Lexington. His particular favorite was a three-story yellow-brick house built sideways close to the street. An archway gave entrance to a flagstone path leading to a Moorish fountain and a rose garden, beneath a splendid two-tiered piazza reminiscent of the old planters' homes in Charleston. Since Wendell had never seen anyone coming in or going out, he liked to imagine that the owners had stored siege provisions in the wine cellar, vowing never to emerge until more propitious times. Judging from the condition of the neighborhood, they were in for a long wait.

Several blocks later Wendell pulled over in front of a corner grocery store. An elderly man in a blood-stained apron was stooped over to sweep up a glittering puzzle of glass slivers from his store-front window. He worked with painstaking care, as if at each step he feared a fall, his own bones as brittle as glass. On the next street a steel ball swung like a pendulum into the side of a burnt-out building, sending a thick reddish cloud drifting out over the houses to float in at the windows and coat everything with a gritty patina of brick dust. If the city fathers (mostly lawyers fronting for developers) had their way, much of the distinctive downtown would be demolished and replaced by shiny high-rises that resembled flashcubes—all in the name of progress and urban renewal—and old Lexington would soon be as lost as Atlantis.

In the parking lot of a nearby carry-out place, two teenage girls in sleeveless blouses, wearing tight cut-off blue jeans faded just right in the ass, stood bare-footed beside a big motorcycle, running their fingers over the black leather seat and the scarlet egg-shaped gas tank. The booted owner of the bike, a slit-eyed man with long tangled blond hair, who looked like a cross between Jesus and a weasel, sat on his turquoise helmet and rubbed his back against the brick wall of the liquor store. He stretched his legs on the gravel and smiled up at the girls with all the wisdom a head-full of hash can bring. Sure, he could take them for a ride.

A sad-eyed collie stood on the curb, looked both ways, then slowly crossed the street with its head down. Wendell followed the dog across and walked up onto the paint-eaten porch of a seedy apartment house. A wrinkled old duffer in a battered hat rocked in the sun by the front door gumming a hamburger. Dangling between his legs was a pink plastic fly swatter, which he waved at a passing matron, dropping his burger in the process. He didn't seem to miss it, so Wendell let it go.

"Does Grady Shifflet live here?" Wendell shouted, assuming he was hard of hearing.

The old man peered up and worked his lips a little, probably more from the aftertaste of the catsup than from a desire to speak. His pajama tops were dark with sweat stains at the armpits. His chest was so collapsed, his arms so skinny, his belly so slack, it seemed as if he were being sucked slowly back into the jaws of his rocking chair. He began to blink furiously from the glare of the sun, showing a toothless grin and a slight head movement which could have indicated a nod yes or a shake no, but didn't say a word. As Wendell walked past, the old man turned his head and spat on the porch, mumbling something unintelligible.

Inside the front door the names taped on the busted metal mail-boxes were too faded to read; junk mail was spread all over the floor. Wendell stooped down and looked for Shifflet's name on the few personal letters buried in the pile of sales offers, get rich quick schemes, flyers from Reverend Ike promising fortunes to the faithful, position papers and family portraits from the political campaign, a few magazines—*Gun Digest, True Detective, Modern Romance*—and lots of collection notices. In all that jumble, there was nothing for Grady.

He soccer-kicked at the pile with a sweeping motion of his foot and started up the stairs. The bannister felt like it was held in place by twine and one of the steps had rotted away completely, providing an unnerving view of the steps below descending into the dark cellar. At the landing he headed down a long unlit hall with a window at the far end. A line of light was visible beneath one door. None of the doors had numbers, but the places where they once were had left legible outlines on the dust-crusted wood.

At the end of the hallway, his eyes stinging from the fumes of a disinfectant, he found Shifflet's door. He hesitated for a moment, his heart pounding out jazz improvisations at a crazy rate, then knocked. The sound hardly reverberated inside, as if the whole place were packed with cotton. He knocked again and got no response; he had an uncanny feeling that someone was pressed against an inner wall listening.

Leaving a room is a simple matter of shutting the door firmly behind you, but entering a forbidden room is subtle and takes nerve. For some thieves the thrill comes from the forced entry. Wendell slipped his American Express card from his wallet and wedged it against the bolt, which gave way so easily he wondered if the door had been locked. Before he opened any further he bent his head, attending to whatever unseen presences might be lurking in the room. Then he sucked in a gulp of air, let his heart simmer down, and pushed the door open quickly to minimize squeaking. He took a long swift step forward, another hurried waltz step to the side, and brought the door to a snickering close. He exhaled with a sigh of satisfaction. A stealthy move. Wendell felt like a detective.

Once inside he wasn't sure what he was looking for. He doubted that he would find anything that would be of help, and he knew he was risking arrest. All he needed to make his reputation as a class operator was a trip to Eddyville for breaking and entering. Once word of that got around, nobody would even offer him divorce cases.

The shades were down and everything was dark. He couldn't tell if the bulky shapes against the far wall were bodies or furniture, so he started feeling his way along, staring out into the murky room and waiting for his eyes to adjust. Drifters like Grady, without a friend in the world, often die alone in their rooms and their bodies aren't discovered until the neighbors start complaining about the smell. With his next step he kicked a dead soldier which scooted across the floor and cracked into a metal leg of the bed, spun back against the wall, and smacked into another bottle. So much for stealth. Nothing moved on the bed.

He picked up a throw rug, so rotten it came apart in his hands, and crammed it against the bottom of the door. Then he flipped on the light. The blue glass fixture was half-filled with a dark pile of dead bugs, permitting only a feeble glow on the ceiling. He walked slowly across the room to see what was on top of the bed. He stopped a few feet away and bent forward, peering to be sure. It was a twisted heap of old blankets.

He tugged at the bottom of the shade beside the bed; it tore at the side in a curved rip that looked like a laughing mouth in profile. The sun slanted through the gap in a band of spun rays that made the thousands of dust motes, floating in soft suspension, sparkle. He pulled back the cluster of blankets on the bed, exposing a piss-ringed mattress the color of a used coffee filter. On a small striped pillow spilling feathers from one end, he noted a dark oily spot where Grady's head must have lain and lifted a curlicue of grey hair for inspection.

Wendell stooped to look under the bed. Out of a gash in the mattress cruddy brown wads of stuffing seeped between broken slats and ruptured springs. On the floor he saw one shoe chewed away at the toe, a scattering of tiny black rat turds, flurs of lint in profusion, some burnt-out matches, and a blackened spoon. Beside the bed a sofa had fallen on its face, feet in the air. One spring, coiling out like an intestinal secret, had punched through the burlap stretched across the bottom. Against the far wall, beneath a plastic-framed picture of Christ on the cross, was an antique hair trunk with broken hinges. As Wendell walked over for a closer look, a miracle happened: the picture changed, and there *He* was, walking on the water.

The silence of the room was oppressive. Wendell felt his shoulder muscles stiffen, the dust drying in his throat. He tried, without success, to stifle a sneeze. The few sounds that filtered in from outside—a baby crying, a woman screaming, a car backfiring—all broke off abruptly, leaving no echo. The air stank from an unholy combination of unwashed dishes, un-flushed toilets, and un-emptied garbage. He went to the window, draped with spider webs like dingy curtains, and tried to open it, but it was too warped to budge. Between the closed window and the screen a trapped fly, who had forgotten that the way out is the way in, bumped drunkenly against the cracked pane.

On the wall a poster had popped its tape and curled back into itself. Wendell unrolled it like a scroll, the once glossy paper almost splitting in his hands, and beheld Sophia Loren rising from the sea in a black blouse that clung to her breasts. We have one thing in common, he thought, admitting a furtive affinity with the lonely man he was trying to find.

He opened the closet door and walked face-first into a cobweb whose filaments stuck to his forehead. He found a tweed sports jacket oozing white silk out one sleeve, and a black umbrella folded upside down like a bat. Otherwise the closet was empty, except for the hairy-legged spiders tucked in obscure corners to wait until he left. He inspected their intricate webs as if searching for an answer. Then he stepped back and firmly closed the door.

The floor of the bathroom was cluttered with chunks of plaster that had fallen from a jagged hole in the ceiling. A dirty pink girdle was slung like a saddle over the rim of the tub, which tilted toward him at an angle because one of its clawfeet was shattered. When he stepped forward, three cockroaches zithered out from under a slab of plaster and made a many-legged dash for the drain. He turned a tap over the sink, hoping to wipe the grime from his eyes, but what came out was so rusty it was useless. A square of cardboard above the sink marked where the mirror should have been—the poor bastard couldn't even get a look at himself.

The lidless toilet was streaked with filth. His stomach clenched as he forced himself to peer at the green copper ball floating in the slimy chamber. He glanced at the dark brown water and pushed the handle to flush. A few air bubbles popped on the surface, intensifying the smell. He got out quickly and shut the door.

In the kitchen an assortment of chipped dishes was souring in the sink. The refrigerator door hung open like an idiot's lip. Inside were a plastic bottle of orange juice which hissed when he unscrewed the lid, a vermilion onion spreading its tentacles, and a shriveled potato whose eyes were popping out of their sockets. The garbage can lay on its side, strewing its contents.

He spread some old newspapers on the torn linoleum of the kitchen floor. Trying to ignore the unmistakable odor of dead fish, he dumped the garbage on the papers: mostly bottles, bones, eggshells, coffee grounds, and beer cans. At the bottom of the pile he found a threadbare washcloth that might have been stained with blood, but he couldn't be sure. It was wrapped around a milk carton which fascinated one fearless fly who continued to cling to the side even as Wendell lifted it up and unfolded the collapsed cardboard top. When he turned the carton upside down, out fell two dead mice, both with broken necks.

Wendell gave an involuntary laugh that sounded more like a bark of disgust. He rolled the garbage in the papers on the floor and jammed the mess into the can. What the fuck am I doing, he wondered, spending a goddamn afternoon picking over some wino's garbage? He hadn't found anything to connect Shifflet with the horse killing; he couldn't even be sure that this was his room. It didn't look like anybody had lived there for a long time. All he had learned, as if he didn't already know it, was that Grady was just one more poor forlorn soul who probably meant nothing to nobody.

On his way out of the room, he bumped into a blotchy-faced woman in a baggy shirt and a cranberry-red sweater out at the elbows. She scowled at him with her arms folded across her chest. Her nervous greedy eyes seemed suspicious of each other. Wendell had learned that this kind of woman could be trouble. She knew he had been in Grady's room and she was ready to take personal offense. Probably her own room was about all she had left, so she was primed to defend her territory. She would be touchy about anything she might construe as disrespectful.

"Why was you messin' around in that room? You ain't got no business bein' in there, an' you know it. I'm gonna call the law on you if you don't get on outta here right now, you hear?" Her voice became more harsh and raspy as she talked.

"I'm a friend of Grady's." Wendell lacked the heart to come up with an elaborate lie. "Have you seen him around lately?"

"You are, huh?" She grew more challenging as she saw his defensiveness. "He ain't got no friends and he don't live here no more. And even if he did have friends, they wouldn't look like you. What are you, a cop? What's he done this time?"

"It's nothing serious, ma'am," he said, hoping she would assume he was a cop. "I'd just like to talk to him."

"That's what they all say, 'I'd just like to talk to him,' then he disappears for a while. Well I ain't seen him. You won't find nothin' here. So get on out of where you don't belong."

Wendell eased past her and hurried down the stairs, almost falling on the missing step. The old geezer on the porch had his head back, his neck lolling on the sharp top of the rocking chair and his mouth wide open. He wasn't dead—because the dead don't snore.

5

The address Louie had given for Russell and Julian was on Jefferson, an integrated street—whites on one end, blacks on the other—that ran parallel to North Broadway. The white end was lined with clunkers and junkers, incestuous offspring, mostly, of the Chevy family, with bare-chested men in oil-stained jeans up to their elbows in recalcitrant machinery. A small cinder-strewn playground enclosed by a ten-foot steel-and-wire-mesh fence marked the beginning of the black section—a run-down neighborhood of corner bars, shotgun houses, and a cement-block Holiness church with a blue neon cross on the roof. Almost all the houses were one-story three-room unpainted clapboard shacks, each with a small collapsing front porch and a torn screen door which led to the living room, then the bedroom, then the kitchen. Someone firing a double-barrell at the front door could send a hail of deadly pellets into every corner of those three rooms, transforming the shack into a shooting gallery. Shotgun houses.

Wendell parked in front of number 139; the place next door had its meager innards spread on the sidewalk for all to see in the shameful autopsy of dispossession and public auction. He walked up on the porch and knocked on the rattling screen door. He was sure he heard sounds from the bedroom, but no one made any effort to respond. He knocked again, harder, trying to peer through the screen into the living room. All he could see was a couch against the far wall with a slip cover and pink blanket cascading from it onto the wooden floor.

Wendell gave the door an impatient pounding, calling out, "Anybody home?" A low groan from the next room, the squeak of bedsprings easing up, the thump of bony feet on the floor. A tall black woman in a frayed yellow bathrobe, which she held closed with one hand at her throat, came to the door. She had remarkably skinny legs. Although she stood only a few feet away, he could not see her clearly because of the rust-clogged screen between them.

"Yeah?" she asked with obvious irritation.

"Are Russell and Julian here?"

"Who?"

"Russell and Julian."

"Russell and Julian?"

"Yes. I'd like to talk to them."

"They ain't here."

"When do you expect them?"

"Say what?"

"When will Russell and Julian be here?"

"They ain't here."

"I know. But when will they be back?"

"Who you?"

"My name is Wendell Clay."

"Does Russell know you?"

"No. But I'd like to ask him a few questions."

"What kinda questions?"

"I'd like to ask *him*."

"I don't know nothin' about it."

"About what?"

"I don't know nobody name Russell."

"I thought you said he lived here."

"Who tole you that? They is a lie. Nobody name Russell be here."

She may have been enjoying the run-around, but all Wendell felt was irritation. He was about to give up when he heard the sound of heavy footsteps from the back of the house. Past the head of the woman in the doorway he saw a man standing in the shadows.

"Who that, baby?" the man growled.

"Some honkey say he want to talk to Russell and Julian. I say I don't know no Russell and Julian."

"Yeah. I heard you." He nudged the woman aside and stepped up to the screen. He was so big Wendell had to look up at him.

"What do you want with Julian?"

"I was just telling your wife here..."

"She's not my wife."

"Look. All I want is to ask some guys a few questions. Do you know where I could find either Russell or Julian? I was told they live here."

"Do you know Julian?"

"No. I just want to talk to him."

"Then why are you calling him by his first name?"

Wendell was dumbfounded. Why did everybody have to be so touchy? He was simply using first names because that was how they had been referred to at Sycamore Springs Farm.

"I'm sorry," he apologized. "I'm looking for Russell Williams and Julian Harrison."

"Julian's not here."

"What about Russell Williams?"

"You a cop?"

"No."

"What are you?"

"I'm a private investigator."

"Investigatin' what?"

"I'm working on a case for Brad Davis."

"Is that right? If you're not a pig, Russell will talk to you."

"Good. Does that mean I can see him now?"

"It do."

"Well, go get him," Wendell demanded, throwing aside his last shred of patience.

"Don't give me orders or we don't talk."

"You're Russell."

"You got it, Jack. What do you want?"

"I understand you worked for Mr. Davis."

Russell looked at him with impassive eyes, leaning heavily against the flimsy door so that his forearms pressed against the screen. He had a scooped-out place where his left bicep should have been; a pink jagged scar ran down the depression. He contemplated Wendell with mistrust, waiting for him to reveal his intentions.

"Somebody shot Devil Dancer this morning," Wendell announced bluntly.

"That was a fine horse."

Wendell was struck by the honest admiration in Russell's voice.

"I understand you're back from Vietnam," he said, hoping to establish some rapport.

"Yeah, I'm back, but I don't belong."

"You don't feel at home?"

"Stateside is bullshit, man. Robots ripping off zombies. What these creeps need is a good firefight to open their eyes and pucker their assholes. If you don't know what I'm talkin' about, I can't break it down for you."

"I've been to war too," Wendell said.

"We've all been to war," Russell acknowledged bitterly. "But we didn't all come back."

"That's right. You've probably had a hard time finding a decent job."

"There are no *decent* jobs, man. In this town you can shovel horse-shit or dump garbage. Take your pick."

"Is that why you quit working at Sycamore Springs?"

"Don't jive with me, man. You know damn well that me an Julian was fired. What kinda action you runnin' here?"

"Like I said, I'm trying to find out about this horse shooting."

"So first thing you go look for the nearest nigger. Shit, man, I don't have to talk to you."

"No, you don't. But look, don't take it personally. My job is to talk to all the men who used to work for Mr. Davis, make sure there were no hard feelings, you see?"

Russell glared at Wendell with cold-eyed intensity, not speaking, but seeming to gather in size until he filled the doorway.

"Back off, Jack," he said in a throaty whisper. *"Didi mao.* Get the fuck off my porch!"

Wendell saw no choice but to do what the man said. Why couldn't he learn to keep his cool, to use an assumed name and a false profession, and discover what he needed to know by indirect means? So far, he was proving to be a piss-poor detective. Scratch Russell.

6

Wendell sat in his car and pondered what to do next. In a vacant lot across the street three black girls wearing identical flower-print dresses were dancing in a ring around a tilted metal pole, stripped of its tetherball, which dangled its frayed cord in the breeze. Very faintly he could hear them singing an old, old song:

Ring around the rosies
A pocket full of posies
Ashes, ashes, we all fall down

They all dropped to the ground and giggled.

As Wendell returned along Jefferson Street, he recognized someone in a gathering of men on the sidewalk in front of a cement-block bar. Eddie Orleans, once a shifty option-running quarterback for Dunbar High, was a long-time friend from Wendell's football days. Even though high school sports were segregated back then, the better athletes found ways to compete on summer playgrounds. He was the only person in the black community Wendell knew well enough to ask for information. Eddie was notorious in Lexington: a jack-of-all trades (some said a man-of-all-cons) who played the horses, ran a handbook on the side, and always seemed to have a wad of cash to lend—at a reasonable interest. That was how he got his nickname, "Money." His arrival anywhere in the black sections of town often prompted somebody to say, "Here come that money man."

Money conducted a boxing and karate clinic for boys, sending some tough young street fighters on to the Golden Gloves. Wendell had heard that he was connected with the local numbers and prostitution rings; rumor also had it that a certain local loan shark named Roger Withers wanted Money's ass on ice. Nothing had come of that; perhaps Withers had heard the story of how Money was sent to Eddyville for five years. Money was a master of martial arts and the way he told the tale was deceptively simple: "I was walkin' down the street an' I saw four cops beatin' up on my buddy, so I had to disable them." Nobody messed with Money.

When Wendell pulled over to the curb Money looked up and gave him a nod of greeting. He walked over to the car.

"Park yo ride in the side street, my man, they'll ticket you out here."

He did as he was told, while Money went back to his friends and called, "Come on over here, Wendell, and meet some of the bros."

Wendell was introduced all around, fumbling through the esoteric grips, handshakes, and palm slaps. It was all very confusing, but nobody seemed hostile.

"We all feel real good today," Money announced, looking surprisingly serious. "Everything is copasetic."

"Thas right," a short chubby-faced man affirmed. "Money is buyin'."

"Good," Wendell said, smiling at the circle of men.

"We havin' us a good time, takin' the sun an' shootin' the breeze," Money said, breaking into a satisfied grin that showed his gold fillings. "Now Wendell here has got hisself a real position. You know what this man do? Private detective, like on the TV. Got nothin' but rich clients who want him to find their diamonds. An' every night he sleep on satin sheets with a different woman. Ain't that right?"

Money's eyes sparkled with his own imaginative vision.

"Sounds good," Wendell said. "When do I start?"

The men chuckled and admitted they wouldn't mind having that kind of life.

"I could sure do that gig," a tall copper-colored man in a floppy hat said. "Be my own man. Keep my own time. Make all that money. Oh yeah. I could play a long time on that."

Wendell wondered what the men would think if he told them that a typical day consisted of slouching for hours on end in his car, eating candy bars and sipping tepid coffee from a thermos bottle and pissing into a wide-mouthed canning jar because he didn't dare leave his stakeout, while he waited for it to get dark enough to go peek in windows. Sometimes, like a real he-man, he even shouldered down doors and shot from the hip with his trusty instamatic camera. Other times he pawed through some poor slob's garbage.

He told them about Devil Dancer.

When he got to the part about trying to talk to Russell and Julian, a burly man with a droopy-eyed hound dog expression interrupted. "What you want to talk to them for?" he demanded. "They wouldn't shoot nobody's horse."

"Hell they wouldn't," Money fired back, a knowing glint in his eyes. "It all depend on the kind of horse you talkin' 'bout."

"Thas right. It do," a flat-nosed man with a long scar on his cheek said, shaking his bristling Afro. "It depend on the horse."

That got a couple of the men joking about do-rooms and the jones man.

"I'm not saying they did anything," Wendell said, letting the drug allusions slide. "I need to talk to them because they used to work for Brad Davis out at Sycamore Springs. Any of you men know where I might find Julian Harrison?"

"He be around," Money said with certainty. "Now Russell, that's one moody dude. He come back from Viet Nam real mean, but don't let that scare you—he rile cool. Julian's a different breeda cat. Some of the bros got no concept, but Julian he always *thinkin'*. He always askin' why. Tell you what. I say you want to see him, he talk to you."

As Money spoke two leggy women came sashaying around the corner, wearing brightly flowered summer dresses that were clingy at the waist and tended to ride up their thighs as they walked. They both were carrying laundry bags and talking with great animation. As they passed, Money reached out and patted the nearest one on the back.

"Where you goin', baby," Money crooned. "You're lookin' real good, you know. You ever need anything, Money's your man."

"You watch your mouth, Eddie Orleans, you hear?" the woman said with exaggerated seriousness. "An' keep yo hands to yo self." Then she set her body to jiggling a little and gave him a slow sardonic once-over. "But if I ever need any *little* thing, I'll keep *you* in mind." She blinked her big eyes and gave him a pronounced hip roll, strutting on down the sidewalk in jaunty full-juiced stride.

"I hear you talkin'," Money said, watching her action. "An' I see you shakin'." Then he turned to the men and said, "Oh, Lordy, there goes my heart. That's nice. So round an' firm an' fully packed. I'd walk a mile for *that*."

"Thas real nice," one of the men agreed. "But you got yo own at home."

"Keep that dog down," the scarfaced man warned. "You too old to tomcat."

"I'm not never gonna be too old," Money boasted playfully. "When that dog starts barkin', it's time to go huntin'. But I know what that sister wants—she's after finance, not romance. Me, I want *love*." Money had a way of saying "love" as if it had eight syllables.

Wendell watched the women go down the street until they turned a corner and went out of sight. Their way of walking waved a flag that commanded any man's allegiance—a licorishly sweet hip-swishing saunter that focused the attention until you thought you had discovered the exact center of the world.

Wendell could have stood there all day listening to Money spin out his rap, but he knew he had to pull himself away before he passed out. Although it was only mid-afternoon, he'd already had a long day and he was beat.

"Money," he said, putting a hand on his shoulder, "you're looking good." He ran an admiring eye over his impeccably pressed slacks, puff-sleeved silk shirt, and wide-brimmed black hat with a silver band. "It was good to see you again. I appreciate your putting a good word in for me with Julian. Let's get together for a drink sometime soon."

"I keep myself in life's fashionables," Money said, obviously pleased to be complimented on his clothes. "Prestige is something I got just by the threads I wear. You know what they say, man, 'If you got the name, play the game; if you got the rep, dress the role.'"

He hesitated a moment to scan Wendell's outfit then spoke again, "A man of your stature ought to dress the part. They got a display sale on silk underwear out at the Mall now. Got some real snazzy shirts, too. Go treat yourself and see if the chicks don't appreciate it."

Money wasn't putting him on; he was offering serious advice. Wendell didn't know what to say, no one had ever suggested that he ought to buy silk underwear before. "Glad to have met y'all," he said, raising a hand to the men in a parting gesture of good will.

"Say, where you livin' at, Wendell?" Money asked, walking beside him to his car.

"Out at Idle Hour Apartments." Wendell handed Money his card and reminded him to get in touch with Julian.

"Oh, man, that's no place to live. Nothin' but wall-to-wall carpetin' and wienies on the rotisserie, right?"

"Not quite," Wendell chuckled.

"Come on in here where the people live. Lexington is a nice-nasty town, dependin' on who you is an' who you know an' what color yo skin happen to be, but me an' the bros is happy today."

"I used to live downtown. Maybe I will move back."

"You do that." Money paused, appraising Wendell once more. "You ever thought of findin' yoself a nice sapphire to enrich yo life?"

"No, I haven't," he lied. He wasn't sure if Money was kidding him or not.

"Well, think about it now," Money said in a confiding voice. "You know there are two types of men, Wendell, those who know how to fuck pussy and those who don't. There are masters and there is riff-raff. The best place for a master, my man, is downtown."

They smirked at each other—two masters—and shook hands.

"You take it easy there, Money."

"I take it as it comes," Money replied smoothly. "That the only way."

Wendell grinned at him, waved again to the men, who didn't pay any notice, climbed into his car, and turned onto Jefferson. Money put one finger to his hat brim as he went by and made some remark to his friends. They all laughed.

7

When Wendell had turned forty several years before, one of his friends had quipped, "You're on the back nine now." That was how he felt, sweating in the mid-afternoon heat, exhausted and ineffectual, as if he'd been hiking up endless fairways beneath a relentless sun and three-putting every green. He had hardly begun his investigation, yet already he was so disoriented he didn't know what to do next. As he drove along, trying to decide where to go, his eyes began to play tricks on him. The street seemed to darken, as though a black cloud covered the sun, and then white specs danced in his sight. He felt a rush of dizziness and a splitting pain in his skull. He pulled over and bent forward to rest his head on the steering wheel, but when he shut his eyes everything started to spin. All those beers with Carl, on top of the bourbons with Brad Davis, had given him one hell of a hangover. He needed to get out of the heat, go back to his apartment, and take a nap.

When he woke up long shadows crawled across the room and a parking lot light glimmered outside the window. He turned on the television, hoping to hear what they had to say about Devil Dancer on the local evening news, but it was already too late for Walter Cronkite's grandfatherly recitation of bad tidings. Instead Porter Wagoner was strumming his guitar in his cowboy suit and singing about the girl he left back home with all the good folks in the lovely hills. Then a loud-mouthed used-car salesman came on, waving his hands in the air and promising to practically give his cars away. "Bring the little woman in with you," he weedled obscenely, "and we'll dicker." Wendell went to the bathroom and splashed cold water on his face and chest, shaved again quickly, combed his hair, put on some casual clothes, and started over to the Winn-Dixie to pick up the *Lexington Leader*.

As he stepped into the parking lot he saw a familiar green VW station wagon. He walked over and looked in the open window on the driver's side. Judging from the clutter, she was the kind of woman who used her car as an extension of her purse. Up on the dash he noticed a small pile of letters and cards; he reached in as casually as possible and flipped them over with his index finger to see the address:

Anna Crane

Apartment #5

Idle Hour Apartments

Lexington, Kentucky 40502

Wendell strolled over to the building, double-checked the mailboxes to make sure, climbed up a metal flight of steps that smelled of cat sperm, and rang the buzzer. Someone had wedged a note under the nameplate on the door: "Gone hunting Don." This is a mistake, he thought, but he went ahead and rang the buzzer again. Muffled splashing sounds came from inside; he heard feet slapping on the floor, a safety latch being pulled back. The door swung open and Anna, wrapped in a fuzzy white towel and with her hair lathered, stood before him, dripping.

"Oh. It's you." She looked at him with a quizzical half-smile as if she were waiting for a punch line.

"Are you busy?" The question was already out of his mouth before he realized how absurd it was.

"It's just that you caught me in a peculiar situation. I'm expecting someone."

Wendell's eyes shifted for a second from Anna to the note on the door. "I think this is for you," he said, handing it to her.

Anna glanced at the note, pouted a moment, then crumpled it up and tossed it aside.

"I guess I'm not expecting anyone," she said. "He's gone hunting."

"For what?" Wendell blurted out. "Nothing's in season."

"He doesn't care."

"He could get caught."

"Not Don. He always uses a bow and arrow."

Wendell didn't know what to say to that. He tried to picture the kind of man who would hunt out of season with a bow and arrow.

"You were taking a shower," he said solemnly, feeling foolish and out of place. But his tongue-tied awkwardness worked to his advantage, because Anna began to tease him.

"What gave you your first clue?" she smirked, shifting her weight to one hip so that the towel stressed her curves.

"The puddle at your feet," he said, smiling his most winsome smile.

"Fantastic!" Anna cackled. "I can see I don't need to ask if you've found out who shot Devil Dancer."

"No Ma'am."

"Well, don't sweat it." She flashed her dark eyes across his face. "You'll find what you want. What's your name, anyway?"

"Wendell Clay."

"Wendell Clay of *the* Clays?"

"On the black sheep side. My great-great-great grandfather, Ezekiel Clay, was one of the early settlers in Boonesboro. He got killed by the Indians."

"You're putting me on."

"No, I'm not, that's the honest truth," he said in his broadest Kentucky drawl.

She looked him over once again, smiled flirtatiously, and replied in a voice that mocked his, "Well come on in, Wendell Clay, and sit yourself down a spell while I finish my shower. It'll only take a minute. All I've got to do is rinse my hair."

Wendell thought there was no mistaking the invitation in her smile, but as soon as he entered the room she turned around and walked slowly toward the bathroom, giving him a glimpse of long tan legs and slim calves beneath the easy sway of the white towel.

He closed and locked the apartment door behind him, nearly tripping over a fancy candy-striped ten-speed bicycle parked inside the entrance. The living room had very little furniture and lots of plants. Pots of ivy and honeysuckle hung suspended from the ceiling; cactuses like candelabra and ferns like fountains rose from sturdy wooden tubs along the walls. All the windows were lined with flowers, mostly garlands. Through the glass doors he saw rows of flowerpots on the balcony. Two long-haired white cats were curled up in a pile of fluff on one of a matching pair of large beanbag cushions. The black horns of a bull were nailed on one wall above a painting of a matador being tossed over a bull's head. On another wall a travel poster, with "Off to Crete" in script at the bottom, depicted white stone columns by a sea of cobalt blue.

Two fancy gilded birdcages swung slightly from the ceiling in one corner. A dove was cooing inside one of them; in the other were two birds which looked like some unusual variety.

"Are those parakeets?" Wendell called out toward the bathroom door, his voice sounding raw in his throat.

"A pair of what?" Anna shouted back from the shower.

"I was asking, are those parakeets."

"I can't hear you. If you want to talk, open the door."

Wendell felt a heady mix of giddy elation and nervous anticipation. His most treasured erotic wish, nurtured by countless B movies and noir novels, was that one day a beautiful woman would invite him to share her shower.

Wendell opened the bathroom door slowly, half-expecting Anna to be standing on the bathmat waiting for him. Instead he found himself looking at a multi-colored shower curtain decorated with sea creatures, shells, and twining seaweed.

"What did you want?" Anna asked loudly, not realizing Wendell had stepped into the bathroom. "I couldn't hear you."

"It was nothing, really. I wondered if those birds you have are parakeets." The word sounded silly and vaguely risqué as he said it.

Anna peered around the edge of the shower curtain and gazed inquisitively at Wendell, letting her eyes linger.

"You should try this shower," she suggested. "I'm almost done."

Anna made her remarks in a matter-of-fact voice before she withdrew again behind the curtain, leaving Wendell to decide if "I'm almost done" meant, "Wait until I've finished" or "Hurry up and join me." He stared for a moment at the swirling underwater world of the shower curtain, as if searching for an answer.

Obeying an irresistible impulse he undressed quickly, like an athlete eager to take the field, then he pulled back the curtain and stepped inside.

Anna was standing with her face to the shower, rinsing her hair and scrubbing her back with a long-handled brush. As he reached out to touch her the water hitting her soapy hair and shoulders ricocheted into his eyes, so that when she turned around he must have looked like a lazy little boy rubbing his sleep-sewn eyes. She made a funny sound in her throat that might have been a laugh and handed him a washcloth to wipe away the stinging soap. By the time he could open his eyes again, she was standing with one leg up on the edge of the tub, lathering her crotch. He was determined not to burst out in obvious erection, since probably to Anna a body was a body, but as he watched the fine-sprayed shower water sluicing off her shoulders, drawing the soapsuds down between her breasts, beading on her bush and running in rivulets along her legs, his cock uncrimped, swelling to firmness with jubilant blood. She lowered her eyes to witness the transfiguration, then placing her hands beneath her breasts she lifted them gently toward him and said, "Do my breasts."

He did, soaping them with his bare hands until both nipples responded. She, in turn, took her long soft-bristled brush and lightly scratched along his thighs, prodding between them to buff his balls and run dozens of soapy nylon fingers over his exuberant penis. He dropped the soap and reached out to hug her. Her alluring eyes glanced up at him for a moment, but before he could bend to kiss her, she lowered her head and pulled back, resting her hands lightly on his arms, and when she spoke there was no hint of passion in her voice.

"I'm all done," she said calmly and stepped out of the shower. "You can stay in there as long as you like. There's a dry towel in the rack by the sink."

Wendell had an urge to rip aside the curtain and take her right there on the bathroom floor, but Anna's offer to stay as long as he liked challenged him to act nonchalant. He went ahead and finished washing, trying not to think about what erotic delights might be waiting for him in the next room. Suddenly he got another dizzy spell, everything darkened and fireflies danced in his head. Then the tub jumped up and slammed him on the head.

By the time Anna arrived Wendell was sitting in a foggy daze rubbing the back of his neck. With Anna's help he walked slowly to her bedroom. He eased himself down onto her waterbed, which surged back and forth from the sudden weight, rocking him until he felt woozy again. Anna wiped the sweat from his face with a wet washcloth and dried him off with a towel.

Wendell lay back, squinting from the pain that flamed up his neck and across his skull, which soon subsided into a dull ache that throbbed when he tried to move. He remained motionless while Anna, wearing a black bra and panties, covered him with a large blue beach towel sporting a dolphin design. She lay back on the bed beside him. For a few minutes there was only the sound of breathing.

"Could you fix me a drink?" Wendell asked.

"Sure, what would you like?"

"Do you have any bourbon?"

"No. How about some fruit juice? I've got some dynamite dope. Want to try some? It could help you to relax."

Wendell doubted if marijuana was what his doctor would have prescribed, but he nodded his assent. Anna came back with a tall glass of orange juice and a small plastic bag. She hunted up a sheaf of rolling papers from her dresser and proceeded to pack and roll a fat joint in what struck Wendell as astonishing speed.

She took a deep drag that made the tip glow. Then she smiled, exhaled with a sigh, and whispered, "My stomach just growled," as if she were conveying privileged information. She set the joint in Wendell's mouth and watched with amusement while he took a few tentative puffs.

"Hold it in your lungs," she instructed. "The longer you keep it in your lungs, the better the high."

She took another cheek-denting drag to show how it was done. After a few more tries he got the hang of it.

Suddenly he remembered sharing a cigarette with a Marine in his outfit after a long day of fighting on Saipan. They were sitting in a Chamorro cemetery, next to a Shinto shrine, their backs propped against a pile of sandbags. Wendell couldn't remember the guy's face or name, but he had an image of the glow of the cigarette in the dark, and he remembered loving the taste while fearing at the same time that a stray Jap might use the red tip as a target.

When the joint became so small it was hard to hold, Anna came up with a little clip shaped like an alligator and showed Wendell how to use it. Because he was too groggy to be steady, he knocked a small grain of red-hot coal onto his chest, which Anna quickly flicked away with her fingernail.

Wendell didn't think the grass was having any effect. He was expecting something like the muddled euphoria of alcohol, yet as far as he could tell he didn't feel a bit different.

"I don't think that one took," he said. "Maybe we should try another one."

"Don't you feel *anything?*"

"All I feel is dry in the throat." He took a satisfying swallow of orange juice. "Maybe we should try another one."

She gave a husky laugh.

"Do you feel anything?" he asked.

"Sure. I feel it from the first toke. Just wait. That's real Colombian cannabis. Believe me, it works."

He picked up the small dark-green alligator clip and started to examine it. He thought at first it was some kind of exotic miniature clothespin, a souvenir from Mexico or Florida. As he scrutinized it more closely he saw clearly that the tiny replica was designed for exactly the purpose it was being put to. He felt proud of himself for making this deduction. He liked to look closely and analyze things and figure out their significance.

He became aware that someone was laughing at him from far away. He turned his head slowly and discerned that it was Anna.

"What's so funny?"

"You," she chortled.

"What's so funny about me? I'm just looking at this...alligator."

"You big dummy, you're as high as a kite. You've been looking at that roach for ten minutes. Staring at it like it held all the secrets of the universe. How do you feel?"

Now that she mentioned it, he did feel different. The pain in his head and at the back of his neck hadn't gone away, but it did seem more remote, and there was a strange new sensation of soothing heat prickling his scalp. Watching the ebb and flow of Anna's breasts, Wendell felt a warmth all the way down to his groin.

Anna noted the modest tent pole lifting in the middle of the beach towel. She reached over and touched the tip, like a chef proud of a successful soufflé, then lay back again, smiling to herself, leaving one hand edged against his thigh. Cautiously Wendell tried to move toward her, but the slightest shifting of his head brought back the pain. Keeping his head frozen in place, he ventured five fingers onto her arm, gently brushing the smooth skin of her inner wrist. He let his fingertips play up and down her ribs then he slid his hand across her bra and touched the top of her breast. It was hard to tell where silk ended and skin began, yet there was no mistaking the way her nipple firmed to his touch. He could smell her dark fragrant hair and the faint soap scent clinging to her flesh. She lay back, breathing softly, and let him caress her.

After a few minutes Anna sat up with her head tilted to one side as if she were listening to subtle signals from the next room. She reached over and took one corner of the beach towel and, in one sweeping motion, tossed it to the floor. She eyed his insurgent cock (the way high divers look down at the water) before dipping her head and kissing the crimson crown with her warm full-lipped mouth, flicking it with her tongue. Then she ran her tongue around the shaft and down to the root, first with the fluttering lightness of a butterfly's wing, then much harder until he gasped with pleasure. She came back to the crown and in one swift movement took all of him in her mouth, squeezing with her lips and shoving her thrumming tongue against his veins. He could feel a hank of her damp hair passing back and forth across his belly as her mouth moved in long sweet reaches, teasing his blood to ecstasy.

Precisely at the point when he couldn't hold back any longer, she gave a last subtle thrust with her tongue, which sent a tingle quivering down his spine, and jerked her head away. Instantly he came in a powerful orgasm that seemed to compress his body in a giant hand. Despite all his years of sexual activity, Wendell had never experienced anything so intense before; his whole body buzzed and simmered.

Completely spent, he lay listless as dust waiting for his lurching heart to leave his throat and revert to its normal slug-a-slug in his chest. He felt smug and satisfied, marveling at Anna's skill and his own spunk. She sat beside him on the bed with the casual languor of a cat, keeping her own counsel. There was a long eye-averting silence before she spoke.

"What I just did for you, I don't do for everybody, you know," she said, answering an accusation he hadn't thought of making.

"I'm glad you did," he said, smiling gratitude. "Why did you?"

"You never quit playing detective, do you? Why did I invite you in? I don't know why. I don't always have reasons for the things I do. I try to stay free in my head and if it feels right to me, I do it. I go with the flow. There's no why about it."

He reached over and touched her thigh. "Can I do anything for you?" It was a gallant offer, although in truth he didn't have the strength.

"No," she replied a little too loudly. "Don't start anything you can't finish."

"That was great," he said, patting her thigh. "I really loved it."

"I know you did," she said without sarcasm. "I know I give great head, but don't take it too seriously, OK? That brings on bad trips. Just relax."

Even though he was already about as relaxed as he could get, she kept talking to him in a soothing yet strangely aloof voice: "Let your muscles go all floppy and droopy like a soggy dishcloth. Just relax and go to sleep."

She picked the towel up off the floor and spread it over him like a blanket. Then she rolled away, the waterbed rocked gently, and soon Wendell was asleep as Anna had commanded.

PART TWO

1

Wendell woke to the strange sensation of a cat scraping its rough tongue up his sweaty armpit. When he pushed her away she hopped gracefully onto his belly, making him say "Ouff." The cat circled, purring all the while, before pouring herself into a warm puddle of tickling fur that weighed on his stomach like a stone. His skull felt like a pressure cooker about to pop its lid, his muscles like mush. When he tried to lift his head a stiletto of pain stabbed the nape of his neck. He lay back, too sore to move, and listened to the birds celebrating the new day.

Wendell's present misery reminded him of a recent trip to his doctor, a grossly overweight man who came into the consulting room wheezing. There was something unnerving about your doctor being sick, rather like your tailor being naked.

"Looks like you've got a summer cold," Wendell volunteered.

"Well, your blood sugar and cholesterol counts are too high," the doctor replied.

"What does that mean? Am I dying?"

"Aren't we all?"

"How high is too high?"

"What most men our age have," he said, putting Wendell in a statistical group he had no desire to join. "Don't worry, your body is deteriorating at the normal rate. You should still have a few good years left."

The doctor, who always struck him as half stoic and half sadist, kept a straight face which did nothing to put him at ease. Wendell was already a hypochondriac; every morning he made a memento mori of his mirror as he noted with alarm everything from his softening gut and doubling chin to sore throats, stiff muscles, and furtive pains. The last thing he wanted to be reminded of was his mortality.

"If you'd prefer cancer," the doctor said, blowing his nose and toying with Wendell's anxieties, "smoke three packs a day and seek employment in the asbestos industry."

This time the doctor smiled and patted Wendell on the back, urging him to exercise more, drink less—the usual good advice that only made the patient feel guilty.

"Keep breathing," the doctor entreated as Wendell paid his bill. "Be well, be well."

Now the pain in his neck gave Wendell a new worry. Maybe his spinal cord was damaged. He felt so leaden it wasn't hard to fantasize about creeping paralysis.

After a while his meandering thoughts came to rest upon Anna. What had the previous night meant to her? Was he a one-night stand-in for the guy who didn't show, or was this the start of something? He had a vivid heart-clenching image of the swift way she had turned her head the moment before his orgasm. How had she anticipated him to the split second? Suddenly he had an overpowering urge to fuck her to a frenzy, to bring her to the boiling point and keep her there, staying in control until the time came to push her over the edge. How quickly his feelings of gratitude had turned into a desire for revenge!

The problem with emotions was that they didn't speak American; you never knew for sure exactly what they were telling you. Why had Anna responded to him? No doubt he had won her over by the masterful way he had handled himself in the shower! Who could say? It was all a delicate balance—your nose falls off and nobody loves you. Laura left him for another man. He was the one who had cheated on Kathy. Why doesn't love last? Some women wanted a sensitive soulmate who braked for butterflies, others a distant daddy they had to bend over backwards to please. It would be scatter-brained folly to put his heart on his sleeve when it came to Anna, but come nightfall Wendell knew he would be back at her door begging for more.

The whole male and female question was not only more complex than he thought, it was more complex than he *could* think, and since trying to think about it befuddled him, he decided that it was time to get out of bed and go fix some breakfast. He put water on to boil while he searched the kitchen in vain for instant coffee, finally settling for some tea with clear instructions on the side that any Chinese could read. Rather than waking him up, the tea relaxed his lazy muscles even more. His clothes were in a damp heap on the bathroom floor where he had dropped them. They felt clammy and stuck to his skin. He should have gone back to his own place and changed; instead, he searched Anna's apartment. Although she had a Sycamore Springs connection, he wasn't at all thinking of the case. Rather there was something so elusive about her that he wanted further clues to her true identity.

Her closet was a kaleidoscope of beautiful dresses and blouses, everything from scant miniskirts to low-cut dresses of other eras laced with sequins and beads. Wendell couldn't resist touching the fabrics and bending his nose to their witching blend of perfumes. Her dresser drawers were filled with silken underthings that slipped like water between his fingers. She had every kind of bra imaginable and her panties clustered in colorful disarray like a bouquet of wildflowers. The bottom drawer was empty. He stared at it for a long moment, reminded somehow of Laura.

Underneath a cement-block and plank bookcase, which held more flowerpots than paperbacks, he found a photo album that he leafed through with impulsive curiosity. One showed Anna standing by some grazing horses, with a bull staring at her in the middle distance, and a ruined castle on a hill in the background. In another she was riding within a stone-walled paddock about to jump her horse over a steeplechase water barrier. Others were of Anna being poled down a flower-banked stream in a flat-bottomed boat by a boy wearing what looked like a Cub Scout cap, or on a wide green manicured lawn looking up at the spire of a Gothic cathedral, or walking into the balcony-lined courtyard of a pub whose ornately lettered sign proclaimed The George. Wendell wondered how long ago it was that she had been in England.

At the back of the album, among a group of five-by-seven posed pictures, he found a series of more provocative shots, beginning with beach ball and bikini and ending with Anna nude on a velvet rug, which looked like layouts for a *Playboy* centerfold. She certainly had the body for it. He gave the last photo a minute scrutiny, wondering what Hugh Heffner could have found fault with. Maybe she didn't look pliant enough to be a bunny. She had a sternness in her smile, at once inviting and intimidating, that said sex with me will be at on my terms.

Back at his own apartment he showered and changed clothes, ground his morning coffee, fixed some cereal, fed the cat, and sat out on the balcony in the sun to ponder what he should do next. There was no lack of people to talk to. He had enough names to keep him going from door to door for weeks, filling up notebook after notebook with more information than he ever wanted about Brad Davis and Sycamore Springs Farm, and still not be one step closer to finding out who shot Devil Dancer. The problem was he simply wasn't certain he was following a warm trail. He even wondered whether there *was* a warm trail. No doubt lots of people, for one reason or another, didn't like Davis, some might even be capable of killing his horse, but what did that prove? If everybody with a motive committed murder, we'd all be homicides. For a horseman it was an all-too-common occurrence to have to put down one of his thoroughbreds—a badly broken leg, a failed kidney, all the ills that horseflesh is heir to—but only someone deeply troubled would be capable of shooting a prize stallion for no apparent reason. And if the killer was compelled by irrational motives, how was he supposed to reason out a method of finding him? After all, wasn't the definition of insanity something that didn't make sense?

When a crime was committed, one of the first things you did was look for someone who had broken their normal pattern of life. Grady's disappearance was suspicious, but that poor bastard had drifter written all over him. Grady's normal pattern was to go to the Mecca Bar every day, drink until he ran out of money, then find a job to make a few bucks so he could get drunk again. There were no secrets in that pattern. The world was filled with Grady Shifflets.

I know him, Wendell suddenly realized, putting the name together with the face he had seen playing pool at The Upstart Crow and at Keeneland scavaging the ground for unclaimed stubs (some guys, called "stoopers," made a living that way, but probably Grady was as bad at that as he was at everything else). He had also seen him at the Columbia Steak House, where Grady had been a dishwasher, the hopeless occupation of so many lost and lonely men.

Wendell decided to check out Julian and make a bigger effort to track down Grady. He also planned to hunt up his old friend Cliff Hargis, and to interview Charlene and Lily. Finally, he'd have to have a frank talk with Brad Davis, a man who did not like to show his weaknesses; but if he wanted to find out who killed his horse, he was going to have to put aside his arrogance and pride and reveal much more about his life. Most of all, he had to be specific about his gambling debts and the solvency of Sycamore Springs. Was the

Mafia involved? If so, who should he talk to? Conor? The man was a walking encyclopedia of underworld lore. Wendell doubted if Devil Dancer had been picked out at random—even crazies think they have a reason—so he had to go on the assumption that the killer believed he was getting back at Davis for some real or imagined wrong. Only Brad Davis knew for sure which men he had insulted or injured, stepped on or snubbed.

2

Wendell drove into downtown Lexington, parked on Short Street, and walked over to the Mecca Bar to check for Grady. Only a few men were inside. Grady wasn't among them and neither was Conor. The place smelled of spilled beer and trapped tobacco smoke. Wendell's throat felt so dusty he took a stool and asked for a mug on draft.

"You was in here yesterday, right?" the bartender said, pointing at Wendell with his cigarette. "I seen you talking to Conor."

"That was me. Tell him when you see him that I came by. I'm looking for Grady Shifflet. Has he been in today?"

"Naw. I ain't seen him in two, three days. He's a real regular around here, but he ain't been by lately. I see him, I'll tell him you're looking for him."

The bartender went down to the other end of the bar, leaving Wendell to sip his beer and eavesdrop on two endomorphs, beer-bellies pressed against the bar, swap dirty jokes. The man speaking slurred his words as though they tasted greasy.

"You hear the one about the guy who goes into the store and buys three merkins—blond, brunette, and redhead? The salesman says, 'Shall I wrap them for you, sir?' and the guy says, 'No, that's all right, I'll eat them here.'"

They both roared, shaking their blubber like sea lions, and guzzled down their beers.

The bartender came back with a fresh round, a cigarette slanting down from the corner of his mouth. He put his elbow on the bar, tilted his head and shut one baggy eye against the rising spiral of smoke, and spoke to Wendell in a soft voice.

"You know, this used to be a nice place. A bunch of regular guys. Now, I don't know, seems like it's becoming a lousy place. All the creeps in town come in here. The other day a guy wanders in with a wooden duck. You know, a decoy. He sets the duck down on the bar and says, 'Gimme two beers, one for me and one for my duck.'"

He stabbed out his cigarette butt on the inside edge of a beer mug, glancing over at Wendell to see if he had any response. Then he grabbed a handful of glasses and started washing, dunking them in sudsy water and hot water before setting them upside down on a soggy towel beside the sink.

"I nearly got robbed in here a few months ago. Did you read about that?"

"I think I missed it. What happened?"

The bartender raised his right eyebrow in surprise, as if no one could possibly not know the details of this particular robbery; then he leaned a little closer, his breath reeking of whiskey and nicotine. While he spoke a fresh cigarette fluttered on his lips like a bobbin by a boat dock.

"This guy looked kinda funny when he came in the bar—he musta been doped up, his eyes weren't right—and he asked for a bag of chips. He put the bag in one pocket and pulls a gun from the other pocket. When he done that I grabbed my Lugar from under the counter and started shooting. My first shot hit the cash register. That cost me three-hundred dollars. My next shot nailed him as he was going out the door. He fell dead on Short Street."

He paused at that point and scowled. A muscle knotted and unknotted in his cheek.

"Now I got bells on the doors and iron bars on all the windows. I had to get an unlisted number after that because lots of people who read about it in the paper were calling up to congratulate me for killing that 'dirty nigger'—which wasn't the way I felt about it, because I don't happen to be prejudice'. The colored can drink in here if that's what they want, just like the white. I don't want trouble, that's all."

"You're lucky to be alive to tell that story." Wendell wondered what he would have done in a similar situation.

"Listen, I spent twenty-eight months overseas, marched all over Europe—I was in the Battle of the Bulge and I never got a wound, not even a scratch. So I come back to the States and try to make an honest dollar and I get shot. Yeah, didn't I show you? The guy got a shot in while I was blowing the brains out of my cash register. Here's the scar, see. That's not bad. But if it had hit me over here, I'm dead. What is that, a couple of inches? That close. Otherwise, there's somebody else here pouring your beer."

"You guys shoulda seen what Buddy Hargis done the other day," the fat man chipped in. "He fired his shotgun at the side of his trailer, to see what it would do, and the crazy fucker blowed a hole in her as big as my head. I said, 'Buddy, what'd you expect with double aught buck?' It looked like he taken a big can opener to the side of that thing. I swear."

"Buddy Hargis, is he any relation to Cliff Hargis?" Wendell interjected.

"First cousin, I think, why?"

"Cliff and I grew up together. Do you happen to know where he lives?"

"Buddy probably would. He's out there at Such-and-Such Estates off the Paris Pike."

Wendell knew the trailer park he was referring to.

"Here, I got his number," the fat man said.

"Thanks, I owe you one."

Then the other fat man offered to tell the story about the traveling salesman and the spastic girl, but Wendell said he had some people to see, paid for everybody's beer, and left.

Across the street, a wild-eyed man with turbulent hair was foisting leaflets on all and sundry and chanting in a scratchy voice, "Change your life." On the steps nearby a drunk was attempting to eat an ice cream cone, which wavered in front of his face before it fell. Watching him trying to pick it up, Wendell knew how he felt.

Wendell decided to drive a few blocks to the pawnshop to see if Grady might have tried to hock anything recently. If he did, maybe he left an address. Rosenberg's Pawnshop on Vine Street was plastered with a hodge-podge of posters and signs. The most prominent said **1000 GUNS**. The front window featured a fancy display of handguns arrayed according to size. There were pistols suitably designed for the shoulder holster, the purse, or the school knapsack. Inside, guitars hung like Kentucky hams from the back wall. Beneath the glass countertops a museum of cameras, watches, and pocket calculators were deployed in semi-circles. All the missing items from miles around had a way of eventually ending up at Rosenberg's. The pawnbroker eyed Wendell as if he were a stoplight and gave him two words of his time: "Yes," he knew Grady; "No," he hadn't pawned anything. Only the chime above the door said goodbye.

3

Before Wendell had the car keys out of his pocket someone in a maroon El Dorado honked, slammed on the brakes, shifted into reverse, and came whining back beside him. Money lowered the tinted window on the passenger side, leaned across the spacious leopard-skin seat, and shouted, "Right after you go yesterday, Julian came by. I told him you want to see him. He say that cool. Talk to you any time. He livin' with his chick over at three two six Deweese Street. He see you today if you be free."

Wendell's thanks were lost in the screech of tires. A blue cloud of exhaust fumes hung where Money's car had been.

Although he doubted that anything would come of questioning the man, Wendell decided to look up Julian while he had a chance. After that there was plenty of time to locate Cliff Hargis. Even if his investigation failed, he planned to tell Brad Davis in detail how he had followed every possible path, dead ends and all.

A light-brown woman with a frizzy halo of reddish hair answered his knock. She studied him from behind her granny glasses before bringing him into the stuffy front room and calling out for Julian. Wendell sat down on an army cot piled with cushions. On the opposite wall, above a sophisticated stereo with flanking speakers, a carved African mask as big as a halved watermelon hung from an outsized nail. A panther with human features: slit eyes smoldering, snubbed-back nostrils scenting prey, gaping mouth flaunting incisors. Nevertheless the mask's total effect was not threatening, rather suggesting attentiveness to spirit voices and ancestral drums. Wendell almost expected it to begin to dance on the wall.

Julian was a well-built man of medium height wearing a purple turtleneck sweater, patched bluejeans, and a pair of run-down sandals that flapped as he walked. He had a slight limp, as if he were nursing a bum knee. A maroon beret floated on top of his resilient black hair. He scrutinized Wendell through gold-rimmed glasses, wiped a hand across his mustache, and widened his mouth into a friendly smile.

"Bring us some beers, honey," he called, unfolding a wooden chair for Wendell. "That's Althea," he said, nodding his head toward the kitchen.

Althea came back with the beers, then she excused herself and went into the back of the house where she began scolding a child.

"Don't drop it. Hey, if you drop my stuff I'm gonna hurt you." They heard something fall and now Althea was really angry. "Didn't I tell you to stay on that bed? Get back up there before I smack you good, you hear? Now I'm gettin' tired of this. I don't understand this kind of foolishness."

Julian sat forward on his chair and listened sharply, trying to hear what the child was saying in defense. By the time Althea was done scolding, the child was crying. Julian scowled and closed the door. Then he sat down, pulled the tab on his beer can, and started to talk.

"Money said you wanted to see me about workin' on that horse farm. I was only there maybe two weeks. Can't tell you much from that. Me an' Russell needed bread so we put time in out there. But it seems they got this lab—I didn't know horse farms had those. Listen, I'm gonna be straight with you—Money said it was cool so I'll say it direct—I needed the bread to score, an' that lab looked real temptin'. I come back from the Nam with a monkey on my back that woulda made King Kong feel small. Over there shit was as common as beer cans in a vacant lot. Kids who shoulda been in grade school would stand outside the base an' trade you *bach bien* for candy bars. I come home with one hell of a jones. So that's the story—Davis caught us checkin' out his lab an' he fired us. We didn't take nothin', but the man could see it comin'."

"I appreciate your honesty." Wendell was pleasantly surprised by Julian's apparent frankness. "I want to be honest with you too. I'm making a routine check on all the personnel that Mr. Davis let go recently. I'd certainly be grateful for anything you could say that might help me out." He felt sure he had started off on the right foot this time.

"I can tell you this," Julian said with an ironic smile, "it wasn't me. I admired the hell outa that horse—had a paddock all to himself, his only job was to service some mares, that horse had himself a life. I don't groove on this Davis dude, y'understand, he kicked me off his farm. But he coulda given me an' Russell some real grief. He coulda called the cops an' made accusations, y'know, so I got no hard feelins. Hey, if I got it on about somebody, he's gonna hear about it from me in person, to his face. I get down on a dude, I don't shoot his horse; that's the kinda symbolic shit honkies is into."

"Don't get me wrong," Wendell said. "I just wondered if you saw or heard anything that might give me a lead. Like that last remark you made, what did you mean by that?"

"Oh, man, if you wanna get deep, I'll get deep. Listen, I was in the fuckin' Nam. I saw it all. I was a Marine. Thought I was a real bad cat so I joined up to improve my rep. Wanted to kill me some gooks an' pass out their ears to the kids on my street. I was all physical then, all muscle. You hit me, I hit you back twice as hard. I played football, never learned the rules, somebody come at me I come at him, rammed them with my head like a crazy goat. I didn't tackle people, I smashed into them. In boot camp we're out on the drill field with our bayonets an' the sergeant shouts, 'Scumbags, there are two types of Marines, the quick and the dead, which are you?' an' we holler back, 'The quick! The quick!' Then he says, 'What is the spirit of the bayonet?' an' we shout, 'To kill! To kill!' Oh yeah, killin', that was gonna be my thing."

As Julian spoke Wendell recalled a dusty Parris Island parade ground, and a raggedy ass recruit with a shaved head yelling gung-ho slogans for his sadistic hard charger of a DI.

"Do they still wake you up by shouting, 'OK, shitheads! Drop your cocks and grab your socks'?" Wendell asked, grinning in spite of himself.

"Oh, hell, yes," Julian laughed. "You were in the Corps too?"

Wendell nodded.

"Then you know what I'm talkin'." Julian glanced at Wendell with respect.

"I know," Wendell said. "But go ahead, I'm listening."

"I was in Indian County two months before I wised up. At first, it was my old life all over again, only deadlier. Somebody shoots at me, I fired my piece on a go=go back at them. I even asked to walk point. I was lookin' for trouble. We spent a lotta time by a river over there, drinkin' 33 beer an' smokin' joints soaked in opium an' watchin' the sampans slidin' along, checkin' them out for Charlie. The dudes would get bored, y'know, take pot shots for the hell of it at the boats on the river an' at the water buffalo on the far shore. Then some things happened. One time I saw a little girl get shot off the bow of one of them boats an' into the water. Some asshole squeezed off a round, only wanted to scare the kid, y'know, make her jump, but the stupid fuck hit her by mistake." Julian grinned bleakly, staring at his sandals. "Grease one."

Julian stood up to go for some more beer. As soon as he was gone Wendell found himself reliving things he thought he had repressed for good. He was back on Saipan. After three weeks of fighting to the northernmost tip, it was all over except for a few grim games of

Flush the Sniper, pitting flame throwers and satchel charges against little men in mustard-colored uniforms making a final stand in tree or cave. Wendell had taken part in the house-to-house fighting for Garapan, and he had seen the grisly results of the Japs' last gasp banzai charge, where high on *sake* and screaming "Malines die," they had attacked with bayonets tied to bamboo sticks. Many of them had taken the easy way out; he had seen body after body with the right hand gone and the chest blown away. As he trudged through the foot-deep chalky dust on the way to Marpi Point, a pale-faced Marine had stopped him and said, "You don't want to go up there. It's too awful."

When he reached the cliffs overlooking the sea, what Wendell saw on the tortuous jumble of volcanic rocks two-hundred feet below beggared description. Fired by patriotic zeal and an insane fear of what the victors would do to them, the Japanese civilians on Saipan were committing mass suicide. There was nothing that could be done to make them stop. With horrid fascination Wendell watched three kimono-clad women who sat by the sea and combed their luxuriant hair before joining hands and wading slowly into the deepening water. He saw their hair streaming on the waves. Then he doubled over and vomited into the dusty grass.

Wendell came out of his reverie with a start. He had no idea how much time had passed. He could hear Julian in another room talking to Althea. The child was no longer crying and Althea was laughing. Wendell wondered what had triggered his flood of memory. Was it something Julian had said? Or was it that crying child? In a moment Julian came back. When he sat down he was smiling, but as soon as he started talking again, the smile vanished.

"The incident that really set me off happened one very hot day when we were out humpin' the boonies to give the VC something to shoot at—no shit, that was our strategy, that was Search and Destroy, that was how we were suppose' to win the war. Anyway, we made some heavy contact, so we called for air support an' hunkered down in the mud an' waited for the gun ships. They got there real quick, I'll say that, an' started blastin' up the jungle in fronta us. They cut loose with their rockets an' cannons an' just wasted everything in sight. Incredible damage. Then there was a lull an' my buddy stood up an' took off his helmet to wave it at the last Cobra comin' over. I shouted at him to keep his head down, but it was too late. The pilot hosed him down with his miniguns an' napalmed our position. My buddy got it in the face an' he toppled back into the hole on top of me. Saved me from the napalm. He didn't die right away, an' there wasn't a goddamn thing I could do because we had used up all the morphine the night before to get high. Gawd, that sounded so bad, man dyin'.

"I picked up my buddy's helmet an' started cryin' an' cussin' at him. 'What the fuck do you think your helmet's for?' I shouted at him. 'To protect your brains, stupid. It's a fuckin' brain bucket. You wear a helmet to save your head. If you don't save your head you lose your ass.' I kept sayin' stuff like that an' damn if I didn't start thinkin', 'Hey, ain't that the truth! They wouldn'ta gone to all the trouble makin' steel pots if brains weren't worth savin', right?' No foolin', it got me thinkin'—about the war an' about my life. It occurred to me out there in that stinkin' hole with my dead buddy spillin' his that brains were to think with. Smart, huh?"

Wendell nodded: he had seen the way soldiers react after a battle, wandering around in a trance gazing vacantly at the dead or staring off into outer space.

"I used to hate my helmet," Wendell said, nervously crackling the beer can in his hand. "But there were times when I would have crammed my whole body inside one if I could."

"I know I'm not the first dude to learn that war is Hell," Julian said. He leaned forward in his chair and began to gesture emphatically. "After my buddy got hit everything started to look different. When

I tried to protest they laid this rap on me about 'selective ordinance' an' 'dispersal patterns' an' 'collateral damage' an' 'friendly fire.' O man, they really laid the words on me. I was in Saigon, an' I'm walkin' down Tu Do Street an' I see all these bar girls with flowers in their hair an' PX transistors held up to their ears waitin' in line outside the movie house to go see *Gone With the Wind.* An' I'm thinkin, 'Oh man, that's heavy. The Man controls the words an' the images—he's gonna abstract you so far away from your own asshole you ain't never gonna find your way home.' Then I pass this little store. Got a hand-lettered sign in the window that said: LAUNDRY COKE GET SCREWED. That got to me. Like we'd dropped thousands of tons of bombs on Hanoi an' billions of words an' images an' dollars on Saigon, which city was really bein' destroyed?"

From what Wendell had heard about the South Vietnamese, he doubted if Saigon needed any lessons on corruption from the U.S., but he let Julian have his say. Yet as Julian's monologue continued, Wendell grew increasingly restless. He had a case to investigate, and ever since he was a boy he had always started to fidget whenever he felt a sermon coming on. But an old inarticulate sense of soldierly solidarity asserted itself, and so he forced himself to pay attention. Julian's problem was he didn't know when to quit. Wendell knew all about that. When he had returned from the Pacific with a samurai sword in his seabag and a few superficial wounds in aesthetic places, all he had wanted to do for weeks was swap war stories with other vets. But that quickly wore off, and for the past twenty years he hadn't even wanted to think about the things he'd seen. He didn't envy the Marines in Vietnam who had to fight without honor and die without glory.

"When I returned home, stateside life seemed irrelevant," Wendell said. "What did they know about what I'd been through? I was set to take part in the invasion of Japan, and the word was that it could cost a million men. When Truman dropped the bomb, I wasn't sorry. I only wished we had had it sooner to drop on Iwo Jima. That fucking place *deserved* the bomb. I was happy to be alive, believe me, but I knew all those Japanese died so that could happen. You end up feeling both grateful and guilty. Why did they die, and not me?"

Wendell was surprised by his own emotional outpouring. His voice almost shook as he spoke of these things. Something had infiltrated his long-standing defenses, causing him to break his self-imposed silence.

"Very well spoken," Julian said, looking at Wendell with admiration. "I'm sorry if I'm monopolizin' this conversation, but this stuff came to me like a revelation, an' I'm tryin' to have it make a difference in the way I live. I don't trust words an' images. I don't believe anything unless I see it with my own eyes, an' then I want to get up close an' touch what I'm lookin' at."

The next moment a child rushed into the room. He appeared to be about four and all he was wearing was a small football jersey that ended at his knees. Althea came to the door and cast a critical eye as the child scrambled onto Julian's lap.

"Leave him be, honey." Julian laughed as he bounced the child on his pumping knees. "Me an' Wendell here been havin' us a good talk."

"Uh Huh. An' I bet I know who's been doin' most of the talkin'."

Althea squinted at Wendell, crossed her arms, and leaned against the door frame to listen.

"What hurts me," Julian continued, "is to see my black people bein' taken in by the con. I see some of the bros wearin' these big Afros out to here, got the gold earring on, a tiki around the neck, wearin' a dashiki, bell bottoms, lavender platform shoes—I say, 'Shit man, where you comin' from? You look like a composite photo of a schizo pimp!' That gets 'em riled, but after they cool off, then we can rap. Nobody in lavender platforms is gonna win a revolution."

Althea shook her head and scolded in mock-seriousness, "Julian, you leave my family out of this."

"I'm not talkin' about your cousin, honey. Don't get me wrong, I'm not like some of the bros who think the gun is the solution. The word with them is 'take ten'—that's ten whites before you die. They shout that out in the streets an' whitey thinks they're talkin' about a coffee break. No. I'm talkin' about winnin' a battle with your own brain. Be real an' you're free, that's my rap. Use your head, I say, that's your shit detector. Black bones fertilize this land, black blood have watered it, be real, be smart, an' it's yours an' your children's children. Don't listen to the words, don't be taken in by the images, that's all a scam, those're just substitutes for bein' alive."

Julian wasn't talking to anyone in the room. He was addressing the mask on the wall as though it were an imaginary black audience. Wendell noticed that Althea kept nodding her head as Julian spoke. At least he had one follower. The child had sat quietly, but now he was attempting an ascent of Julian's chest. Pouting his lower lip, and with a totally absorbed look on his face, he reached out to snatch the beret that danced on Julian's hair just beyond his grasp. Julian tilted his head back and forth in play, then handed him the beret and set him on the floor.

"You're quite a speaker," Wendell said, rising to his feet. "You've given me some things to think about."

"Thank you very much." Julian took Wendell's remarks as a genuine tribute. "In the Marines we were taught how to take care of ourselves in the dark. How to kill with our teeth an' assemble a rifle by touch. A time is comin' when the lights are gonna all go out. An' then a blind black man is gonna lead us. Things is gonna turn upside down an' all around then, I can see that plain, but my black people are gonna come out all right. Whitey, I don't know about. He's gotta learn to live in the dark, an' I don't think he can."

4

For a man who held words suspect, Julian had no trouble speaking. Wendell was impressed by some of his notions, but as many a would-be prophet he seemed to wager too much on apocalypse: like the followers of that end-of-the-world cult of the last century who, on the designated day, donned white robes and climbed to their housetops to greet the King of Kings—only to make a sheepish descent the next morning to review their math. Nevertheless, meeting with Julian and Russell had served its purpose: Wendell now felt sure that neither was involved in the shooting. So far he was doing an outstanding job of finding out who *didn't* kill Devil Dancer. Several million people in Kentucky didn't pull that trigger, was he destined to spend the rest of his life talking to them one by one and clearing them of suspicion? Could all this talk be designed as diversion, luring him in the wrong directions? He needed to pick what appeared to be a promising trail and follow it until it led somewhere or petered out. Who knows? Maybe he could get lucky: like the hunter who tracked the black bear and discovered Mammoth Cave.

Wendell wasn't ready to admit that he was lost. He remembered the story his father told about what Daniel Boone said when asked if he had ever been lost in the forests of Kentucky: "I can't say as ever I was lost," Boone replied, "but I was *bewildered* once for three days."

Wendell located a pay phone at the Transylvania student center and called Buddy Hargis, who gave him the address of his cousin. Cliff Hargis lived in a carriage house on an alley behind one of the palatial homes on Second Street. Surely he would have some inside information about Devil Dancer. Wendell knocked on a smaller door cut into huge double-doors built to accommodate a four-in-hand.

"A face from the past," Wendell said when he saw his old friend.

There was an awkward silence before Cliff spoke.

"Wendell, long time no see. I didn't recognize you at first. How have you been, ol' buddy? Is something wrong?"

"Do I look that bad?"

"I've seen worse," Cliff remarked sardonically. "What have you been up to these days? You still painting houses?"

"I'm a detective."

"Yeah, and I'm an astronaut."

"No, I'm serious. I really am."

"That's interesting. What's my offense? Say, this wouldn't be about me and..."

"It's not about you. It's something else. I thought maybe you could help."

"Try me."

The completely remodeled carriage house had a cathedral ceiling topped by a stained-glass skylight. A second floor balcony ran around the three sides where bedrooms replaced the old haylofts. Cliff, a man who took pride in craftsmanship of all sorts, had refinished the antique furniture himself. Wendell had last seen his high school friend several years ago when he had painted his father's house.

"You worked for Brad Davis, right?"

"Until we had a little falling out."

"What was the problem?"

"Hey, this is about Devil Dancer isn't it? Who are *you* working for?"

"Davis, who did you think?"

"And he asked you to talk to *me*?"

"No. Brad's groom Louie mentioned you. This is my idea. I wondered what you could tell me about Devil Dancer and Brad's operation."

"Let me get this straight, you're investigating your client—your old high school pal, the guy who hired you!"

"He's your pal too; we hung out together, remember, and played on the same team."

"Yeah, but all I did was block, you were the guy who got to catch passes and score touchdowns...and drop some too," Cliff added, winking to get his goat.

"Tell me how you came to work for Brad," Wendell urged. "Did you two keep in touch?"

"Not really, but I'd see him around town. It was more a spur of the moment thing. My folks aren't from the Iroquois Hunt Club set, but my daddy sure knew horses and so do I. I ran into him a few years back and offered my services. You know Brad, he thinks he can do it all; he doesn't even have a farm manager and he ignores his trainer; he put me in charge of the breeding shed, and for a while there he stayed out of my way."

"What kind of horse was Devil Dancer?"

"Magnificent! As fine a stallion as I've ever seen. You couldn't fault him, his conformation was perfect. And he knew it too. He loved to show off for a crowd. He'd stand there with that regal curl to his neck, just like a chessboard knight, and soak in all the adoration. He was the equine American dream. I'll never forget that horse. Never. Did you ever see him?"

"I saw him win the Blue Grass Stakes. Louie showed him to me once. When I came to his stall Devil Dancer poked his head out and nickered like he was glad to see me."

Wendell remembered Devil Dancer's large, lambent eyes, how the horse had gazed at him for a sustained moment, first one eye, then the other, before gobbling down a carrot and snuffing his face with a nose as soft as velvet. He felt his warm breath on his hand. Devil Dancer was a big strapping dude capable of killing a man with one kick, yet with Wendell he had been friendly and gentle. Who could shoot such a superb animal?

"He was like that," Cliff admitted, "he played favorites. There were people he liked on first sight and people he didn't. He was sensitive, moody, you could definitely hurt his feelings and he had a mischievous streak."

"How was he in the breeding shed?"

"At first he was too much of a stud; he was so aggressive he'd savage some of those mares. It was all we could do to control him. I'll tell you he was a randy rogue, a real rank stallion, with too much tool for the job. We put a pad on the mare's back, a muzzle on him, and we always used the big roll to keep him from doing too much damage, and still he'd sometimes lunge at those mares and drive them into the wall. We needed six men to help him do his thing."

Wendell had lived in the Bluegrass long enough to know exactly what went on in the breeding shed. Talk about unnatural acts! Foreplay was a study in frustration as the poor teaser pony first got the mare in heat; then she was led into the breeding shed with one leg hobbled and a twitch twisting her lip; next came the stallion, all washed and ready, with men on both sides to guide his penis and keep him from toppling off the mare's back. Seconds later he'd flag his tail to signal that the deed was done and the happy couple were separated as quickly as possible. Wendell also knew about the big roll, a kind of padded rolling pin that was positioned between a prodigiously endowed stallion and the mare's vagina to limit penetration.

"Was he a difficult horse?"

"Hot bloods are high-strung by nature. He had a fiery temperament; he was fractious, spooky as hell, and very territorial. He'd chase anything—a bird, a squirrel—that came into his paddock. He was skittish, headstrong, he'd throw a tantrum if you didn't give him a carrot when he wanted one. He'd pin back his ears and look sulky. When he did that, watch out. Hell yes, he could be incorrigible, a real brat. But he was a great horse, a very spirited individual with a lot of ability and heart. When he was in a good mood, he was as playful as a puppy."

"Did he stamp his get?"

"I'll take a rain check on that one."

"What do you mean?"

"At first, no problem. I suppose you follow the primo sales like everybody else in Kentucky. Devil Dancer's yearlings used to fetch top dollar at Keeneland. You looked at them and you saw their daddy. They all had that swagger, even when they were standing still, that fire in the eye. Who wouldn't pay hard cash for horseflesh like that?"

"But what?"

"Man, you maybe don't want to get into this. I don't know if you noticed, but last month there were only three Devil Dancer yearlings at Keeneland, and even though Davis had a sexy exercise girl in a tight tanktop and satin hotpants walk them around the arena they still didn't bring much."

"So he's deeper in the hole than I thought."

"You know what they say about how to make a small fortune in the horse business?"

"Tell me."

"Start out with a large fortune." Cliff gave Wendell a sardonic smile as the punch line registered. "I don't keep the guy's accounts, so I can't crunch the numbers for you, but my guess is that Davis is deeper in debt than even *he* thinks!"

"The death of Devil Dancer will ruin him," Wendell said, acknowledging that an entire Kentucky kingdom could depend on the potency of a single horse. "Is that why you quit, because you saw what was coming?"

"Hey, I don't turn my back on a man when he's down. But Brad was up to his eyeballs in quicksand and he thought Devil Dancer could pull him out. I didn't."

"What do you mean?"

Cliff paused a moment to consider his next words.

"This has got to be strictly confidential between the two of us. If any of this should ever come out in court, you didn't learn it from me, OK?"

"Sure, it's a deal. I just want to know the whole story."

"Maybe yes and maybe no, but here goes. I don't know what he told you, but Brad Davis is in debt like you wouldn't believe. He owes people in Vegas, he owes people in Lexington, I wouldn't be surprised if he owes people all over the goddamned world. And to pay off his debt he got the bright idea that Devil Dancer was a cash cow that never ran dry. He was selling shares and pledging seasons on that horse left and right."

"Brad told me that Devil Dancer wasn't syndicated."

"He isn't, officially. But Davis is in bed with some silent partners who may be skimming off the top. He's got more scams and sweetheart deals going down than anyone can keep track of. Why that horse was as highly leveraged as junk bonds. But Brad wasn't worried. He thought Devil Dancer would always be there to bail him out."

"What finally made you quit?"

"At first I went along with it all," Cliff explained, looking over at Wendell for understanding. "The money was good and handling horses was what I did best, and so when Brad began to extend the book on Devil Dancer I figured, hell, why not, he loves his work, a few more trips to the breeding shed can't hurt. But about halfway through last season Devil Dancer began to change. Instead of raring to go he'd stand around, toeing the floor with one foot and acting disinterested, his heart wasn't in it anymore. He'd traipse down to the breeding shed, taking his sweet time, not even willing to try. Right in the middle of the season he had become a shy breeder who couldn't raise his stick, and when he did he mostly shot blanks. It was taking more covers for the mares to catch and time was running out. Devil Dancer even wore a cock ring during breeding season so nothing was wasted."

Wendell knew that stallions, even some who weren't good performers in the breeding shed, had a tendency to masturbate, by slapping their penis against their stomach, when they were alone in their paddock.

"Brad was losing it," Cliff continued. "If the banks ever called in his loans, he'd take a bath, and his prime collateral couldn't cut the mustard anymore. I pleaded with him to give Devil Dancer a break, let him rest in his paddock and get his spunk back, but Davis told me, 'He's here to breed and by god that's what he's gonna do.' That's when I quit. I haven't seen Brad since."

"So who do you think shot Devil Dancer? One of Davis's creditors?"

"It's possible; I really don't know. If you wanted to wreck the guy, financially speaking, and make sure he stayed wrecked, that would probably be a good way to do it."

"These 'silent partners' you spoke of, what do you know about them?"

"One is a pretty unsavory character."

"Who's that?"

Cliff studied Wendell a moment, deciding if he really wanted to pursue the matter.

"A guy named John Lane."

"What makes you suspect him?"

"He looked the part. Some gangsters actually dress like the ones in movies. This guy drove a cream-colored Impala with tinted windows and he had on a shiny suit, a silk shirt with matching tie, two-tone wingtip shoes, the whole outfit—complete with diamond accessories."

"When did you see him?"

"He came out to the farm. He and Davis had an animated discussion."

"Was there anybody with him?"

"Now that you mention it, yeah. Two thugs, big guys, they sat in the car."

"Do you know their names?"

"No, thank God. I'm glad I don't. I tell you, it was all too much for me. I already know more than I should. Devil Dancer was a pawn in a pyramid scheme that was about to collapse. I'm glad I won't be around when the dust settles. If I were you, I'd get out while you can."

Cliff's face tightened when he gave this last piece of advice.

"I didn't realize the story was so complicated."

"More than we'll ever know," Cliff asserted. "Brad Davis doesn't keep a paper shredder in his office to hide his charitable contributions."

"What a tangled web we weave," Wendell remarked under his breath.

"At least some of us do," Cliff replied. "As for me, I've had enough to last me a lifetime."

Wendell's head was whirling as he tried to absorb all the information Cliff had provided that put the case in a multitude of new perspectives. Why had Davis hired him in the first place if he had so much to hide? Maybe Louie, when he said that it was all "bad news," was trying to tell him something. On the drive back to his apartment, Wendell tried to sort out a vertiginous rush of disconnected thoughts about Brad Davis and Devil Dancer.

5

A man with a shotgun stopped Wendell at the gate of Sycamore Spring Farm, eyed him like a spider on his sleeve, then telephoned to the main house for confirmation before waving him through. On the winding drive to the house Wendell pulled over for a moment to watch some sunken-headed mares grazing. The way they kept their noses to the grass seemed to bring the wide green field into focus, as if each were saying, "Here. Here. This is the best spot. Bow your head and be nourished." In contrast, their spindly legged foals rolled their glossy coats on the rough ground or kicked up their heels and cavorted around the spacious pasture, romping off this way and that, up hill and down dale, with random bursts of speed.

When he got to the main house Wendell parked his car and walked up the steps to the portico. A guard sat in a metal chair propped against a pillar with a rifle in his lap.

"Who are you?" Wendell asked, beating him to the draw.

The guard sneered like a horse tasting a tight bit, and his face reddened in anger. He wanted to speak, but his opening line had been stolen. He sat there, red as a beet, his lips crimped in scorn, going through a kind of crisis. Wendell would have laughed if it hadn't been for the latent danger of the situation. How touchy some people could be. Finally, like a man who had dislodged a piece of meat stuck in his windpipe, his face subsided to fleshy pink.

"Name's Calvin," he said with a submissive grin. "Mr. Davis is inside."

Davis stood at the front door looking surly.

"Wendell, where in hell have you been? I called your apartment last night and you weren't home. I hope you can explain yourself. I hired a detective, you know, not a playboy."

Now it was Wendell's turn to feel flabbergasted. Brad's sarcastic crack had come too close for comfort. Could there be another detective following *him?* Before he could respond, Davis clamped a hand on his shoulder and steered him down the walnut-paneled wall, past the fading portraits in their ornate gilt frames, to the den, where they settled into easy chairs.

"Grady Shifflet's missing," Wendell announced. "Nobody's seen him at the Mecca Bar for several days. I went to his room, and the place is a mess. It doesn't look like he's been there for a long time. I've also talked to those two black men you fired. I don't think they had anything to do with it." Wendell decided not to mention his conversation with Cliff.

"No. Those colored boys were not involved. No, sir," Brad said, looking preoccupied. "But what about Grady? Can't you find him?"

"That could be hard." Wendell gestured with both hands for emphasis. "If he's still around, he'll show up at the Mecca Bar. The chances are he's on a drunk, but I think his absence is suspicious. A wino like Grady could go crazy and kill a horse for no good reason."

"You're right," Brad snapped. "There's no telling what a man will do when he's drunk. But I want him found."

Wendell sympathized with Davis' impatience. After all, he was an important person who paid generously and expected Wendell to pick up the scent and hound the culprit down. But was this that kind of case? Like most people, Brad probably assumed the world was orderly, perhaps with brief intervals of chaos, but maybe it wasn't that way at all. Maybe randomness ruled and there was no way to satisfy Brad's logical expectations. Besides, wasn't he withholding information himself that only made Wendell's job more difficult? Unless something was done soon, Brad Davis and Sycamore Spring Farm were facing financial collapse.

"The cops were here this morning." Davis spoke with weary irritation. "They said that *they* didn't know what to do next. I don't know either, but it's not my job to know, am I wrong?"

"A case like this is a tough nut to crack. There are dozens of people I plan to talk with, but so far nothing has clicked. The motive is just not apparent." Wendell waved one hand in the air and looked abstracted. "I keep asking myself why anybody would want to kill Devil Dancer and all I come up with is a blank. What was there to *gain* by killing a horse like that?"

"I know it's a hard case," Brad said. "But that was *my* horse and I want the killer. What do you intend to do today? Can you tell me?"

Wendell stood up, as if to demonstrate his eagerness to get on the job, and began pacing the floor. "I'm going to keep hunting for Grady. And I plan to talk to more of your workers. Right now, if you don't object, I'd like to ask your wife and daughter a few questions. I hate to keep insisting on this, but that shooting might have been to terrorize one of them."

"God damn it," Davis muttered, rising from his chair, "why do you think I've got all these armed guards—to protect *me*?" He stabbed a finger at Wendell's chest and spoke in a menacing tone. "If you find out someone is trying to frighten my family, I want you to come directly to me and tell me the name. Then I want you to forget you ever heard of this case." Davis moved closer until he stood inches away from Wendell. "In fact, regardless of what you find, you work only for me and your information is mine alone. Is that understood?"

"You hired me," Wendell said with obvious annoyance, "and if I find the man, you'll be the first to know. But it's too late for private revenge. A lot of people know who I'm working for, and by now everybody has heard about the case. Don't take the law into your own hands."

"OK, OK, let's drop that for now." Davis curled his upper lip in a gesture maybe his best friend called a smile. "Let's just say that if you find him, justice will be done."

It wasn't the kind of promise Wendell wanted to hear. Davis had a big dramatic face that illustrated in large startling lines his powerful feelings. Right now he looked as if he wanted to head down to the local saloon and shoot it out with the black hats. Wendell wondered if Brad might have been a successful Kentucky politician. He had the requisite look of rugged frontier honesty, a deep manly certainty in his voice, and an ability to believe in the righteousness of his fluctuating moods and opinions. If he did find out who killed Devil Dancer, Wendell pitied the poor bastard who would have to face the wrath of Brad Davis.

Wendell requested again to speak with Charlene and Lily. Brad was reluctant, but finally he agreed, leaving the room to call them himself. The maid brought Wendell a drink.

"As long as Jim Bean keeps making bourbon, life will go on," Charlene said in a wry throaty voice as she stepped down into the den.

Wendell hurried to his feet, blinking from the pain in his neck caused by the sudden movement. Charlene must have thought he was already a little tipsy, or even winking at her, because she arched her eyebrows in mild surprise and repressed a smile. Davis and his daughter followed Charlene into the room. He made the necessary introductions, gave Wendell an expression both troubled and threatening, and left.

Lily, who appeared to be about twenty, had a wealth of rippling blond hair, large blue forget-me-not eyes, a prim nose, and lips that were parted just enough to show the tips of her upper teeth and locate her dimples. Her mouth was ready to laugh at the next joke, but her eyes remembered some old injury.

She looked like a wholesome country girl in her blue jeans, white halter top, and leather sandals. Her deep tennis tan and matching muscle tone exuded health and vitality. He wondered if the shooting of Devil Dancer was the closest she had ever come to tragedy; then he recalled that she had lost her mother when she was a girl. That was one of the ironies of having an attractive face and a luminous smile: everyone assumed your life was all sweetness and light.

No one would accuse Charlene Davis of innocence. All her gestures bespoke polish and sophistication. She had a quality of watchfulness in her eyes that was disconcerting in its unblinking worldliness. She was one of those women Wendell's ex-wife Laura would have described as "well-preserved." Dressed in a richly-textured leather midi-skirt, a fluffy pink sweater, a white leather vest decorated with small multi-colored feathers, and white leather boots, she might have been the lonesome cowboy's dream girl—yet somehow her outfit didn't look at all Western. There was no sense of the great outdoors in the way she wore her clothes; rather it was clear that she was a woman who could wear leathers, sweaters, and feathers to pre-Derby galas and presidential dinners, changing the world's ideas about fashion. Her burnished chestnut hair was veined with gold; her green eyes, flecked with a hint of hazel, were set in a faint network of wrinkles, so symmetrical they enhanced her appeal, suggesting that here was a woman who had faced life directly. She had a pouty turned-down kiss-me mouth.

Charlene, from all reports, was the centerpiece of the entire horsey set, the belle of every ball, the one the others counted on to establish the tone of any event she attended. She was the one who might dance on the table, jump in the fountain, or tell the risque story people remembered the next day. When she was at a party, the idea of high society seemed to be mankind's most inspired invention. She could make a bunch of pampered people with hyphenated names, sampling the pâté and sipping flutes of champagne, feel as if they were the very pinnacle of civilization. She was the ideal horseman's wife, and when Brad Davis picked her after the death of his first wife, he must have made his choice with at least as much deliberation as he had ever put into buying a prime thoroughbred or deciding which mare to breed with what stallion. She, in turn, played her part so skillfully there was never any question of spontaneity. Her life was clearly a work of studied choice as well—a self-conscious designing of costumes, practicing of gestures, and rehearsing of lines. She may have been the artifice upon which Bob Davis depended, but she was artifice raised to the level of artistry.

"I'm sorry to trouble both of you ladies at a time like this," he said gallantly. "But I need to ask you some questions. I want to be frank from the start: there is a possibility that whoever shot Devil Dancer did it to get back at one of you."

Lily blanched; Charlene didn't show any emotion; he might as well have been informing her that her car needed an oil change. Wendell thought it would be best to begin his questioning with her, giving Lily time to compose herself.

Wendell and Charlene sat down in two easy chairs near the fireplace. As she was lighting a cigarette an Irish setter came in, flopped on its side, and began beating its tail on the throw rug in front of the hearth. Charlene started cooing to the dog in a voice that made Wendell wonder if he should excuse himself. Then she reached out and scratched the folds of fur under the dog's throat, causing it to close its eyes in delight. Wendell watched her hands attentively; she was wearing a gold wristwatch so thin it looked as if it had been painted on and an emerald ring a few shades lighter than her eyes. Finally she looked over, stopped stroking the dog, blew smoke in his direction, and smiled a grieving smile.

"I'm listening," she said.

"I assume you've already considered the threat of what I mentioned, Mrs. Davis," Wendell said rather formally. "Maybe the best procedure now would be for you to share your thoughts with me. I realize this must be a very difficult time for you; all I ask is that you make every effort to talk straight with me. Tell me your major suspicions, if you have any, as well as your minor fears. Is there anyone who might want to do you harm?"

Charlene fixed her eyes on his face, apparently watching him more closely than she was listening to what he had to say. She wore a sardonic expression, as though she were on the verge of a sarcastic remark, but her response was in keeping with the gravity of the situation.

"I appreciate your directness, Wendell—you don't mind if I call you 'Wendell,' do you?"

"Not at all, ma'am. I'd prefer it."

"Good. And you can call me Charlene. We might as well be on a first name basis, since you are asking me to share the secrets of my life. It *has* occurred to me that someone might want to revenge himself on me by shooting our best horse, and I've gone in great detail over incidents from my past to ask who might be demented enough to do such a thing. I assure you I've known some very crazy people in my time, but none of them would be capable of this." She glanced up as if she expected him to shake his head in agreement. "There are people who may hold grudges against me, but I don't think shooting a horse is the way they would choose to get even. For one thing, I have never been emotionally attached to my husband's horses the way many wives around here are. Of course I cheer for them at the track, and I'm very excited when we win, but on a day-to-day basis I don't spend time with the horses, I don't know most of them by name." She tossed her wrist as if she were dealing cards, sending her emerald flashing. "Though I must admit I did know Devil Dancer. I had no trouble recognizing *him*. He was easily the most gorgeous animal I've ever seen. A walking work of art. I feel terrible that he was killed, such a senseless waste, but I don't take it personally, do you understand?" She tilted her head and smiled at him. "I feel sorry for my husband and the horse-racing world, not for myself. Anyone who wanted to hurt me would know that killing Devil Dancer wouldn't be the way to do it."

"You're probably right. I hope you don't think it's merely idle curiosity if I go ahead and ask you to name some names."

"I'll try to be cooperative, Wendell, but frankly I think you're barking up the wrong tree."

Charlene noted the ash on her cigarette with a critical eye, tapped it into a small brass tray shaped like a horseshoe, and reached out with her toe to nudge the dog sleeping at her feet. When she continued she spoke in a soft voice that was as intimate as a touch.

"As you probably know, my husband and I are invited to a lot of parties, and both of us like to drink, and sometimes I feel uninhibited and do unusual things—I dance, I sing, whatever pleases me. Usually no harm is done, and the next day, when I read in the Society page that I was the star of a party, I'm too hungover to remember. As you can imagine, men make advances at these parties, and on occasion I suppose I respond more than I should. I don't mean anything by it, but feelings do get hurt. Maybe I have to say a few blunt words, or maybe a face is slapped. The normal round of recriminations and regrets. But I keep getting asked back to all the parties, so I don't imagine I've ever done anything too outrageous."

Charlene had an actress's ability to focus emotion in various parts of her face. A slight fluttering of her long eyelashes, compressing of her lips, or lifting of her chin could suggest a world of feeling. It was fascinating to watch her speak, and difficult not to believe her every word; yet Wendell doubted that her flirtations had stopped with a few stolen kisses.

She gazed at him with sharp glittering eyes, smiled capriciously, and remarked, "I'm afraid my reputation for decadence is on the wane."

"I read about you at Anita Madden's last Derby-eve bash," Wendell said. "The pictures didn't do you justice."

"Nothing bad, I trust," she replied, giving him a glance that acknowledged his compliment. "I'll admit to anything, except my age. Most of the time I prefer to stay as far from the Madden crowd as possible, but Anita does put on quite a party. She's knows how to entertain hundreds of guests while having a good time herself. I admire her facility."

One evening Wendell had torn a pair of slacks climbing an apple tree to spy on Charlene at the Madden's celebrated annual baccanal. The extravaganza had a different theme each year and the guests were expected to dress and act accordingly. This one was based on the James Bond movie, *Goldfinger*. The Madden's poolside was decorated in a gold-bullion motif to suggest the interior of Fort Knox; a metallic-gray Austin Martin, a gorgeous golden girl draped on the hood, was prominently displayed in front of the bandstand. The men wore black tuxedos and the women strapless silk gowns; each couple was given a black derby hat as a party favor to throw at each other. As a special surprise a Piper Cub flew over, and out of it parachuted none other than Joey Heatherton, dressed as Pussy Galore in a tight leather jumpsuit; she proceeded to slink to the mike and sing the movie's title song before blending into the crowd.

As the evening progressed, the atmosphere became more sensual. The band, improvising on the contrapuntal popping of champagne corks, picked up the beat; mermaids (on loan from a local sorority), who had been lolling on an artificial island in the pool, swam to shore, doffed their wigs and golden-scaled tails, and began to frolic with the guests. The glitzy party as a whole depressed Wendell, perhaps because he wasn't invited; there was something unutterably sad in the frantic way everybody tried so hard to have a good time. He wondered how Charlene felt as he watched her dance with man after man and then go home alone.

Wendell pressed his luck and asked her to mention names. She was reluctant, although she did allude to her difficulties with a prominent person in the horse-breeding business, a notorious lecher who was known to proposition women in no uncertain terms. She insisted, however, that he was of no significance and made Wendell promise not to reopen old wounds by looking him up. "I'm grateful for your discretion, Wendell. You've been tactful throughout this interview, and I appreciate it. I sincerely want the killer of Devil Dancer caught; that's why I've been as cooperative as possible. If I've shown any hesitation, it's because you were hired by my husband, and I wanted to be sure I could trust you. How shall I put it? Brad and I aren't as close as we used to be, do you understand? We lead our own lives—I have my own office, secretary, and activities. My husband would certainly disapprove of certain facets of my life if he knew about them. So I'm taking a risk by being open with you. I am a woman who relies on her impulses and emotions, Wendell, and I feel sure that you're a good and honest man."

If she was acting, it was a splendid performance. Wendell wanted to believe in the sincerity of her statement, which hardly amounted to a full confession, but he also knew she might be trying to charm him because she regretted her candor. Wasn't she hinting at the very infidelities Brad had suspected? Nevertheless, at that moment, Wendell really did believe himself to be a good and honest man— and a brave one, too. He knew he would like the case better if he could pretend he was working for her.

"What about Brad's gambling? What can you tell me about that?"

"Not very much, I'm afraid. I don't like Las Vegas. I don't gamble and never ask how much he lost. Of course if he's won, I hear the whole story."

"From what I've learned, he owes some people at Caesar's Palace a lot of money."

"All I can say is they treat us very well there. Brad knows the Host, he's a Kentucky boy who used to work at the Beverly Hills Club in Newport, and so we usually stay for free."

Brad must have been a high roller, Wendell noted, to be comped by the casino.

"Do you happen to know a man named John Lane?"

"No, I don't believe so, why?"

"I think he's tied in to the money Brad owes, but I'm not sure just how. Have you ever seen anyone threaten your husband? Have *you* ever received any strange calls?"

"I'm not aware of any threats Brad's received. Speaking for myself, I'm more liberal than most people—Kentucky can be such a provincial place—so I get my share of crank calls and warped letters from the local bigots. An attractive woman sometimes receives unwanted communications from strange men. That's one of the reasons why I have a secretary, to screen me from unnecessary attentions. But nothing unusual has happened to me recently."

Charlene's weary smile indicated that the interview was over. She snuffed her cigarette in the ashtray and rose to her feet, extending her right hand. Wendell stood and held her hand longer than he should have and thanked her for her time. They exchanged a direct gaze that felt vaguely conspiratorial. Then she turned and walked out with the Irish setter at her heels. He heard her call Lily from the hallway and order the maid to bring her a Valium.

Lily came in a moment later with an expectant look on her face. As soon as they were seated Wendell apologized for frightening her earlier and explained again that there was a remote chance that someone had killed Devil Dancer for revenge. He asked her if she knew of anyone who resented her and might want to get even.

She listened closely, as if memorizing every word. When she spoke it was clear she comprehended the danger.

"I'll try to be helpful, but I don't want to accuse anybody. I suppose I have some enemies, though that's probably too strong a word. I'm not the most popular girl in school, you know. People are envious of me because of Daddy's money, the horse farm, other things. Also I get asked out often, and most of those dates I turn down. I know you're supposed to be very careful with the frail male ego, but if somebody asks me out and I don't want to go, I don't invent a thousand excuses. I simply tell them I don't want to go. As you can imagine, I get accused of being a snob, a flirt, a tease, and worse. That's one thing Charlene and I have in common. I trust she's been telling you similar stories."

"What does your father think?" Wendell asked. Lily was more savvy about her sheltered world than he had at first assumed.

"Daddy would be happy if I refused everybody. He never approves of anyone I bring home. He says, 'You've brought some real dogs though these doors.' Nobody is good enough for his daughter. He's very big on breeding, you know. I suppose if I ever broke my leg he'd take me out in the pasture and shoot me."

"What kind of man does your father have in mind?" Wendell asked, troubled by Lily's inopportune analogy.

"Prince Charles would be about right for him—though not for me—and failing that, a boy from one of the better horse farms. But I don't want that either."

"You don't want to stay in the Bluegrass?"

"Oh, I love horses. I had planned to transfer to Vassar this year to study music and art history, but Daddy promised me that I could pick a foal in the spring and raise it myself. He said I could race it when the time came, if I didn't put on too much weight."

There didn't seem to be much danger of that. She was as slim and limber as a willow wand. Prince Charles didn't know what he was missing.

"I don't want the kind of life my father and Charlene and their friends have. They smoke and drink and everybody laughs real loud, but nobody seems very happy. You look at them closely and you can feel that their lives are being gnawed from the inside—their faces say, 'I'm not satisfied with who I am or where I'm going.' I shouldn't be so critical," she said, fidgeting.

Wendell assured her that she could be as critical as she liked and he would respect her confidence. He was impressed by her acute perceptions. She had a lilting musical voice that probably could make the phone book sound like fine poetry. With her looks and that voice she could have gone through life mouthing silly nothings and nobody would have complained. Instead she was a sensitive young woman who used her own eyes. Wendell asked about long-term relationships and if any of the men she had rejected had been a problem.

"I hardly dated in high school, and not much happened during my freshman year at Transy, but in the Fall of my sophomore year my roommate Susie and I spent an afternoon cutting four inches off our skirts. Suddenly, we both were popular. One night after a very late date we were both very drunk and Susie said to me, 'We're swans, Lily, we're swans! Last year we were ugly ducklings, but now we're swans.'"

Although Wendell doubted if Lily had ever been an ugly duckling, he did ask her about her boyfriends.

"I went out with a K.A. until Kent State and Cambodia."

"What happened?"

"He didn't like my major."

"What was that?"

"Stop The War. We broke up after I got tear-gassed at a protest march on the U.K. campus. Daddy didn't approve either; he says we're fighting in Vietnam for the same reason we fought the Civil War—the North invaded the South."

"Were there any hard feelings?"

"Not really. He went his own way and I went mine."

"What about since then?"

"I'm not very interested in college guys right now."

"What happens when you say no?"

"Usually, after I've turned somebody down, they get the message. A few guys keep calling, but I like them okay, so we talk on the phone. Sometimes I do get crazy calls. The kind that think they're being clever if they disguise their voice or play a record without talking. I hate those calls, but I forget them. There are kids at Transy who think I'm a prude; they might try to scare me. You know a lot of them get off on the Dracula bit—bat T-shirts, plastic vampire teeth—Transy has its share of oddballs."

Lily unfolded her hands and began tapping her chin with her finger.

"Daddy has been drinking a lot (last Christmas he came home so drunk he couldn't put up the tree), and Charlene and I haven't been getting along too well lately. He's a strange man, my father. I'm a mess, too. I have been since mother died."

"That must have been rough. Would you like to talk about it?"

Wendell's best qualification for being a detective was the attentive sympathy in his eyes that told people he truly listened to what they had to say. Although he was brought up a Methodist, so many of his high school friends used to confide in him that his mother once told him, "With all these confessions you hear, you should have been a priest."

"It was my fault," Lily said in a shaky voice. "I was down in the office when the phone rang. Daddy had gone to Louisville. It was this crazy woman who slurred all her words. I couldn't make sense of what she was saying; I assumed she was a drunk with a wrong number, so I hung up. About fifteen minutes later she called again, and this time she spoke a little more clearly—it was mother, she'd had a stroke. I called the hospital immediately, but by the time the ambulance arrived, she was dead."

She looked at Wendell, her eyes shiny, her lips parted slightly as if to ask, "Why?"

"Do you believe in dreams?" she asked suddenly. "Dreams are so mysterious; it's like all day we weave and at night everything unravels. Not long ago my mother came to me in a dream. 'Mother,' I cried, 'you're alive! You didn't die!' But she just gave me the saddest look I've ever seen and said, 'We all have to die sometime, Lily.' I don't know why I'm talking about all this; Tom says I ought to put wheels on my mother's coffin, I get so much mileage out of her death."

"Who's Tom?"

"Oh, well, he's a professor at Transy."

Wendell could tell by her expression that he had hit upon a topic Lily wasn't about to discuss. Curious that she could talk about the death of her mother without the same reluctance.

"You said earlier that your father was a strange man. Has anything happened here lately, before Devil Dancer was killed, to make you think that?"

"We're all pretty strange, when you get right down to it. There was a situation, a few weeks ago, some men came out to the farm. I didn't like them. They were threatening Dad."

"What did they look like?"

"They were big, three men. One in a shiny suit, another dressed like a biker. You know, boots, blue jeans, sleeveless jacket, tattoos. He had a funny earring, a paperclip or something. The other guy wore slacks and a polo shirt. He had a nasty grin."

"Did they threaten your father physically?"

"No, they never touched him. The biker looked like he wanted to hit him and Daddy looked afraid. I noticed, because I've never seen my father act frightened before."

Wendell didn't ask Lily any more loaded questions; he would save those for Brad Davis. Instead he encouraged her to talk about college and her future plans. Unlike her stepmother, she didn't want to party away her life. She was interested in the arts and serious about her studies; in part, Wendell assumed, because she was involved with one of her professors.

"I enjoyed talking to you, Lily," he said. "I appreciate your candor. I just hope I can figure out soon what kind of nut might be crazy enough to shoot a horse."

"Or a person," Lily said, facing the bitter idea that her own life could be in jeopardy.

Wendell urged her not to worry, since her father had the grounds very well protected.

She grasped what he was saying so quickly that once again he wondered how, when he first met her, he had assumed she was naive. Right now she looked the picture of awareness.

"You're a remarkable young woman, Lily," Wendell said, struggling to find some words that might be comforting. "I'm sure you'll learn to live with what has happened to you."

"I've already learned a lot that I wish I hadn't. I suspect that I'm too strong to ask for help, and too weak to live without it."

She took his hand and smiled weakly—it was a brave attempt, but as soon as he was gone he knew that she would cry.

6

Wendell left the den and walked out on a rear patio overlooking a kidney-shaped swimming pool. A plastic swan drifted with the breeze in the middle of the sparkling turquoise water. On closer inspection, it proved to be a chlorine dispenser. A guard was sprawled out in a deck chair, his gun leaning against an exercise bicycle. He told Wendell that Brad Davis had gone down to the office and directed him toward a tanbark path through the woods.

The bending path came out on a hillside overlooking the back part of the farm. The office, half-hidden by a thick hedge of hibiscus, was a long one-story stone cottage with a steep shingled roof topped with a copper cupola that sported a ceramic stork. Behind it he could see the training track swirling with dust devils. In the infield there was a willow-lined pond where real swans preened. A jockey, standing up in the stirrups, cantered his mount around the far turn; another stallion with flattened ears hoofed the tattered earth and danced in place while his rider, crouched over his neck, whispered sweet nothings to soothe him.

The cottage had two doors. Gold-lettered signs identified the office and the lab. The knocker was a brass horse's head; Wendell lifted the iron ring in its mouth and let it fall. Someone said "come in." Pictures of horses lined the walls. A peroxide-blond secretary in a sleeveless pink sweater was on the phone trying to mollify an owner of a broodmare who had booked a cover from Devil Dancer. She gave Wendell a look, which suggested she had lunched on green persimmons, and pressed a button. Brad Davis appeared at a door Wendell hadn't noticed because it, too, was covered with photos of thoroughbreds.

"Come on inside," Davis ordered.

The office was twice the size of the reception room and paneled in wood a violin maker might envy. A wide bay window enabled Brad to lean back in his sumptuous leather chair and prop his feet up on a desk as big as a pool table, watching his horses prance around the practice track and hearing his own heart thud to the pulse beat of their hooves.

"We've got to discuss your gambling debts," Wendell said, hoping to impress Brad with his no-nonsense approach. "Lily saw some men talking to you who didn't look very friendly."

"Yeah, it's embarrassing, but true. Three men came out here and I told them I was a stand-up guy and that I would pay what I owe."

"What did they look like?"

"The one who did the talking was a natty dresser. He said his name was John Lane, but he looked Italian—olive complexion, silver-streaked slicked-back hair, his left eyelid drooped."

Brad himself, Wendell noted, was a master of the classy casual look—half snob, half slob—with his chambray shirt unbuttoned to the hair on his chest and a blue nylon windbreaker slung over his shoulder.

"What about the others?"

"They were thugs. One wore a jean jacket hacked off at the shoulders; he had a shaved head the size of an oak stump, bushy eyebrows, a mustache like a Turkish wrestler, no neck..."

"And a ring in his nose."

"You know him."

"Unfortunately."

"The other was big, but not as big. He didn't say a word the whole time; he just stood as still as a stone and gave me this hard stare. A scary guy, very intimidating."

A man who could make Brad cower was not somebody Wendell wanted to meet.

"Did you catch his name?"

"Vinnie, I think that was it."

"Did they threaten you?"

"Not exactly. They didn't lay a finger on me. They just flexed their tattoos."

"What did this John Lane say?"

"He was a very cool customer. He said we understand you owe a marker and that you're making a diligent effort to pay it off. He said he wanted to know if I had a plan and whether I was working on it, and if I didn't, maybe he could help me out. He said his line was public relations and short-term unserviced loans."

"Sure, they could loan you the dough, but then they'd bust your balls with the vigorish. You'd exchange one problem for a bigger one. Did you tell them you had a plan?"

"I told them about Devil Dancer and all the stud fees I'd be collecting in the spring."

"Did they buy it?"

"I believe so, yes. They left shortly afterward."

"And they didn't say anything that was directly threatening?"

"Only in a veiled sort of way. Lane said I had a nice place here, a nice family, and that it would be a shame to lose it. Do you actually think *they* shot Devil Dancer?"

"Don't you? Why didn't you tell me this before?"

"I don't know. It's humiliating, you know, to lose so much money; it's nothing I want to talk about; I really didn't relate the one thing with the other."

"I think it's a real possibility. I'm not much of a gambler myself, but I was a truck driver and I know that Teamster money built Caesar's Palace and that the mob uses the Central States Pension Fund as its piggy bank. I don't know which mob these guys represent—it could be Pittsburg, it could be Cleveland—and I don't know exactly what their game is. Probably it's in their interest to keep you dangling on the line; the casino can write off your unpaid marker on their tax return, then have some designated thugs collect it to add to the skim. If that's the case, you're the goose that laid the golden egg and worth more to them alive."

"But what if they want to ruin me and take my farm?"

"That's another ball game. I sure as hell hope that isn't the case."

"Can't you find out?"

"I'll try. It could be dangerous. I could get my nose put out of joint by sticking it where it doesn't belong. I'd like to live a long life, you know. I'd hate to think that all those social security payments were in vain. Maybe if I can find out who this John Lane is I can also figure what the mob is up to. On the other hand, your first impulse that this has nothing to do with Devil Dancer might be valid, there's that to consider."

"I don't know. You suggest we're finally on the right track, and then you turn around and say maybe not. Don't forget there *is* a right track. That was a real horse I buried yesterday."

"Tell me more about how you got into this, Brad. When did it start?" Wendell wanted to ease Davis away from the issue of the Mafia for a moment and get him talking about his gambling. He needed to know how much he owed and how serious the problem truly was.

"You can't own a horse farm and not be a gambler. This is a great luck business, only a fortunate few make significant money. And if you want to make big bucks, you've got to be willing to test your luck. What's the point if you know you're going to win? You're not really a gambler unless you're willing to risk it all. It's ecstasy or nothing. Luck is a lady and she don't favor the faint of heart, no sir. You've got to show her you're all man."

"If horses are already such a big gamble, why take more risks?"

"It's in my blood, I suppose. Kentucky thrives on vice. I've always needed some kind of a thrill to add a little edge to my life."

Wendell had an uncanny sense that he and Brad were remembering at that moment the same event from their boyhood. The game was to break into a strange house in the middle of the night, drink a beer from the refrigerator, leave the empties on the kitchen table. One summer they did this at several houses and were never caught.

"Remember Newport?" Wendell asked, recalling an episode when the seniors on the football team went to a town whose name was synonymous with gambling in Kentucky.

"Do I!" Brad's eyes lighted up. "That's really where I got my start."

"You smuggled a squirt gun into the burlesque show and shot the stripper."

"Oh, hell, yes, I remember. She squatted in front of me and I couldn't resist." Brad's eyes had a sleepy expression and his sensual mouth smiled. The mere mention of high school sports and adolescent pranks seemed to induce a longing for cheering crowds and pliant cheerleaders. "Then we went to Vivian's down on Second Street and I broke my maiden, what a night!"

Like many a river town, Newport had a long history of catering to the depraved tastes and illicit urges of the flotsam and jetsam the western waters brought its way. Cincinnati, directly across the Ohio, eventually cleaned up its act, but Newport, a shabby little town of 30,000, made vice its major business and gained notoriety as Sin City. During Prohibition, Kentucky whiskey and Ohio thirst met in Newport's speakeasies; when drinking became legal again, the big money was in gambling. York and Monmouth Streets were lined with seedy clip joints and strip clubs, while up in the hills behind town swanky casinos courted the high rollers. The convention business in Cincinnati prospered once word spread that a good time was a short taxi ride away. It wasn't long before Sam Tucker, on behalf of the Cleveland Syndicate, realized that the only thing lacking was a little organization, so about 1940 the mob moved in. Owners who didn't wise up and sell out were treated to what the locals called dingdonging: if some rough stuff didn't work, their establishments were torched and they were left with a pile of ashes and no choice. By 1950 the mob was firmly entrenched, the town's constabulary was on retainer, and Newport was the biggest gambling center in the country east of Las Vegas.

Brad and Wendell had revisited Newport after the war and blown their wads in more ways than one. But Wendell soon tired of bust-out joints and B-girls, and he couldn't afford the casinos, so he stopped going. Brad, however, was on his way to becoming a degenerate gambler. He told Wendell he spent time at the crap tables in the sleazy Sapphire Room on the second floor of the Glenn Hotel; razzle-dazzle was especially popular, a multiple dice game where the stakes doubled with each successive bet; the point was to dangle an enormous payoff in front of a sucker's nose and keep him playing until he'd lost all his money. Those who preferred not to participate sometimes woke up in the back alley with a sore jaw and empty pockets.

Once it dawned on him that razzle-dazzle was all sizzle and no steak, Brad visited the Beverley Hills Club—a plush casino with a gourmet restaurant, a celebrity floor show, and a gaming room as large as a basketball court—to test his skill at cards. He had played a lot of poker during the war and fancied himself a good enough judge of character to call a bluff. And his wife Liz liked the big-name entertainers: Frank and Dean made the scene; Pearl Bailey sang the blues; Jimmy Durante cracked wise; and Liberace in a sequined tuxedo tickled the ivories with bejeweled fingers and flung his hands in the air like startled birds. Then Brad saw Sean Connery as James Bond in *Casino Royale* and decided he should try his luck at baccarat.

"I became a black-chip bettor," Brad told Wendell. "Cash or chips, to me it was only play money and I did my best to have fun with it."

"How did you make out? Did you lose a lot?"

"I played it safe. Sometimes I won big. I never lost more than I could afford."

Wendell doubted if black-chip betting at baccarat could be termed safe, but what Brad could afford was considerably more than the average man.

"When did you start going to Vegas?"

"About the time George Ratterman went to sleep in May and woke up in April." Brad crinkled his eyes at Wendell; they both knew the joke and the story.

Back in 1961 the good citizens of Newport decided to clean up their town; they convinced George Ratterman, a former Cleveland Browns quarterback, to run for sheriff on a reform ticket; one night in May he was lured to a hotel by a trusted friend to meet with Tito Carinci, a former football player and part owner of the notorious Glenn Hotel, who supposedly wanted to quit the rackets; as they drank and talked, George was slipped a Mickey Finn and pirated across the river to Tito's third-floor apartment at the Glenn Hotel, whose other owner, Marty Buccieri, ordered April Flowers to cut short her striptease at the Tropicana Club and report to Tito's bedroom where a drugged Ratterman and a hired photographer were waiting. Next came a call to the police station. Three of Sin City's finest were shocked to find frail April, in lurid deshabille, wrapped in the Valentino embrace of groggy George and proceeded to press charges. Fortunately, the irate citizenry were too savvy to fall for so blatant a badger game, especially when it was revealed in court that the Commonwealth's Attorney had arranged ahead-of-time for the photographer. Ratterman was duly acquitted and elected; during his term as sheriff the whorehouses, handbooks, bust-out joints, and casinos were shut down and most of the mobsters and their minions moved on to greener pastures in the Bahamas or Las Vegas.

"I tell you," Brad said, "the first time I visited Caesar's Palace it was like Old Kentucky Home Week. They gave me top-of-the-line treatment; everything was 'free gratis', as they say."

"But you know how that works," Wendell interjected. "They give you free food and drinks and a room and you proceed to lose your shirt and pay for the casino."

"Yeah, that's right. They treat you like a king so you'll spend like one."

"What's the big appeal of baccarat? I watched a game once at Caesar's Palace, nobody seemed to be having a good time."

Wendell remembered the tight-lipped, joyless faces of the players as the velvet-voiced croupier in a gray tuxedo kept everyone informed of the on-going situation and the cards slipped out of the shoe like esoterica from an oracle. Maybe it was the frenetic pace of baccarat that made it so addictive, where fate was decided swiftly by the turn of a card and the player had very little control because the rules were set. Why would a domineering man like Brad want that?

"It's a seductive trap," Davis admitted with a shake of his head. "I tell you the adrenalin rush is tremendous; you get a heady sense of omnipotence, as if all things were possible, and you're a big spender with money to burn, a player, a goddamned pioneer! And when you're not on a roll, there's a giddy thrill in losing it all, in taking one false step, and down the slippery slope you slide. The more I lost at Caesar's, the more excited I became, so I bet more and lost more. I was in a fucking free fall, and damn if I didn't feel exhilarated, like I was some kind of hero. I hadn't felt that way since the Pacific when I pulled my plane out of a tailspin."

Wendell looked at Davis with concern; he had never seen him so enthused and eloquent. It was almost frightening the way talk about gambling fired him up.

"How bad was the damage, Brad? How much did you lose?"

"I may be a high roller, Wendell, but I'm not a whale. They've never cut off my credit." He seemed inordinately proud of this fact. "But this last time it was Tap City, I'll tell you."

Although Davis couldn't bring himself to admit exactly how much he had lost, Wendell was sure that it was a considerable sum, even for him. He also knew that to tell Brad to stop gambling would be like asking a beaver to stop chewing on bark.

"Maybe you wanted to lose, there's that to consider."

"Why would I want to do that?"

"Well, you've had a lot handed to you in your life. Maybe you wanted to throw it all away and find out who you were without it."

"You're dead wrong."

"Am I now?"

Brad fidgeted impatiently, a man with no taste for repartee. Then he started tapping his foot restlessly, as if he were late for an appointment. Wendell knew the interview was over. They parted on Wendell's promise to check into the Mafia angle and call tomorrow.

As Wendell drove back to Lexington he couldn't help mulling over what he had learned about Brad's gambling addiction. For the life of him he didn't understand the allure. It was a flamboyant sham of a city where only the ersatz was authentic; a neon Babylon where grandmas in stretch pants and sneakers spent hours at the slots, pulling for a trifecta of cherries and a crescendo of silver coins. The city's over-the-top opulence was designed to compel the suckers to go slack jawed and say "Ah," leaving them too bamboozled to notice the steady flow of untraceable cash into the mob's coffers. Why would anyone prefer the bordello baroque of Las Vegas to the aesthetic pleasures of a lush bluegrass horse farm? Why, Wendell wondered, would Brad Davis want to throw all that away and let his fate ride on the random turn of a card?

7

After he returned to his apartment, Wendell was so exhausted that he took a nap. When he woke up, the sun was down to the level of the trees. He felt dizzy as he hobbled to the bathroom but splashing cold water on his face seemed to help. He was enormously hungry, more than a little horny, and anxious to see Anna again. Although he had learned a lot during the day, Wendell wanted to wait until the morning to decide on his next move; besides, he couldn't get Anna out of his mind. Devil Dancer may have lost his sexual drive, but Wendell felt primed. Just the thought of her filled him with longing. She had an allure that helped him forget about Laura. What a chump he was when it came to women! One good blowjob and he was smitten.

Wendell showered and shaved and made a special effort to look presentable, putting on a new navy blue golf shirt with a tiny yellow alligator on the pocket and his best pressed slacks. He dressed with nervous haste, like a teenager on his first date. To clear his head and steady his hands he poured himself a glass of Southern Comfort on the rocks. The first swallow burned all the way down to the pit of his stomach; the others restored his confidence.

Anna's door was opened by a jockey-sized hippie with gelid blue eyes and hair tied back in a ponytail. He was bare to the waist, only wearing a pair of cut-off jeans. Without a word he stepped aside to let Wendell pass, looking all the while as if he were in on a private joke. He went into the bedroom, exchanged muffled words with

Anna, came back out, still shirtless, but now carrying a shiny guitar and a green parka and with an army surplus knapsack slung over his shoulder. He kept that smug look on his face as he barged out the door.

Anna appeared a moment later in faded jeans with polka dot patches on the knees and a voluminous light blue man's work shirt that hung down to her thighs.

"Oh, hi," she said in a breathy voice.

Wendell stepped forward to kiss her, but she turned her head slightly at the last moment so he only brushed her cheek.

"You've been drinking."

"A few beers here and there. A little pick-me-up before I came. Yes."

Anna gave Wendell a wry sidelong smile.

"Who's your friend?" Wendell asked.

"Why do you want to know?"

"I just wondered, that's all."

"That's Woody."

"Does he live around here?"

"Yes, he does. He lives here."

"In Idle Hour Apartments?"

"Woody lives with me."

"Somehow he doesn't seem like your type."

"What do you know about my type?"

"Sorry," he said, waving goodbye to his confidence. "Tact is not my strong point."

"Exactly what is your strong point?" Anna asked mockingly, doing an exaggerated imitation of his voice, "Ahm jus' wonderin', thas awl."

"You like to tease me."

"It's not hard to do. Woody's a good friend. He doesn't live here all the time. He works with the miners down in Pikeville. He stays with me when he's in town."

"I hope I didn't scare him away."

"Don't flatter yourself. You're glad he's gone. Woody doesn't mind. If he wants to bring somebody here, I leave. We have an arrangement. Woody's sweet. You'd like him."

Wendell doubted if he would like sweet Woody. Ever since she had walked into the room he had wanted to hold her. She had the slow studied movements of a woman aware of the power of her body. No matter her stance, she was always on display.

He was getting ready to allude to last evening, hoping to pick up where they left off, when Anna gave him a coy look and said, "We were pretty naughty. That was nice."

"Naughty is hardly the word," Wendell laughed.

"Are you feeling better?"

"Than what?"

"Than you did last night."

"Last night was great."

"No. I mean your head."

"Sure, it still hurts. It hurt like hell this morning. I've never fainted like that before."

Anna didn't appear to want a medical report, so he changed the subject.

"I'm starved," Wendell announced. "Would you like to have dinner with me tonight?"

"Why not?" Anna flicked her eyes at him. "I love to eat out. Where do you want to go?"

"How about Stanley Demos's Coach House?"

She nodded her head vaguely, pursed her lips and looked distant and moody for a moment, then walked into the bedroom to change.

She was gone a long time. While he waited Wendell inspected the spackled plaster walls, counted the cracks in the ceiling, and noted the puddle of water under the air conditioner.

Anna returned in a full-length red skirt circled by flounces. On top she wore a short-sleeved black silk jacket with three ornate silver clasps down the front. Her hair was piled high and held a diadem of sparkling pearls. She had golden hoop earrings, a gold medallion on her necklace, bracelets on each arm, and conspicuous rings on several fingers. Wendell glanced at her feet to see if there were bells on her toes. He felt absurdly under-dressed in his sports shirt and slacks, but since nothing in his closet went with Anna's exotic outfit anyway, he would simply have to make the best of it.

The red-brick restaurant, a one-story pseudo-colonial affair was on South Broadway not far from The Red Mile racecourse. The columned portico in front featured four plaster of Paris statues of black-faced jockeys, each holding a ring in his outstretched hand to hitch your horse on. Lithographs of famous stallions lined the walls of the cherry-paneled main dining room. After an animated conversation with the waiter about the merits of various entrees, Anna finally decided to have what Wendell was having. The sommelier, a sipping cup on a silver chain around his neck, poured the appropriate wines in apropos glasses: A very dry Chardonnay for the shrimp cocktail and Caesar Salad; a robust Cabernet Sauvignon for the Chateaubriand in a brandy-laced mushroom sauce. All this would cost a fortune, but Wendell wanted to impress Anna with his down-home version of savoir-faire.

"This Devil Dancer killing has me baffled," Wendell confessed. "I just don't know for sure where to turn?"

"I've been thinking about it too," Anna said, gazing back at him with troubled eyes. "Please, can't we talk about something less depressing?"

In an effort to set aside his brooding on the case, Wendell tried to lighten things up by telling a few tales about his childhood.

"I grew up in Athens, Kentucky, a town so small that instead of a fire department they had a lawn sprinkler. The biggest thing that ever happened there was the year they built the sewer and two married women in town ran off with ditch diggers. Afterwards there was a saying in town that went, 'We really got screwed on that sewer job—and we weren't the only ones!'"

Anna laughed. "How old a dirty old man are you?"

"Forty-four," Wendell said, choosing a number he thought he could get away with.

"Married?"

"Divorced."

"Everybody's divorced. The first one is always hard."

"The second is worse."

"I'll never marry. What's the point if you're only going to split up? I want to be free to move on."

Wendell squirmed in his chair—apparently that was her credo. They were both silent until the waiter brought their shrimp cocktail. Anna stared down at the tulip-shaped glass for a moment and then started talking in a confessional rush.

"I'm an orphan. My foster parents live in New York, upper East Side, that's where I grew up. They also have a farm in the Catskills and a place in Florida. My father is a corporate lawyer. He's very rich. Daddy makes the money and Mother spends it. That's their life. I wasn't at home much myself. They sent me away to school. First I went to Barlow School. That was nice. We all skied down the hill to class every morning and at noon we took the chairlift back up for lunch. I had a crush on my English teacher; one time I came up to him at registration and whispered in his ear, 'I have this fantasy of fucking you.'"

"How old were you?"

"I was thirteen and he was thirty-two."

"What happened?"

"What do you think? I told my girl friend about it and she tattled on me to the headmaster. The teacher was fired and I was sent home. Mother was very upset. She and Daddy decided to send me to a Swiss finishing school. They thought it would be very proper and that I could keep up with my skiing. By the time my parents came for me in December I had put a blond streak in my hair, started smoking, and taken to drinking Daiquiris. And the ski instructor there taught me more than how to ski. When Mother saw me she burst into tears."

Before Anna went on with her story, she picked a shrimp up with her fingers and sucked the tangy red cocktail sauce.

"The next school they sent me to was Miss Porter's. I started smoking dope there and I got pregnant. I was fifteen. I guess I was pretty crazy as a kid. One day my mother and I were driving and my mother said, 'The only difference between you and a prostitute is that they get paid for it.' When she said that I slapped her. Poor Mother could only say, 'I'm going to tell your father,' and of course I shot back, 'He's not my father.'"

Anna paused a moment before she added, "Daddy arranged for the abortion."

"How did you feel about that?"

She hesitated for a moment. "I wasn't sorry."

"How did your father feel?"

"Poor Daddy," Anna said tenderly. "He was furious at the time, but a few months later he came into my room drunk one night and started talking to me about how unhappy he was with Mother. Then he got very quiet and touched me."

"What did you do?"

"I hit him too." Anna laughed at the crazy symmetry of it all. "He cried and apologized. I told him to forget it, but he kept buying me expensive presents and giving me money. I saved the money, left the presents on my bed, and ran away from home."

Wendell listened to Anna's story with a mixture of fascination and repulsion. He had never known anyone like her before, and whatever her life had been, he wanted to find out how she became who she was.

"Did you hate your father after that?"

"Daddy? Of course not. He's a sweet man and I love him. I had heard that exciting things were happening in California and I wanted to see for myself. You know that song:

If you're going to San Francisco
Be sure to wear some flowers in your hair.

Well, I wanted to be there. It was great. We'd go to Golden Gate Park, listen to the Grateful Dead, and get stoned. I remember one time I was listening to live Airplane, lying on the grass watching the clouds go by. It was beautiful."

"An afternoon of Jefferson Airplane doesn't sound like my idea of a good time," he said.

"Why not?" Anna asked with a quizzical smile.

"I grew up on crooners myself."

"Ba ba ba boo, strangers in the night, that sort of thing?"

"You've got it," Wendell laughed.

"Daddy knew Vic Damone, does that turn you on? Personally, I found him a bore. He thought Las Vegas was Heaven."

"So does Brad Davis."

Anna didn't respond to his remark; instead she glanced at him searchingly for a moment and went on with her story.

"You'll never guess who I met in Santa Barbara," she said.

"Tell me."

"Charlie!"

"Charlie?" All Wendell could think of was Julian talking about the Viet Cong.

"Charles Manson. This was before helter-skelter came down. I was fascinated by his name, 'man' 'son', man's son." She waved one hand as if to shape the words of his name in the air. "Son of man, right? At the time that was very heavy for me. Like he was some kind of prophet. He really did believe in love, but he abused his gift and blew it. He writes to me sometimes. They let him send letters from prison."

"What are they like?"

"Weird."

"Could I see one?'"

"You're curious about everything, aren't you? Charlie said that I should never show his letters to anyone, but I don't see what harm it could do."

Wendell felt very uneasy from the moment Anna began to talk about Manson.

"How well did you know him?"

"I met him at a party. He tried to get me to make it with a friend of his. I told him 'no'. He was very upset—like 'no' shouldn't be used in his presence."

"How many times did you see him?"

"Not often. He'd always come on to me real strong about how he had this beautiful thing going that would be perfect for me. I told him 'thanks but no thanks'."

Anna seemed proud of herself for having rejected the offer.

"Later, after Preston and I returned from Mexico, we stopped by the Spahn Ranch one day. What a mess! Busted dune buggies all over the place and grungy girls running around in dirty underwear. It reminded me of the poverty I saw in Mexico."

"I was in Mexico once," Wendell said. "What was that like?"

"Preston, the guy I went with, dropped out of Stanford, bought a jeep, and decided to be a film maker. What he ended up doing was smuggling dope. I saw it as an adventure. I think I smoked half of his weed before he got a chance to ship it back to the States."

"I've smoked a lot of dope myself," Wendell said with mock bravado.

"Yeah, right," Anna smirked. "Last night."

"The cops in Mexico are something else," she continued. "One morning we saw that all four tires had been stripped off our jeep. In the center of town we saw these kids by the marketplace trying to sell our tires. We found a policeman and he went over and talked to them. At first we thought he was going to arrest them and return our tires, but instead he came back in a minute, shrugged his shoulders, and said, 'Es barato,' and walked away. When Preston tried to take them, they shouted, 'Vayase al carajo, gringo,' picked up the tires, and ran away. Finally we had to get a friend of ours to hunt up the kids and barter with them until he got them back."

Anna had seemed indignant as she told the story, but she cackled with delight when she finished—as if she had to hear her own stories to find out what they meant.

"How long was it before you were busted?"

"How did you know that?"

"It's inevitable. A guy like Preston and a girl like you. People in Mexico take their siestas with one eye open. Everybody knows what everybody else is doing. Whether they do anything about it is another matter."

"The cops found out all right, and of course they wanted a bite of the action. Before long all of Preston's profits were ending up in their pockets. When they learned he couldn't pay any more, they raided our house. They found some dope and acted surprised. Preston gave them his stereo and the jeep and they let him leave. We borrowed some money and flew home."

"You haven't touched your entree," Wendell said, giving Anna an amused look.

"I don't like meat," she confessed.

"You could order something else."

"I'm not really hungry," she said, picking at her salad.

"There's a good vegetarian restaurant across from the university," Wendell said glibly. "Next time we can go there."

"That would be nice. Fresh baked bread and homemade butter is what I like."

"Whatever happened to Preston?"

"Preston's dead. We split after we got back. He wanted to smuggle heroin from Colombia into the States to finance the great movie he always talked about making. His crazy plan was to fill a condom full of heroin, seal it, and swallow it down with ice cream. On the plane trip the rubber broke in his belly and the overdose killed him. The family reported the cause of death as a ruptured appendix." Anna mentioned this last detail with a sardonic frown.

"The ultimate hippie death," Wendell remarked. The whole incongruous episode made him feel depressed. "What happened to you then?"

"I stayed at my friend Michael's horse farm. Then I went to England for a summer with his family. I loved England; it was quiet and gentle compared to Mexico, so cool and formal and precise. English men are such gentlemen. I'd walk down the street and hear things like, 'Hello, lovey, how about a kiss and a cuddle?' In Lexington all I hear is, 'Nice tits'."

"That's not only vulgar, but understated."

"You don't miss much, do you, Mr. Private Eye?"

"Not when it comes to you," Wendell said. "Tell me more about London."

"I only got hassled one time when I was there. This distinguished-looking man in a bowler hat came over and in a very soft cultivated voice offered me ten pounds for my panties."

"Did that bother you?"

"You bet it did. I needed the money. I was furious that I didn't have any panties on!"

Anna tipped her head back and laughed. Then she swallowed some Cabernet Sauvignon as if it were water.

"I don't usually drink," she said, reading Wendell's thoughts. "I don't usually talk this much either. It's not just the wine. It's you, too. You really listen to what I say."

Anna didn't speak with a drunken slur, but now her voice went lower and her stories became more uninhibited.

"Michael was terrific with horses. When I got back from England I went to work on his father's farm. They had a horny stallion there who tried to fuck everything—girls, cars, benches—you name it, he'd try to fuck it. The stable boy had to bring him his oats with a pitchfork in one hand. One time he went for me and everybody panicked. All but Michael. I was cornered by the fence when he ran up with his arms out and hugged that wild horse. It was the bravest act I've ever seen, yet Michael probably didn't think about it twice. He simply loved horses and they loved him. He was great with horses. He didn't like women."

"You have strange friends."

"He really didn't. What I dug were those horses. I get excited when I'm walking a stallion. Have you ever noticed those prim and proper ladies at the track, how they get all hot and bothered when the stallions come by?"

"All this time I thought it was me." There *was* an erotic undercurrent to the world of horses, Wendell had seen it in the dreamy look grooms, both male and female, had when they rubbed down the sleek sides of a thoroughbred or in the smiles of satisfaction on all the flushed faces at the finish of a race.

"I'm serious," Anna said laughing. "I have fantasies about horses. My analyst tells me I'm an Amazon. I won't tell you what I tell him *he* is. I'm into living out my fantasies. Don't you believe in doing what your imagination tells you to?"

As she leaned across the table and refilled her wine glass, Wendell wondered if he should tell Anna about his shower fantasy. When she went on with her story her voice was so intimate and alluring that he could almost feel the warm caress of her breath in his ear.

"Woody and Bruce and I were at this spiffy nightclub in Louisville. The kind with all black waiters and white tablecloths that touch the floor. We were sitting there sipping our drinks and I was very turned on so I asked if I could slip under the table and suck them both off. They didn't mind, so I did. It was *very* exciting. I could imagine their eyes."

Anna must have seen Wendell's expression change, because she began to defend herself.

"They weren't using me. It was my idea. Some day I'm going to buy a big house with rooms for all the men I've made it with. Then they can all be with me and I will love them all."

Anna finished her speech with a sweeping gesture that nearly spilled what little was left of the wine.

Wendell slowly lifted a napkin to his lips, still tasting of mushroom sauce, and looked at Anna with a mixture of dread and desire. He wondered just how large a house she had in mind. Listening to her talk he had felt, at first, a surge of lust, but the more he heard the more the drums of warning sounded at the back of his mind, and he cloyed with it all. The next minute he would turn his eyes to hers and the stream of her stories would flow so smoothly, her face would be so animated, that his fears were forgotten.

Her hair clustered at her forehead like harvest grapes, Anna seemed oblivious to the possibility that she was saying anything unusual. It was as though she was talking to herself alone, and Wendell had somehow overheard her. For the rest of the meal she kept silent, sitting back with her jacket in place while she ate cherries jubilee and sipped her coffee. She looked so lovely and demure that Wendell felt another wave of desire. He was already anticipating going back to Anna's apartment when her eyes brightened and she said, "Let's go someplace funky."

8

Boots Bar, as funky a dive as Lexington had, was on the ground floor of the Scott Hotel, a vaguely Victorian building that emitted an aura of desolation from its isolated placement next to the railroad tracks that severed the city. At one time the hotel had been the favorite of the railroad men, who used to leave their red lanterns burning by the doorway while they went upstairs with their women. The trains and the railway men were all gone now, but the old coot at the desk would still rent a room for the night—or by the hour if your tastes ran that way.

The bar was dense with smoke. The clientele was a mix of U.K. students slumming it, the usual assortment of local yokels and alkies, and a few hillbillies down from eastern Kentucky who had left their coal mines and whiskey stills to go see them some naked women in the wicked city. As naked women go, these were the dregs. Behind their made-up masks of beauty—which looked as if they had been layered on by a drunken undertaker—you could catch the trapped glance of a homely hound-dog face from the country, or the hard-eyed desperation of a plain Jane making a last-ditch effort to market her scant virtues.

In the right front corner of the room, the girls took turns putting records on the scratchy portable, climbing up on a stage the size of a card table, twirling Day-Glo tassels on sequined pasties, and setting their knockers to trembling and their buttocks to twitching. Whoever wasn't dancing was expected to be at the tables hustling drinks. From the rear of the room a fat man, wearing a pork pie hat tipped back on his head and with a cigar fuming from his lips, straddled a folding chair. Although the room was so small he could have been audible with a whisper, he twanged away into a blackjack of a microphone, keeping up a running sewer of commentary.

"Let's give Cindy a big hand, folks. She may be over forty, but she don't swell or tell and she's grateful as hell. When she comes around to your table buy her a drink. She looks like she needs it. She's the original M&M girl—you'll melt in her mouth not in your hand. And now let's hear it for the lovely Nadine, who comes to us from the Green Bay Packers. She started out as a tight end but ended up as a wide receiver. Let's give her a big hand."

Nadine put on her record and started doing a sleepy-time version of the green apple quick step, cranking her right arm as if she were playing an imaginary slot machine. Probably even the front row strokers didn't find anything exciting about the lovely Nadine. At every awkward bump and grind false eyelashes fell out. She looked like a wind-tossed pine tree shedding needles. As she worked up a sweat the paint and powder began to run down her face. At the end of her number she tongued the air—looking like a spoiled little girl mad at her mommy—twirled her tassels as if for takeoff, and rubbed her crotch against the dusty curtain, spilling sequins.

Next Little Enis, the feature attraction, came on stage. He was an undergrown overweight man whose real name was Carlos Toadvine. Wendell remembered him from earlier days, back in the fifties, when he had been an aspiring imitator of Elvis. (You've heard of Elvis the Pelvis: Lexington, Kentucky, proudly presents—Enis...the Penis!). He looked rumpled and haggard. His Elvis-like pompadour was lifeless and lopsided. His small brown eyes appeared to be pressed like two thumbtacks into his skull to keep the jaundiced skin of his cheeks from sliding off his face. But his jaw still jutted out with feisty defiance.

Enis, whose specialty was strumming an upside-down left-handed twelve-string guitar, had toured for a season with Jerry Lee Lewis. He even had his own group, Little Enis and the Tabletoppers, which never made it past Paducah. Nevertheless, Enis was good. Wendell had heard him sing at the old Zebra Lounge on Short Street; back then, he sometimes did Elvis better than Elvis did himself. After that he disappeared from the local scene for several years. Rumor had it that Enis had drunk himself to death; but here he was, considerably the worse for wear, still drinking and singing, yet looking as if one more Elvis hip twist would tear him in half.

It seemed Enis was now a sober man—in thought if not in action. He preferred to talk about his own tragic life than to sing copycat renditions of "Hound Dog" or "Jailhouse Rock".

"I had a heart attack at Comer's," Enis said in his raspy Kentucky drawl. "Passed out in the middle of my set. Down at the morgue Chester Hager pulled the sheet over my head. Well, a little later two nurses come by and they stopped and lifted up the sheet and took a peek at my naked body. And the one nurse said to the other nurse, 'Somebody's lost a dear friend.'"

Good old Enis was as randy as ever. Enis really did have a notorious penis, nicknamed "Old Blue". One time a waitress out at Marty's had whispered to Wendell, "That Enis, he's as heavy-hung as a horse. That little shrimp is one-hundred and forty pounds of dynamite with a nine-inch fuse." She had shaken her head and smiled as if she knew from experience.

Anna seemed bored with the bar, but when Enis came on she perked up and paid attention. He kept rambling on about his life, trying to kill time so he wouldn't have to sing.

"I went to a funeral down in Whitesburg and everybody was gettin' all worked up. They was yellin' and screamin' and rollin' on the floor, when all of a sudden the minister pulled out a six-foot rattlesnake and throwed it in the coffin—that's when I left, fast."

Wendell wondered what kind of reaction Enis expected to receive. Apparently the story came to mind, troubling him in some way, so he said it out. He didn't tell it as a joke, and certainly nobody laughed. In fact the audience was getting restless and starting to wisecrack.

"Play 'Hound Dog,' Enis, somebody who looked like a counter-culture type shouted out.

"I've been singin' for twenty years," Enis said in a morose voice, "and people keep askin' for the same songs. I guess that means they haven't learned anything."

Instead Enis sang a slow song that obviously meant a lot to him about how he had kept the wine but thrown away the roses. The audience continued talking while Enis sang and when he finished only Wendell and Anna clapped. A look of internal torment pinched his face. Wendell's heart hurt to watch him. "This next song," he said, "I'm gonna sing real soft, so I can hear what yah'll are talkin' about."

Wendell wondered if Anna was getting bored again, since the place was so dingy and depressing only a drunken man could stay happy there for long.

All of a sudden Anna called out in a commanding voice, "Play something fast."

Enis shaded his eyes, trying to see through the shoals of tobacco smoke.

"I never refuse a lady," he announced. Then bracing himself for a big effort, he broke into a high-tempo version of "All Shook Up".

Anna sprang to her feet, pulling Wendell by the hand after her to an open space among the tables, where she began to gyrate. Wendell had stopped dancing fast numbers about the time he slipped a disc doing the twist. Anna simply wanted him to stand beside her while she did her shimmy and shake. That was fine with Wendell, who loved to watch sexy dancing. A beautiful woman moving to the serpentine rhythms of her own body was his idea of holy.

Anna raised her hands slowly, twirling them in spirals over her head until they took on a life of their own, holding her head high and turning in a tight circle. Then her body began to roll and revolve beneath her floating hands. As she sped up the people in the bar struggled to their feet to get a better view. They started stamping and clapping and hopping around in a drunken effort to reciprocate her sinuous rhythms. But her ass flashed so fast now no eye could pin it down. Her feet pranced, knees pumping, as she lifted her dress above her waist and let it fall, tossing her arms in graceful swirls toward the ceiling.

As she continued to coil and contort herself, her torso frozen for a moment in a S curve then flowing into another pattern, some men in the room, compelled by her turnings, began to stumble counterclockwise in a ring around her. Finally Anna, completely carried away by her own designs, flipped open the last silver clasp and let her silken jacket fall to the floor. The sight of her glistening breasts brought a collective sigh from the men who all pulled in toward her, but not one dared to step inside her circle. She seemed to dance for herself alone, making love to the music and rubbing her body against the see-through veils of smoke hovering in the air.

Enis had kept his song going as long as he could, but he broke off abruptly in the middle of the refrain and said, "Ahm too plum tard to sing any more," and limped off the stage, painfully bent forward, with one hand on his lower back.

Old sewer-mouth at the microphone didn't even bother to urge the folks to applaud for Enis. He was too busy trying to get Anna up on stage. She shook her head, whispering to Wendell, "Grab my jacket, will you, and get me out of here."

Wendell stooped down, retrieved her jacket, and put it over Anna's shoulders. He forced a path through the crowd of excited men and whisked her to the door, thankful that no one had tried to stop them. Apparently they were so stunned it didn't occur to them to cause any trouble. As Wendell and Anna exited, the man at the mike was priming the folks for the special treat of Mary Lou the Dairy Queen, who called for two drunks to come up on the tiny stage with her. The fans were going to love this.

"Far out!" Anna exclaimed, shaking her head.

Wendell wondered if she meant Mary Lou's crude act or her own enticing dance.

9

Back in Anna's apartment Wendell asked to see one of Manson's letters. The entire ghoulish case, as filtered through the media and his fading memory, had an aura of unreality. He thought that perhaps the written words of The Monster himself would help put things in perspective. More importantly, he wondered what Manson had to say to Anna.

She handed him some crumpled papers covered with a childish scrawl that looked at first like an ancient undecipherable script. There were stick-figure doodles around the edges of the pages and complete paragraphs were almost impossible to read; Wendell puzzled out what he could while Anna went into the bedroom to change:

> *for you to read & throw away & if you let any else read this you didn't do what i ask you have not been reading about me there was no family before the DA & news papers had to hook me up to win a court case people came & went from & to that ranch as they wanted i was my law & lived outsede the law & if anyone got down rong i would cut there ears off i never killed no one My reflections did cause other things & other people were efected by me but thats only because i was free & open in my mind my only goal is to be in my place & keep a bunch of mindless fools off my back with a bunch of insane Bull i got enough problys carrying the world confusion as everyone had*

*run off on me all they dont want to face in themselves & thats
only the truth about themselves that they would kill in me rather
than face there own igarence...*

*you lost your real self your playing man now & lost your
real woman years ago—the hole thing is backwards you cant
play new age woman with old age thoughts i wouldnt keep you
in school putting useless garbage in your brains i would put
you in a world garden fixing the earth & useing your bodys
to WORK*

*womans job is to serve her children & keep the Earth but shes
not been on her job—she kicked back on her ass & the money
took over & she lost the balances of air water wild life & even
as her kids die in the street from drugs & Bull Shit she runs her
blam on me...*

*ps ive spent 30 years in prisons pecking the brains of the
men who experienced the pitts & typs of life & have never found
2 realitys the same—even the little words mean different things
to different people*

*reverse everything you think about me & put it back on the
people who put it on me & you will wake up that its just the
word games of the world you live in—everyone judges them
selves in me by me through me but no ones judged me—only i
can do that—*

i am—EASY—you—be as is, as i remain

> *your servent*
> *Charles Manson*

When Wendell finished the letter he felt dizzy and done-in.
There was an uncanny forcefulness to the non-stop flow of ideas,
no matter how crazy they were, that sent his head to spinning so
much he felt a touch of vertigo, as though he were standing out on

a rock overlooking the Red River Gorge. While he read Anna put on satin hotpants and a V-necked T-shirt, set a pile of records going on her stereo, and went into the kitchen to brew some mint tea.

"Reading a letter like that is enough to make me believe in the Devil," Wendell said, as they sat on the large beanbag cushions in the living room. "Why on earth did you write to him?"

"I don't know. I saw an article in a magazine that mentioned what prison he was in, so I thought I'd see what he had to say for himself."

"The man is warped."

"That sure is a kinky letter. I don't think I'll write to him again. I have this fear that he'll write me one that orders me to do something witchy. He's got a weird power, Charlie has."

She paused a moment and ran a hand through her hair absentmindedly.

"He's right about school though," she continued. "It *is* a bunch of mind-games. Three hundred of us sitting on plastic seats in a big hall listening to our professor drone on and on and everybody tries to go to sleep. It's even worse for me, because I've been out of school for years. To have to watch all those small-town middle-class kids going through their identity crisis and a bunch of out-of-it professors wiping their glasses on their ties or fussing with their pipes—what a downer! The whole world is a bummer these days, even Haight-Ashbury is nothing but bicycle shops and junkies. It's just a slum. Nothing is happening. The only excitement I get out of life is breezing around the track on a fast horse—that's the only thrill left."

Wendell gave Anna a close scrutiny—were her final remarks a challenge to him to put a charge back in her life? He reached out and touched her shoulder. She didn't seem to notice, so he began to rub her back lightly through the thin cotton of her shirt. Anna sat quietly, her eyes downcast, oblivious to his hand. He felt a simmering in his blood that encouraged him to persist. He slid off his beanbag cushion and over to hers, putting his arms around her and nuzzling his face in her fragrant hair. Her curls tickled his nose.

He brought his hands up to her neck, feathering his fingers along her throat, nudging her ear lobes, touching her cheeks, and slowly sliding his left hand downward until it rested on her breast. He could feel a soft nipple through the cloth. Putting one hand on her chin, he turned her face toward his and pressed his lips against hers. She looked at him coolly and impassively, neither taking nor refusing the kiss.

Feeling like he was reverting to the backseat wrestling of his senior prom, he kissed her again, holding her face to his while he slipped his hand under her T-shirt and up her back, running his fingers up and down her spine, massaging her neck, rubbing her shoulder blades.

"How does that feel?"

"Nice. Only why don't you do it right? Go get the blue bottle of massage oil from the nightstand and give me a proper back rub."

Wendell got up in a daze and followed Anna's instructions.

Anna slithered out of her shirt, shorts, and underwear, then lay out full-length on the living room floor and closed her eyes. Wendell contemplated the smooth brown skin of her back, buttocks, and legs. He poured some oil into his palm and worked on the muscles at the nape of her neck. Soon his own back was sore and his knees ached from kneeling on the hard wooden floor. At first he didn't know how to hold his hands—whether to touch lightly or apply pressure, whether to go fast or slow, pushing to the heart's center or outward to the extremities.

After a period of trial and error he got the knack. He cupped his hands to follow the contours of her body and varied his pressure from softer to harder, feeling for the particular needs of each muscle. Soon his hands were racing exuberantly over the smooth sand dunes of her skin, stroking and skimming, probing and rubbing. He even tried hacking and tapping her flesh with the outside borders of his hands.

All Wendell's efforts were putting Anna to sleep, but they were a sheer stimulus to him. He kept massaging her with one hand while he undressed with the other. When he was completely naked he stretched out on the floor beside her and began to knead her buttocks like bread dough. He inched closer, rubbing her with one hand and himself with the other.

He could hear the blood beating in his ears, and he shivered when his cock, quivering like a hazel rod near hidden water, touched her cool hip. He eased his hand between her thighs and moved it forward until it was pressed against her mound. With vacillating fingers he stroked the tangle of her bush and tried awkwardly to separate the warm, melting folds. He had never experienced difficulty at this stage before, but try as he might she would not let him discover her innermost source.

He felt a wave of anxiety, staring pointlessly at the molasses tumble of her hair. She didn't stir, she didn't even seem to breathe, but the air was thickening with seashell smells rising like incense. He slid his sweaty hands along the floor and rolled her over. Then, heart pounding, he tried to force his way inside her.

"What do you think you're doing?" Anna cried out, glaring daggers at him.

She jumped up and walked quickly to the bathroom, coming back with a towel around her waist.

"Who do you think you're kidding?" Wendell demanded.

She stared at him coldly and said, "Look, if you want to fuck, you should ask me."

Wracked by conflicting emotions, Wendell stood enraged, unable to speak. He felt a tremendous pressure building up; he wanted both to express his anger and explain his anguished frustration and why he acted the way he did, but his tongue had turned to stone. Even if he could have spoken, Anna was in no mood to hear what he had to say. She stepped directly up to him and continued her attack.

"You didn't really want to fuck me. If you wanted to fuck me you would have. You just wanted to play around like I was some kind of toy. What you really wanted was for me to seduce you, that's why you were so gentle, because you think that's how women should seduce men. You didn't want to fuck my cunt, you wanted to fuck my face. That's what men like you want, to be sucked off, because you're all queer at heart."

The blood flamed in his face, his eyes rolled back, and his heart stampeded. Obeying some buried instinctive rage beyond his control, Wendell whipped out his arms, grabbed Anna by the throat, and started squeezing.

In a second he saw the grimace on Anna's face and released his grip just as she brought her knee up sharply into his groin. He staggered away, doubled over in pain, feeling a rush of nausea. He half-expected Anna to hit him over the head with one of her flower pots, but instead she spoke to him in mocking tones, as if she were teasing him again.

"You crazy asshole. You don't know your own self. If you had gotten rough sooner, you could have had your manly fuck."

Wendell straightened up and glowered at her. Her knee had not made full contact with his balls and the pain began to subside.

"Go ahead. Put your hands on my neck," Anna ordered, enjoying her control of the situation and daring him to assert himself again. "Go ahead. Be fierce. You're too gentle. I like you better when you're angry."

Anna placed his hands back on her shoulders, but he had no desire to tighten his fingers and she knew it. Her eyes shone; she was getting a kick out of the scene—at last something exciting was happening. She reached down and caressed his cock. Then standing on tiptoe she lifted one bent leg as gracefully as a ballet dancer and with surprising ease guided him into her. She wrapped both arms around his neck, swung her other leg up around his back, and for a tottering moment he felt her full weight. He took a few faltering steps, his hands gripping her hips, then he managed a kind of controlled collapse onto a beanbag cushion. They both laughed. She mounted him again and started to generate an agile wriggle all her own, crying out like a coxswain, "Keep it up, I'm almost there."

Wendell came just after she spoke, while Anna went on thrusting, making him groan in spite of himself. Then she came in a series of profound contractions that made him flinch. She didn't stop moving until he pressed firmly on her rump to hold her still.

He braced himself, expecting to be put down for coming too soon, but she slipped gently free, gave him a full-mouthed kiss, and walked languidly to the bathroom. When she got to the door she turned around and smiled lazily at him.

"Good night. I'm going to bed."

"Do you want me to stay?"

"No. I think you should go home now," she said, and then added casually, "I'm such a bitch. Sorry I got so upset."

"I don't know what happened to me," Wendell said, his face throbbing. "One minute I'm acting like an adolescent at the drive-in, then I'm the Boston Strangler. It's just that I don't know where in hell you're coming from. You turn me on and off like a radio."

"I know I turn you on," she said. "I can't help it. I like to lure men on. I don't know why. I just know I enjoy it. So what can I say?"

"What about how I feel about you?"

"You don't know how you feel. First you want to fuck me and next you're trying to choke me."

"I don't know why I did that."

"It's no big mystery," she said offhandedly. "Hate is the flip-side of love, right?"

Anna beamed at him as if she were Buddha explaining the universe.

"But I don't hate you."

"A lot of men start out loving me more than I want and end up hating me more than I deserve."

"Well," Wendell said, trying to conceal his bitterness and be philosophical in turn, "it takes all kinds."

"I know," Anna replied, still smiling. "They ask me out."

She turned and went into the bathroom, closing the door.

Wendell stared at the slick spot her body had left upon the floor, watching it evaporate at the edges.

PART THREE

1

The shrill sound of an ambulance made Wendell sit up in bed. Its manic screech got louder before fading away in the direction of Richmond. He always felt a tightening in his chest when a siren broke the silence. One day for me, he thought, one day for me.

As he watched the trembling play of lunar light and tree shadows on the window curtains, he thought of his boyhood days on a farm outside Athens (pronounced A-thins in Kentucky). He evoked a vivid image of the cow barn, tobacco shed, and chicken coops—even the weathered pine siding of the house elaborately patterned with whorls and knotholes. He remembered the pride his father took in the wide-board wood-pegged floors and how he used to stand at the gate at dusk calling the cows with his deep voice, "Come boss. Come boss." He remembered how the hens held their wings out on the hottest days and how the whole family had to stay in the fields stripping tobacco until it became too dark to see the grade. He could almost hear the night sounds of cattle coughing or a restive horse slamming his hoof against the stall with the sharp retort of a pistol shot. They had lost the farm during the Depression, and his father ended up selling feed and seed at a country store while all the kids took turns pumping gas.

At night Wendell and his friends used to go cow-tipping, sneaking up to a sleeping cow and knocking it off its feet with a mighty shove before the poor beast understood what happened. One night out in the pastures he came upon a white horse under a leafy tree in the full moonlight. There was something so haunting about the sight that it terrified him. He stood staring at the horse for a long time, as if petrified. Then silently he backed away and hurried home, feeling strangely subdued. He never went cow-tipping again.

Maybe it was the moonlight that had made him evoke his past, but he was feeling wide awake now and his mind raced with memories. He grew up in a country of rolling hills where a boy's best dream was to grow tall enough to stuff an inflated leather sphere through an iron ring suspended ten feet from the floor, yet somehow his first love had been baseball. Every morning after milking he would throw a rubber ball against a strike zone he had painted on the barn, imagining the day when a line of large men would walk up to the plate, bat in hand, and he would coil back, kick one foot at the sky, whip his left arm forward, and fan them all. He was going to be the new Dizzy Dean. After his family moved, he did pretty well, too. He was the star pitcher of Lafayette High, until Pearl Harbor; all of a sudden, instead of being in the Big Leagues, he was an eighteen-year-old crackerjack Marine island-hopping across the Pacific.

After the war, he attended the University of Kentucky on the G.I. Bill; like many a returning veteran, he was serious about his studies. He worked hard and received good grades, but he couldn't decide what he wanted to do. Then in the summer before his senior year he married Kathy and it was no longer a question of what he wanted, but of what was available.

He hunted up a job in Detroit on the G.M. assembly line. His first day at the plant he went into the restroom and heard a man crying in the water closet. For the life of him he didn't know what the man was crying about. Then a month later, after he had been driven half-crazy by the pounding monotony of the conveyor belt, he found himself in that same toilet bawling his eyes out. The women on the line cried in front of everyone. Not the men. They had feelings that they were ashamed to show, so they wept in the john. Wendell vowed to get off the assembly line and find decent work. He did so well on the plant team that dreams of being in the Big Leagues returned. He pitched a three-hitter in the league championship and a scout for the Tigers offered him a tryout, but the Korean War broke out and he got called up. The next spring, instead of firing his fastball, he was ducking mortars and trying to merge with the mud at the bottom of a foxhole on some godforsaken hill whose number he could no longer recall.

When Wendell returned he found a job as a long-haul trucker driving a diesel rig. His plan was to work during the off-season, then in the spring join up with the Tiger's farm team and show his stuff. But that winter he developed bursitis in his left shoulder from traveling so much with the window open, and that finished his pitching career. Driving a truck for the Teamsters was the dumbest thing he had ever done. He felt like he had just walked in the winning run.

After that came a series of jobs: gas station owner, bartender, chauffeur, night watchman. He even joined in a vacuum cleaner sales program: that was the worst of all, smiling jerks in three-piece suits treating him like a happy robot they wanted to program "can do." They had inspections every morning—tie, shoes, shirt, the whole bit. They sang company pep songs at dinner and handed out merit badges at an awards banquet—all that Boy Scout crap. When it was over he dumped his sales kit in the nearest garbage can and never looked back.

Kathy was upset about that. She had been waitressing and doing other crummy jobs to make ends meet, and the hassle of it all was slowly honeycombing their relationship until there wasn't much left. At the start they had been as happy as two kittens in a clothes drawer, making love like they had invented it; but as the years and the bad breaks accumulated, it seemed as if the only passion they could muster was when they had their weekly fight over whose turn it was to clean the bathroom. Kathy could feel Wendell pulling away from her and retreating back into his shell. "What's gotten into you lately?" she would ask. "Tell me your feelings." "There's nothing to tell," he would say, and return to reading the sports page.

A few weeks later one of Kathy's friends saw Wendell with Gail at the drive-in and the roof blew off. "I know you're laying her," Kathy asserted, her eyes blazing as she paced up and down the living room. "Well, I'm sick of it and I want out. Go see if that doe-eyed dummy will darn your socks." After that it was nothing but recriminations and regrets, locked doors and cutting silences. It was a time of stale kisses, the stench of tears, and finally, the return of keys. Kathy left; he and Gail found out they had only one thing in common; Wendell went through mounting spirals of sorrow and self-hate. Why did he bungle everything he touched? After the divorce settlement, like many a lost soul seeking a new start, he moved to Key West.

That small drinking island with a slight fishing problem had lived off the bleached bones of shipwrecks, hand-rolled cigars, sweet-tasting shrimp called "pink gold," and finally tourists—the flowery shirt, Bermuda shorts crowd, smiling beneath sunglasses, taking pictures of each other, and feasting on conch fritters, yellowtail snapper, and key lime pie. Mingled among these gawking folks with red faces were assorted drug smugglers, the guys who never tucked in their silken shirts, wore Ray Bans and diamond earrings, and parked their power boats at the town dock. Wendell, who simply wanted to fish and forget the past, felt edgy in their presence.

Then he met a man who owned a tour boat in Flamingo, at the tip of the Everglades. Wendell worked for him during high season, telling the visitors about the mangrove swamps and showing them the old Seminole burial ground. He made enough money doing that to take the rest of the year off. Unfortunately, Florida had the best politicians money could buy; by the time the developers with their draglines and dozers were finished draining off water, the coast would be solid condominiums and the Everglades brown grass and cracked mud.

Wendell loved those mysterious swamps and he hated to see them destroyed. He liked to set out in a light canoe, forging a path through the maze of shallow canals. The vast expanse of sawgrass was dotted with small hammocks of trees where the deer hid during the day. He would reach down his hand into the tannic-tinted swamp water and bring up a punky green mass of spongy peat in his fist that he would squeeze again and again and still not wring dry. As filthy as the water looked, it was safe to drink. The swamp survived because of that stuff.

Sometimes he would seek out the ominous shades of the swamp where cypress trees squat in the muck, pink knees protruding from tan waters, Spanish moss and old man's beard hanging in silvery-grey fringes from angular bare limbs spread out as if in lamentation. Often a smoky mist rose from the water, giving everything a ghostly aura, so you had to look sharp to see the cottonmouths hidden in the maidenhair along the bank and the alligators basking in the sun on the muddy shore or sunk in ooze up to their eyeballs. The ones out of the water liked to sleep with their mouths open, letting the hot rays dry their teeth. They always seemed to be dead to the world, but he had seen how they could, when the situation called for it, slither down the bank with lightning speed and swim straight to the spot where the young deer had fallen or the largest gar were feeding. He had a profound respect for an alligator's alert and accurate eye, its uncanny ability to catch the least scent of blood. Once he had learned to detect at a glance their lairs, it seemed as if he couldn't stop seeing them. Before he dove into a swimming pool he always scanned the bottom, and the briefest glimpse of a piece of retread along the highway instantly registered in his mind as "alligator".

After a period of years Wendell left Florida and returned to Lexington, where he worked as a house painter, married Laura, and was happy for a time. He thought about soft lips and last kisses until he fell asleep.

He woke up hours later to a furry head trying to wedge itself under his chin, purring vigorously all the while and kneading his chest. Wendell tried to move his head. It hurt. He could feel the blood pulsing inside his skull and his groin was sore. Anna had certainly put him through his paces. The only danger he had experienced so far as a detective was when an irate husband had threatened him in the parking lot outside a Winn-Dixie with a tire iron. Wendell was grateful he had avoided any violence. After witnessing two wars he had no appetite for macho posturing and mayhem. He had become so tranquil in recent years that Laura used to tease him that he ought to wear rope sandals and carry a staff. Yet last night Anna had brought out the kind of murderous urge he hadn't felt since he had been a Marine in combat. How quickly she had stripped him of his hard-won maturity!

The truth was that Anna puzzled him as much as the crime he was hired to solve. In spite of all his years of experience with women, she made him feel like a complete novice. She had a way of troubling his emotions, sending him slamming like a light plane through turbulence, depleting his resources, throwing him off course, and making him fear that he might lose his bearings forever. Even in memory the image of Anna wrapping her legs around him and crying out in desire stirred him, but what did it all mean? She was like cotton candy, titillating his tastebuds but leaving him with that empty feeling and a toothache. Still he had a mad craving for her he didn't want to resist. He felt as if he were riding a toboggan down a steep wooded hillside with no hope of reversing his direction, yet if he kept his wits about him he might miss the trees. He knew Anna was trouble, but didn't want to dam up all his emotions, nor did he want to let his feelings flow only to watch them vanish in the sands of her impassiveness. At least she had taken his mind off Laura and made him stop moping around and feeling sorry for himself.

His personal credo was that life's two essential facts were sex and death, and that the challenge was to see how much love you could bring to the one and courage to the other. But today the whole man and woman thing baffled him. Why were they drawn together? Why did they pull apart? What he had once thought of as the simple beauties of sexual attraction now struck him as a senseless botch. Instead of nurturing the empathy and care that make love and courage possible, it seemed that men and women lived only to give each other grief.

Wendell knew that brooding about Anna wouldn't get him anywhere; he had to face the fact that the Devil Dancer case had him stumped. Two days of talking to the hired help had produced some tantalizing clues, but where did they lead? Julian's remark about the "symbolic shit" whites were prone to vexed him. What did he mean by that? What might the killing of Devil Dancer symbolize? Was there some kind of hidden meaning? Was Louie trying to tell him something when he said it was all "bad news"? Wasn't there a horse named that once? Because bad new travels fast. Whose horse was it? Sometimes nothing is as invisible as the familiar. Maybe the answer was right under his nose. He had watched a woodpecker stop its hammering and cock its head to one side, attentive to the bug beneath the bark, before resuming its attack. That's what he had to do—concentrate and then decide what leads should be pursued.

The most pressing possibility he needed to investigate was the Mafia angle. Even though Brad wouldn't say how much he had lost in Las Vegas, clearly he had dug himself a deep hole for the mob to bury him in. But how could Brad pay up now that Devil Dancer was dead? Or was that the plan? Did the mob kill Devil Dancer in order to force Davis to surrender his horse farm? Cliff had seen a slick customer at Sycamore Springs who might have been part of a secret syndication of Devil Dancer. Probably he was the same man that Lily saw. Was his real name John Lane? If so, was he the key man, or merely a mob goombah going about his godfather's business? In which case, who was the godfather? With front men running Caesar's Palace and Jimmy Hoffa on parole it was hard to know who was in charge of the Teamsters' pension funds and what the Mafia ties were. Maybe Conor could help. He might know about John Lane. He also might recognize the name of "Vinnie," and he certainly could tell him more about Ed "Bull" Fuller. The problem was that this was a boat Wendell did not want to rock, because he knew he could end up floating along the Kentucky River—face-down.

Wendell resolved to find Grady Shifflet as well. Probably he was off on another drunk. If he had nothing to hide, he'd turn up at the Mecca Bar. When he did Conor would let Wendell know. Meanwhile, he would try to forget about Anna for a while and put all his energy into the case. Maybe if he talked to enough people, searched enough rooms, fingered enough walls, somewhere a concealed panel would slide back and disclose the secret. But who knew where or when? Like his father used to say, "If you don't know where you're going, any road will take you there." Still, he wasn't about to give up. Shooting a horse might not qualify as a homicide, but in a way killing a defenseless animal was worse. Besides, he felt an affinity for Devil Dancer, a sense of obligation. He remembered the thrill of watching his great stretch run and the way the horse had greeted him with a friendly nicker, gazed at him inquisitively, and nuzzled his hand. Baffled as he was, Wendell was also excited by the case; maybe this would be the day he would find what he was looking for.

2

A group of the regulars was sitting at the bar tended by Barney and a guy with a face like an aging cherub named Larry. Wendell walked over and stood behind Conor. As usual he was expounding his philosophy of life, waving a bottle of beer in the air for emphasis as he spoke.

"Hey, Wendell, you old scratch-ass sonofabitch, you snuck up on me. You move like a cat. Maybe a little second-story action might be more your line of work." Conor winked at him with his good eye. "I was just telling the boys my version of the situation. You got to admit these ain't good times. Say, do you know these guys, Wendell? That's Al, this fat guy here is Jesse, and this is my good drinkin' buddy Joe. I got to know Al real good in Eddyville. We both done our own time down there."

Wendell recognized Jesse as one of the obese men who had been in the bar the other day telling dirty jokes; Al was a tall thin-faced man whose eyes were red-rimmed with what looked like a bad case of welder's flash. He kept blinking as if air were too abrasive an element to see in. Joe had lost both of his legs in World War II; now he walked on two wooden peg legs supported by crutches. Every time his government disability check came in, he would cash it and head for the Mecca Bar. He would sit down at one of the tables, unfasten his peg legs, and put them on the floor next to his crutches. Then he would drink himself into oblivion. When the police arrived they would send in two men—one to carry Joe and the other for his wooden legs and crutches.

Wendell listened to the men banter. They could go on all day, on any topic—flying saucers, the perfect car, politics, horses, women, sports, crime—covering a staggering sequence of subjects during a single afternoon. Most bars, the men sat around glumly, staring at their drinks or watching the ball game and mumbling out a half-sentence now and again, but these men loved to talk even more than they loved to drink.

"Still looking for Grady?" Conor asked. "He hasn't been in here since I last saw you."

"Yeah, I'm still looking for him."

"Christ, why bother?" Al asked. "That dingbat is one hopeless case. There ain't nothing he ever did in his life that didn't come out wrong. Take sales, he tried that. You know some guys can sell ice cream to Eskimos, but Grady, he couldn't sell gold bricks for a quarter. He's about the unluckiest guy I know. Some guys could fall into a biffy and come up with a fistful of ten dollar bills. But Grady, one day he'll fall through his pants and hang himself."

"How well do you know Grady, Al?" Wendell asked. "Did he ever talk about his plans?"

"Grady was always talking big," Al said. "He wanted to piss with the big dogs. But that squirt couldn't pee upwind on a calm day. All he did was drift around this city year after year. He'd work as a dishwasher, then he'd go off on a drunk and get fired. Next he'd try to steal something, get caught, and get sent to Eddyville. When he got out, he'd start the cycle all over again. He was always talking about the big jobs he was going to pull, but one time he tried to break into a hardware store, cut his arm on the broken window, and had to turn himself in before he bled to death. That guy, talking about him makes me depressed."

"I can just see him," Conor said, "pulling his pistol in a bank and saying, 'Putem up, mother-sticker, this is a fuck up.'"

"Where does a guy like that go?" Wendell asked when the laughter stopped.

"There are a lot of bridges in this state," Al said. "He could be sleeping off a drunk under any one of them."

"Or he could have croaked," Conor added. "Too many guys like him turn up dead."

"If all you're ever gonna be is a dishwasher, you might as well be dead," Jesse said.

"Now detective, there's a plush job. All you do is show broads your gun and they beat you to the sack, right?" Al gave Wendell an envious grin.

"Don't he wish," Jesse said.

"You got it, Jesse," Wendell replied. "If wishes were horseflesh, we'd all be thoroughbreds."

"Or we'd all get trampled," Conor said, squinting at Wendell.

"Why are you looking for Grady?" Joe asked.

He told them.

"So you're working for Brad Davis," Al said. "Talk about lucky guys, he's one of them. His second wife, Charlene, is a pure sugar scoop. She is one fine filly, and hot to trot, what I hear. That chick, I'd love to pull her legs apart and make a wish."

"Wish in your left hand and shit in your right, Al, and see which one comes true," Conor added morosely.

"What have you heard about Charlene?" Wendell, feeling queasy, gave Al a hostile stare.

"What I hear is that the Davises give parties for the Kentucky football team out at Sycamore Springs."

"That's no big deal," Wendell said. "Brad Davis has always been a big football fan."

"Yeah, but what I hear is that top recruits are brought out there to get a tour of a horse farm and some players usually work there during the summer."

"So, what's the point?"

"The point is that it isn't Brad Davis who arranges all this, it's Charlene. The word is she entertains some players on a more personal basis."

"There are always rumors about what Charlene does at parties." Wendell was becoming increasingly defensive.

"But this isn't at parties," Al said. "And these particular players happen to be black."

"Sounds like Sycamore Springs is a stud farm in more ways than one," Jesse said.

"It's just a rumor." Wendell felt an urge to slam his fist into Jesse's drunken mug.

"You used to play football, didn't you, Wendell?" Jesse asked. "Hey, now I remember, Brad Davis was the quarterback. He threw the pass that you dropped against Bryan Station. He was good. Where did he go to college?"

"Yale," Wendell said. "After the war."

"I've heard of it," Conor remarked. "They make good locks."

"How did you do at the track yesterday?" Al asked Conor.

"I almost had a religious experience in the third race, but he got jammed on the far turn. Then some jailbird gave me a tip on a late good thing. But that damn butt-sprung morning glory was so slow the pinhead riding him collected time and a half."

""Mine got left at the gate," Al said. "That nag's got a future as dog chow."

"I still love Keeneland," Conor asserted. "I wouldn't be a true Kentuckian if I didn't believe that my redeemer was born in a stable."

"You're Irish, aren't you, Conor?" Al asked. "I hear they got no snakes there."

"And none the worse for that," Conor admitted, winking at Wendell. "You are correct, there are no snakes in Ireland—except in the heart." He started to laugh at his own joke, but his laugh misfired into a racking cough.

"Did you have a bad night last night?" Wendell asked.

"No. Last night was good," Conor said. "This morning. That was bad."

"Were you drunk last night?" Wendell asked.

"That I was. It seems I have a problem. My drinking is the result of a total lack of character—and a great thirst."

"You made quite a hit with that dame last night, Conor," Al said, smiling widely. "This broad comes into The Paddock wearing skin-tight gold lamé slacks and a low-cut sweater that barely protected the property and hid nothing of the view. And every time she leans over to suck off her swizzle stick, all the guys groan. Finally, Conor staggers over and very formally he says, 'Madame, if you're going to drown those puppies, I'll take the one with the pink nose.'"

Jesse laughed so hard he blew beer suds across the bar. The others couldn't stop howling. Wendell took the chance to go take a leak.

The men's room at the Mecca Bar was one of those places where the floor was merely an extension of the urinal. Wendell waded in and took his stance, noting on the wall a photo of Annie Oakley with her pistol pointed at his crotch. "Don't look up here," stated the graffiti at eye level, "the joke's in your hand." Going out he saw another one on the bottom of the crapper door that made him laugh—"Beware of limbo dancers."

When he came back the men were talking about the election.

"Well, who are you going to vote for then?" Al demanded.

"I don't know, McGovern, I guess. He looks like he needs the money."

"McGovern?" Al shouted. "He's a horse that won't finish."

"I know he's a loser, but I like him. Scuttle your own canoe, that's my motto."

"At least he'll get us out of Vietnam," Wendell said, thinking suddenly of Julian.

"War. Agh. I wouldn't send a dog to war," Joe said. "Not after what I've seen."

Wendell knew that once the men got worked up about war and politics they could wrangle until midnight, so he guided Conor over to a dark booth away from the bar. He told him about Davis's gambling debts and how a man named John Lane accompanied by "Bull" Fuller and "Vinnie" somebody had visited Sycamore Springs.

"These guys are mobsters, obviously, but whose mob do they work for? Do they freelance, or are they Mafia soldiers? You've got to help me with this."

"There is no such thing as the Mafia, Wendell, and if you call them that, they'll kill you. Those are real rough boys. If Davis owes a marker in Vegas, they can find very creative ways to collect. They would probably sublet the matter. I know guys who might know if they whacked Devil Dancer, but I also know those guys won't talk. See, I know, and they know, a stool pigeon who had his tongue cut out and his head held back until he choked to death on his own blood. I wouldn't want that to happen to me or you. For Dracula, that's OK. Me, I don't drink blood."

"I sure don't want to stick my neck out. My idea of an adventure is drinking a dry martini in a plain glass and falling off the back porch. I don't like to take unnecessary risks, but I need to know what those guys are up to. If Davis is in the hole as much as I think, they might want to take over his farm. You see my problem. What can you tell me about them?"

"Plenty—but if I tell you, you've got bigger problems. I've already been observed by a certain person talking to you. You can't hide things from those kinds of guys."

"Look, I've got to investigate this, whether you help me or not. If you don't let me know what I'm dealing with here, I could get taken for a ride and never come back."

"I feel lousy, not being more help. You know me, I've been threatened before. I scare, but I don't scare easy. But these guys, they threaten you, it's a whole new thing. It's not like one guy giving you a hard time, it's *them*. If you're tougher than the first guy, they got another guy, maybe a bunch of other guys, backing him up, and each is tougher than the one before. I know a guy, they gave him a terrific beating and he still didn't crack, so the day he left the hospital, they jumped him in the parking lot and beat him so bad all his bandages fell off. Lucky he's near the hospital, or he's a dead man. You age quick, those guys come at you. A few seconds with them, you're an old man. I'm telling you, Wendell, drop it. I don't want you nosing around and slipping up. Guys make mistakes. I go to their funerals. The casket is always closed."

"You're a morbid bastard. You wouldn't be trying to frighten me, would you?"

"Damn straight. I may be a fool, but at least I'm not a young fool. You better listen to me. I'm not just alive, I'm *still* alive. That ain't no small accomplishment, the life I've lived."

"I'm not exactly a rookie. I'm pushing fifty."

"I know. I know. But compared to me, see, you're a young man. You want to learn where everything goes. You got a crime here, a puzzle, and you want to find the pattern and put the pieces together. Am I right or am I right? Hell, Wendell, this ain't no game. Nobody sees where nothing goes. What you find is not what you thought you was looking for. You never even know what you mighta done different. You just live until you die, if the limb don't fall."

"Conor, I want to live a long life too. Help me do it. Tell me who these guys are. You must know something about Bull Fuller."

"OK, OK. He's a cop, or at least he used to be, up in Newport. He was in on the Ratterman bust at the Glenn Hotel. He got kicked off the force for treating his girlfriend the way Jerry Lee Lewis treats a piano. The mob uses him as backup sometimes for shakedowns. Who knows what else he's into. He's a mean piece of work and he'd plant you at the drop of a hat."

"Where does he live?"

"He's down here a lot, but I think he still lives in Newport. In the past he's worked as a bouncer at the Kitty Kat Klub, maybe he still does."

"What about John Lane, do you know anything about him?"

"I'm afraid so. I got settled in the state pen in Columbus a few years ago—gave me a chance to catch up on my reading. I shared a cell with Marty "The Closer" Malafissi; he was an enforcer for the Cleveland outfit. Say what you want about a code of silence, these mob guys love to tell their stories. What they have up in Ohio ought to be called The Melting Pot Mob, because you've got the Jewish Boys, the Irish Crew, and the Murray Hill Gang all mixed up in the thing together. This John Lane, his real name is John "Jack the Ripper" Zentko, works mainly for Jack Licavoli and the Youngstown mob. He started out on the goon squad at the Jungle Inn. Then for a while he worked for Sandy Naples and hung out at a place called Satan's Inferno. He got his nickname because he likes to use the knife. Two taps to the back of the head and a slit throat—that's his signature. He fancies himself a ladies man and he craves the best of it; I used to see him gambling at the Beverly Hills; he was once engaged to Martha Raye."

"What did they see in each other?"

"I have my dark suspicions."

"What about this Vinnie, does that ring a bell?"

"It tolls for you, my friend. You're probably talking there about Vinnie "The Vice" Scarbono. You don't want to know how he got his nickname. He does strong arm stuff for Teamsters Vending Workers Local 410-Y; any machine you see in a bar—jukebox, cigarettes, candy—they get a cut."

"So who do you think sent them down here, Jack Licavoli?"

"Could be; but like I said, it's all tangled up there. See, Licavoli works for the Cleveland mob, but the boss, John Scalish, is getting old, so his people are being challenged by an upstart Irish guy named Danny Greene. And on top of that you've got Moe Dalitz and all those mobbed-up Jewish guys who live in Vegas now but still have clout in Ohio and with the Teamsters. So I don't know who sent those guys you mentioned or whether they put a hit on Devil Dancer. My guess is they just wanted to collect some cash and get out; but now that the horse is dead, that's blood on the water to these sharks, and there's no telling what they'll do."

"Are Zentko and Scarbono still around?" Wendell felt compelled to keep asking leading questions, even though they might lead straight off the gang plank and into the deep blue sea.

"I know somebody who might know."

"Will you tell me his name?"

"*Her* name's Caprice Speciale, and she's up in Newport. She's the owner of the Kitty Kat Klub and she owes me a favor. I met her through Sally. She's a real broad, not some twist. She was married to Charles "Chucky Surprise" Cisternero…this summer he got bumped off…"

Conor seemed to choke on his words and looked pained.

"What is it?"

"He was found up in Newport in his bathtub, with a bullet in his forehead, another between his balls, and his throat slit."

"A mob hit."

"Sure, but it's that slit throat that bothers me. That looks like our boy Jack the Ripper."

"How does that tie in?"

"If civil war is starting in Ohio, it could spill over to Newport. Listen, my advice is don't go there; you don't want to walk into the lion's den when the big cats are snarling over scraps."

"I thought the mob got kicked out of Newport years ago after Ratterman was elected."

"The play's still there and so are some of the players; I hear Screw Andrews is out of the slammer and might try to muscle back into the action; they've even renovated the old Beverly Hills and reopened it as a supper club. Sweet Jaysus, Wendell, I've already told you more than you should know. Promise me that if you go to Newport you'll be very careful. These guys, they're motivated; for some it's the money, but for others it's the chance to clip a guy; their idea of a pink slip is an ice pick in the ear. If you don't watch your ass, you'll end up as trunk music in some airport parking lot."

"The way you sound, maybe I should tell the undertaker to expect a customer."

"You never know. I heard about a guy, drinking beer like you and me, who swallowed the flip top tab of his beer can, slit his own throat from the inside, and died on the spot."

Wendell fidgeted a little as Conor told the story, remembering that he had cut his upper lip on a beer can about a month ago.

"I know lots of stories about funny ways guys die," Conor said. "You ever hear of the Hashhouse Kid? That's one for the end book. He was one of the old time con men. A fine man—damn it, they was all good men in them days. He was on the Titanic when it went down."

"A lot of people went down on the Titanic."

"Stop interrupting. The Hashhouse Kid went down on the Titanic, like I said, but he came back up again. He didn't die. He was saved. Later he found out the names of many of the people who *did* die, filed a series of phony baggage claims, and made a killing. The disaster was so confused, the company didn't know who went down and who didn't, the Hashhouse Kid saw an opportunity there, and he took it."

"How did he finally die?" Wendell wondered if Conor was putting him on.

"All his life the Hashhouse Kid was a bachelor. That's how he got his name. He slept in flops and ate only at hash houses, even when he was in the money. He dressed like a bum, too, and drank like a fish. Everybody figured he was gonna burn himself out young. But he didn't. He lived until he was sixty. And then he fell in love. With a social worker, a real looker, still in her twenties. She was gonna reform him. He started dressing neat, eating only in the best restaurants, water his strongest drink. I went to the wedding. It was in an Episcopal church, tuxedos, the works. A very classy affair. The next day I get a phone call. The Hashhouse Kid is dead. He died on his honeymoon night."

"I've heard of that happening," Wendell said. "A guy changes his life, it messes up his whole system. I'm always hearing about guys who die within six months of the time they retire. I'm sorry about the Hashhouse Kid, but what's so special about him dying the way he did?"

"You haven't let me finish the story. I get the call that the Kid's dead; it seems his will called for a brief open-coffin funeral with only his closest friends in attendance; he wanted his body to be cremated and his ashes scattered in the Atlantic. So I go down to the funeral home that same day. About twenty of us are there. We're all sitting around looking glum and exchanging stories about the Kid (he was a real character, he even wrote poetry, he was almost as good a poet as the Sanctimonious Kid), when suddenly he sits up in the coffin! We all damn near have a heart attack at the same time. The Kid wasn't dead! He's sitting up in the coffin, looking groggy and puzzled, like his eyes couldn't quite focus, trying to figure out where he is and what's going on. At first I think he thinks this is still part of the wedding ceremony, cause all of us guys had been at the wedding the day before. That was why he smiled. And when he smiled, we all started smiling too, and we stood up and started over to talk to him, ease him into what has happened. But no sooner do we move in his direction than he notices where he is. He looks down at the coffin, still smiling, still thinking maybe this is some kind of bachelor party and the coffin is some kind of joke, when suddenly the smile vanishes. I realize he's just remembered the part about the honeymoon, about the stroke or whatever it was he had that the doctor (who I heard was more dead than alive himself) had mistakenly pronounced terminal. Then the Kid gets the most agonizing look on his face I've ever seen. His mouth opens as wide as it would go, wider than you'd think a mouth *could* go, and his tongue is sticking out farther than any tongue has a right to reach. It looks like he's screaming at the top of his lungs, only he isn't making a sound. Just that silent scream for a split second, then he jerks his hand up to his throat, looks at us with unspeakable reproach, tucks forward like he's been hit with a sledge hammer, and dies. Instantly. He was dead when he hit the coffin. The next day he was cremated, and his ashes got scattered where he wanted."

Wendell had listened to Conor's story with growing interest. It was such a bizarre tale, he didn't really see that there was much point to it. In fact, he didn't see the point to most of the stories he had heard during the last three days. But it had moved him anyway. It sounded more like somebody's nightmare than something real, yet he didn't think Conor had made it up. That wasn't his style. He liked his stories to be true. Even when they were unbelievable.

"If I listen to any more of your stories, I'll be afraid to get out of bed in the morning. Or go to sleep at night. Every time we talk all I hear are things that leave me more confused than before. You wouldn't be stalling me, would you, to keep me from solving this case?"

"That's a thought," Conor chuckled and gave Wendell a mischievous grin. "Yes sir, that's definitely a thought. Not much of one, though. You know me, I could care less who shot Brad Davis's horse. But I like you, boyo, and I want to see you make good. You started a little late out of the gate, in my opinion, being a detective. You're going to have to make one hell of a stretch run if you want to solve this here case quick enough to get on prime time."

Wendell eyed Conor closely. "Do you know who shot Devil Dancer?"

"I've got a hunch," Carl said, "but it's just a hunch. Young man, I've already told you more than I should have. I don't want to be the one who tells you something you don't really want to know, in the long run. If you must go to Newport, look for Caprice at the Kitty Kat Klub and tell her I sent you. After you've talked to her, if you value your life, don't hang around town and don't try to hunt for Bull Fuller or his friends, understand? You'll be on your own, single o, and you don't want nobody grabbing you by the throat."

"OK, I'll be good. Thanks for your help. You're a life saver."

"That remains to be seen," Conor said morosely.

"I got something for you," Al said to Wendell when he and Conor had returned to the bar. "Did you know that Grady's got a sister, lives here in Lexington? You might look her up. I don't think they're that close. I only heard him mention her once or twice. But it can't hurt to ask."

"What's her name?" Wendell asked excitedly. "Do you know where she lives?"

"Betty something," Joe said. "I used to know her. She lives with a guy named Pete. On North Limestone right before you come to Third Street. It's just past the used bookstore, on the left. A little place with a white picket fence in front."

Wendell knew the bookstore. He could stop by Betty's house and still be in Newport by the early afternoon. He thanked the men for the tip, asked Conor to keep in touch, and paid Barney for the drinks.

"I'll see you guys later," he said on his way out. "Sorry to break up the party."

"I should be going, too," Jesse said. "I gotta go home and do my homework."

"Ah. Don't rush off," Al said. "Take your time. Let your old lady enjoy herself for once."

Everybody roared except Jesse.

"You wanna watch you don't let your mouth overload your asshole, you know that?" His voice lacked the authority of genuine anger.

"Calm down and cool yourself, Jesse," Barney shouted. "I don't want no beefs in my place. If you wanna fight, go out in the street and fight. You guys gimme a pain."

"OK, Barney," Al said. "I'm tired of talking about broads. The fuckin' you get ain't worth the screwin' you take. These days I'm getting laid off more than I'm getting laid anyway."

Jesse hadn't been especially mad. The men always ribbed each other, but Barney had over-reacted to the situation and looked upset. Everybody turned their attention to calming him down. By the time Wendell reached the door, an argument was brewing over who kept his cool the best. Joe was hollering that it was him.

3

In quest of a caffeine pick-me-up, Wendell walked over to a small arcade that had a Coke machine, put his coins in the slot, and a can clattered out. He sat down for a moment in a plastic chair by the door, watching the jerking hips of the pinball players. They played as if their lives depended on it—ecstatic when the machine threw one of its electric fits. In the end, they always lost—they got tired, or bored, or they forgot to concentrate—and the silver ball dropped down the hole. That was his problem, Wendell thought. He needed to clear his head and concentrate, then maybe the clues would connect and the hidden meaning emerge. He was determined to persist, like a safecracker systematically fiddling at a combination lock, until he could feel the tumblers fall into place and the case was cracked open. One step at a time, he told himself, first Grady's sister then on to Newport to talk to Caprice Speciale. That was the plan.

Betty's tiny house was jammed between the bookstore and the bar on the corner. One listless tree drooped in a front yard the size of a sandbox. Two robins pecked haphazardly beside the gravel path. Nailed to the trunk of the tree was a crudely lettered sign that said:

KEEP OUT

BAD DOGS

pete

There was no dog in sight; since the two sidewalls of the house were flush with the neighboring buildings, there wasn't even a dog out of sight, unless he was hiding under the ramshackle porch.

Wendell reached over the picket fence, released the catch on the gate, and swung it open on a rusty hinge. He walked cautiously up onto a porch so fragile his footsteps seemed to shake the house and rapped lightly on the door, fearing that the vibration might shatter the windowpane. He stood motionless, listening, not hearing any sounds, but after a long pause the dirty linen curtain was pulled aside slightly and he found himself looking into a hollow-eyed ghostly face with high cheek bones and a chin that tapered to a point.

"What?" the woman asked in a strained voice.

"I'm a friend of Grady's," he said, hoping for the best.

"You a law?" She glared at him with wary eyes.

"No. Like I said, I'm a friend. I'm a drinking buddy from the Mecca Bar," Wendell shouted so that she could hear. "I borrowed some money from him a while ago, and I'd like to pay it back. If you'll be seeing him soon, maybe I could leave the money with you."

"How much?" She studied his face as if trying to read the fine print on his forehead.

"Fifty dollars." Wendell picked what he guessed would be a reasonable figure.

He heard her slide back a bolt, turn a lock, and then the door swung open.

"I know yer lyin', Grady never had no fifty dollars to lend to nobody in his life. I don't have any notion about where he is, but I'll talk to you. I got nothin' better to do."

She mumbled these remarks as she led him into a low-ceilinged sour-smelling room cluttered with a broken-legged couch, two small wooden chairs, an out-sized outdated TV set, and a card table with a checkerboard design on the top. A picture of John Kennedy, apparently torn from of a magazine, was scotch-taped to the wall.

"My name is Wendell Clay, Mrs..."

"Jist call me Betty."

"I'd like to ask you a few questions if it won't put you to any trouble."

"Trouble! Lord, you couldn't put me to no more trouble than I already got." She shook her head and compressed her lips.

She sat down in a chair facing him, looking washed-out and worried. Her swollen-veined hands fidgeted in her lap as if she were trying to pick the polka dots off her dress.

"Jist look at me," she said in a parched voice, lifting one withered hand up to the wrinkled skin at her throat. "Look at me and you tell me how serious it is. I look terrible. I feel terrible, too. It's a hard life on a woman, for a fact. I can't do but so much anymore before ahm pure tard. I feel like somethin' the cat dragged in."

Wendell searched his mind for consoling words to say, but the truth was she did look bad. She was painfully thin; her skin had a sickly sallow color; her small pale-blue watery eyes stared with trapped desperation from behind the faint purple cobweb of crooked veins that netted her face. Her upper lip seemed to be feeding on the lower from sheer deprivation.

"I been tard all my life," she continued. "I never thought there was nothin' permanent wrong a right smart piece of rest won't fix, but the doctor jist tole me different. Hit's luke."

"What?"

"Luke-ah-ke-mah. Doctor tole me yesterday."

She announced this with a plain matter-of-factness that Wendell found much more disturbing than if she had wept or raved. He couldn't think of an appropriate response. What do you say to someone who has just been handed a death warrant?

"I can't tell you how sorry I am, but none of those things are as fatal as they used to be," he said, trying to sound upbeat. "They're getting closer to a cure for cancer every day."

"Not for Luke, they ain't. They got it now so if you take all their medicines you start to feel better; you even sometimes get to feelin' good; but then you die anyway. Them medicines, I can't afford'em, an' they don't do much good. No sir, it's all up with me. I got an eaten cancer in the blood so it won't be long now before I'll be gone. An' I'll tell you something else, I ain't that sorry. Hit's gettin' so I can't hardly walk. If it gets any worse, I'd jist as soon be dead."

Wendell felt his face twist into a grimace that was probably a mirror image of Betty's own agonized expression.

"A body can't take but only so much," she said, looking more frail than ever. "Hit's a wonder I got this far. I come from a good-sized family, but me an' Grady is the only ones left now. I lost my little sister Opal to the flux, an' two of my brothers got theirselves shot dead in the Depression—Clayton for joinin' the union, an' Elroy over that Whitaker gal, Tesse Sue; Cecil was kilt in the war; Lester passed away last year."

Betty recited her list of disasters as if it were an assignment she had memorized for school. Wendell hoped she wouldn't go on. If there were fourteen children in her family, he was afraid he might burst out laughing or screaming. Even tragedy can be redundant.

"Do you ever see Grady?"

"When we was kids me an' Grady was real close. After Mama nigh lost half her blood havin' Opal she never did get all the way better. I had to take care of the kids. I'm the only mama they ever really knowed. My daddy couldn't farm much after the flood of 19 and 27 brought in all that mud an' then we got tractored out anyway. Back when I was a baby 'Devil' John Wright come up our holler with gold in his hand an' my granddaddy signed... He didn't sign, he made his mark. I been to school myself, though I can't but barely sign my name. Granddaddy never had no schoolin'. But when he seen that gold he put his mark on what we called a 'long deed' an' sold all his mineral rights for fifty cents an acre. He never had no cash money, so he reckoned it was fine by him if they wanted to mine under his land. He didn't know nary a nothin' about no strip minin'. They didn't have that then. But they did when my daddy owned the farm. One day a bulldozer come to the holler an' tore up everything; they come right through where our people was laid to rest. I like to go crazy when I think of that. They knocked down all them trees up back of the house, an' the next big rain washed us right down into the creek. Grady an' me slept in a junked Chevy all the rest of that year. Then Daddy started workin' for them coal companies—Black Mountain, Fordson, Peabody—he worked for a bunch of 'em an' we moved around from company town to company town. One winter when the mines was shut down an' they put us out we most froze to death; we lived on nothin' but pinto beans, corn bread, an' bulldog gravy. We never had no decent meals, us kids. An' you can't do without food."

Wendell had grown up in the thirties, so he knew what hard times were all about, but it was all too clear that Betty's life had been nothing but hard times.

"Whereabouts were you and Grady raised?"

"We weren't from anywhere. Jist from near there. We growed up on Hell for Certain Creek after the flood. Then we moved around some, mainly in Harlan an' Leslie counties. We lived in Greazy an' Brutus, on Flat Creek an' Hurricane Creek—I can't recollect whereall we lived, but it was no life. Hit was considerable violent in them days. There must a been several killings, I don't know. My memory don't serve me. I believe there was, yes. Now I recalls all them funerals. They shot that sheriff, Sheriff Daniels. Them Jones and Hightower boys got blamed. Then the sheriff over in Knox shot that Simms fella when he tried to come an' make a speech. He was jist a boy, Simms was, but I hear tell he was a real fine speaker. There was a plenty more, nobody knows how many. The company brung in them gun thugs from Chicago an' those niggers from

Alabama who jist got theirselves kilt. I found one. Nigger left on a spoil bank beside Looney Creek. He was deader than hell. Oh Lordy, it was jist terrible."

Wendell had vague boyhood memories of "Bloody Harlan County," but he didn't remember the story—something about communists and writers and the United Mine Workers.

"I growed up hatin' those yaller dogs an' scabs, but that didn't make me feel any better findin' that body. Somewhere in there we moved to Hazard. Hit was me, Grady, an' Daddy then, they both worked in the mines. Daddy was a good coal man, but Grady, he didn't take to it, so he off an' enlisted. He was in the navy, but they discharged him dishonorable—to this day I don't know what he done that was so wrong. After that, he got footsy an' jist started in driftin'."

"Could Grady have gone back to your home in Hazard?" Wendell asked, trying to get Betty ahead of her story.

"I don't think Grady ever would want to go back there. He never were a homebody an' he hated those mines. He got real bitter about how much money them owners had. Some of them bosses got independent rich overnight, seems like. Grady used to say he wished he was an owner with an air-cooled car, then he could tell everybody to go to Hell, an' the Devil take the hindmost. Can't say as I blame him neither. While we was livin' off script an' pilin' up debts at the company store, they was buildin' big houses above the town. When I see them highfalutin' houses an' when I think how them mines is filled with dead men's bones, I get bitter, too. There's always some folks what wants a whole lot of everything for doin' a little bit a nothin'. Grady got so mad he even shot a man in a fight, killed him, too. Grady was up for willful murder, but he got left off. Nobody liked that foreign fella he killed."

Betty's story startled Wendell. He had assumed that violence was not a part of Grady's character. From all reports, he sounded like too weak and defeated a man to pull a trigger.

"Did Grady get into fights very often? Did he carry a gun?" Wendell hoped his sudden questions wouldn't alarm Betty, who thus far had been more than willing to talk.

"Grady? No. Grady never carried no gun. That fella that died got kilt with his own gun. My Daddy, now he had a gun, called it his John L. Lewis Peacemaker. I might not oughta say this, but he's dead now, so I don't see that it much matters, but I do believe he used it a few times too. He was real strong for the union. I don't know what you want to talk to Grady about, but he warn't no violent man. He sometimes got real hot inside, he'd get so hot I thought he'd explode, but jist for that one time, I never heard nary a nothin' about him even bein' in a fight. Good thing, too; Grady's no fighter. I whupped him all the time when we was kids."

"What sort of things got Grady mad?"

"Grady was always, like I say, mad at the bosses. He had sharp memories of what happened to our Daddy. He'd get down on the niggers more than most folks I'd say. Where we lived in Leslie County niggers was only there to serve the white people of the town. Mostly all he was to us was a shoeshine boy. They had their own place to live set up by the town—this street was called 'Back Street' because they lived there—as long as he stayed there, he was said to be a good man. When Grady come to Lexington he took on terrible about how the niggers was steppin' outa line. He never done nary a thing about it, far as I know, but he jist burned inside. He wanted every place to have a Back Street. He didn't think this race mixin' was right."

Wendell wondered how Grady kept his head on straight, working on a horse farm side by side with the black grooms. Could he have fumed for years and then finally exploded, directing his anger at a horse instead of at the blacks he apparently hated? That sounded farfetched, but possible. Or did Grady associate Brad Davis with the arrogant bosses of his youth? Grady was beginning to look like a serious suspect. But that merely complicated the problem, because he had no idea where Grady might be. Wendell asked Betty if her brother had any other relatives.

"Grady never was big on family. He'd go years at a time without ever settin' foot inside our home. When Daddy got crippled in that slide an' ended up workin' as a slate picker, Grady never even knowed it until almost a year. Sometimes he'd be in the pokey— them laws was always puttin' him in jail for jist nothin'—but most of the time he'd be goin' every whichaway some. He hasn't got real good sense, I don't believe. Grady, he tries, but he's jist as sorry as most men, you can't count on 'em. He couldn't hardly make the standards at school. He never got above sixth. Some years we didn't even go cause we didn't have no decent clothes. Course I done even worse, but I had a household to run when I was barely eight. I ain't sayin' I done any better'n Grady. I've done some real dumb things. Got married when I was thirteen. Everybody tole me nothin' good would ever come of it—didn't neither—but I was too young to not know no better, so I done it anyhow. Soon as I had his baby, he up an' left me. I tole you I was dumb. If I knew where that baby was, I'd tell you, but the truth is I don't. Cause I give my own precious baby up for adoption an' run off to De-troit."

A drawn distraught look made Betty's face appear even more haggard. She lifted bent fingers to her cheek and touched a red spot below her right eye where the blood vessels had broken. If she continued to talk about her life, Wendell felt totally unprepared to console her. How was he to cope with all this random intimacy, the tragic stories people tell each other? Why couldn't she just tell him what he needed to know so he could be on his way to Newport? Why did she, like so many people, seem to have a terrible need to lay bare her soul to a stranger?

"At sixteen I was a whore in De-troit. This was the Depression an' everything was dirt cheap. A woman's body was one of the cheapest things of all. I'd a been dead a long time ago if a strange thing hadn't happened. One day this little preacher man—he wasn't hardly but five foot tall—tole me that I had a friend in Jesus. Well, sir, I laughed at him, and I blew smoke in his face. When I did that he didn't even blink, but I seen that he was weepin' (it might a been just the smoke from my cigarette), but I figured he was weepin' for me. Mama was long dead an' Daddy wasn't no weepin' man, so I'd never had nobody weep for me before. After he left I got out my Bible an' I wrote in it 'Jesus Loves Me.' That were a fine feelin', to write that. I quit bein' a whore an' I come back home an' become a mother for Grady an' his brothers. Nobody could tell me where my baby had gone, an' I never have heard to this day. I don't hold by religion so much anymores. I figure when you die, you die. But that little man did save my life, an' ahm grateful to this day. I can't tell how low in Jesus misery I had sunk in De-troit. It was pure livin' Hell, an' that's the truth. Down. Down. I been there."

Betty's eyes were filled with remorse. If she were a country singer, she'd probably have enough material from her own life to make her fortune in Nashville. Perhaps she and Little Enis ought to collaborate on some sad songs. Wendell knew that he wasn't much closer to finding Grady than before, only now he had a notion that finding him might be the key to everything.

"I'm sorry about your illness," he said with empathy. "I do hope you get well."

"I'm sorry, too. Seems like you never do come out on top, not in this life. Yet the last is gonna be first. Jesus said that. An' the Bible says His ways are not like our'n. I just don't know the why of it, I surely don't. I may be crazy, but it does seem like there ought to be some justice in this world. I don't care what you do or how much you do in this life, you're gonna have loved ones who is unhappy an' that's gonna hurt your heart. People don't find their proper happiness on this earth. I feel real bad fearful about that."

Betty lifted a distracted hand to her hair and fidgeted with a grey strand, while she turned her head to one side and stared at the floor as if she were pondering something.

"Just because we all die," she said, looking directly at Wendell, "that don't mean it's right. An' just because we all live, that don't mean it's worth it. I think animals is more happy than people. I can't be sure, but they act like they don't worry about a thing. I've been poor all my life, an' sometimes I wish I would not have lived, but we're all poor in the end. You can't get no poorer than dead."

Betty wasn't talking out of self-pity, but rather in an attempt to put into words what she felt about dying. Wendell listened to her with respect and didn't try to offer any pat homilies.

"Maybe you should go back to the Cumberlands," he suggested. "I'm sure you could find some of your people up there. You shouldn't have to face this alone." Whoever "Pete" was, Wendell felt certain he wasn't anyone who could be depended on.

"I'd surely like to go back. I don't like it here. The sky is too far away. I remember well the way it useta was when I was a growin' girl an' that country was kinda virgin. Now they have teetotally destroyed the part I knowed best. But I'd like to be buried in Hazard beside my daddy. Poor man, he wasted as he went. His lungs fulled up with fluid an' he drowned. When he died we laid him out in his work shirt just like he always were when he was workin' an' we put silver dollars on his eyes. Then we stood around the coffin an' sung a song askin' Death to pass us over for another year. Maybe I'll find a little preacher man down there who'll save me from the torment before I die. I don't guess, but maybe."

Wendell's chest was tight. He had a thorn in his throat and couldn't speak. Repressing tears, he took Betty by the hand and thanked her for her time. Only at the door did he remember to give her his card in case Grady showed up.

4

The Kitty Kat Klub in Newport occupied a once-elegant Victorian mansion on an out-of-the-way street near the river; the grand portico had been torn down in favor of an incongruous cement-block and glass extension that reached to the sidewalk. Flanking the front door were two tall sputtering neon signs, one showing a pointy-titted stripper in profile and the other a grotesquely grinning cat sticking its paw into a bubbly goblet of champagne. The bartender, a florid-faced man with a Bill Haley kiss curl on his forehead, gave Wendell the once-over as he entered and nodded toward a stool.

"What's your pleasure, pal?" His voice was laden with phony bonhomie.

"Give me a dark beer on draft."

"Aw, you gotta want more than that," the bartender said, implying an item not listed on the menu. "You see anything you like, just ask."

"How many girls do you have here?"

"How many do you need?"

Wendell enjoyed a thirst-quenching swig of beer and didn't reply. He figured it would be wise to check out the situation before he asked to see Caprice. The inside of the Kitty Kat Klub was as incongruous as the exterior; the large front parlor of the old palatial house had been turned into a go-go bar. Against the far wall was a makeshift stage, bathed in an aurora borealis of flashing strobe lights, where a leggy girl, her hair flared out in a fright wig and wearing a G-string, spiked heels, and a forced smile, was tossing her body to the disco sound. A scattering of customers —mainly glum, overweight men—fingered their beer glasses and stared at the dancer with no sign of desire. A henna-headed waitress wove her way among the tables, spilling drinks and giggles. Cupids protruded from the corners of the rococo ceiling and an ornate chandelier's long crystal bangles still sparkled despite a lowering pall of tobacco smoke.

A stale-cheese odor made Wendell aware that someone had sidled up to him at the bar. Turning, he saw a sparse armpit of a goatee and a set of depthless baby-blue drugged-out eyes.

"I'll give you three uppers if you'll buy me a pitcher of beer." The gangly teenager spoke in a whiny voice that set his nerves on edge.

"You shouldn't talk that way to strangers," Wendell said softly. "I could be a narc?"

"So bust me. Bust me!" the boy shouted, drawing the attention of everyone in the room.

The bartender was now studying him suspiciously. Wendell wondered if he should explain that he wasn't a narc, merely a poor detective up in Newport on an unwanted assignment that could get him killed. Instead he asked for a refill and pondered his next move.

A stripper in a leopard-skin costume strutted on stage and proceeded to get down to the bare essentials; the previous dancer slipped into a robe and took a seat beside Wendell at the bar. She set a cigarette on her lips and looked his way until it dawned on him that he should light it.

"Do you come here often?" she asked, as if she didn't know.

"I'll bet you say that to all the guys," Wendell replied, aware that roles had been reversed.

"Only you." She tapped her cigarette so that some ash landed on his slacks. "What are you doing here anyway?"

"Whatever comes my way."

"You can do me, if you want." Her mouth attempted a weak grin, failed, and fell into a frown. Her face was so caked with makeup that it looked like a child's finger painting.

"How does that work?" he asked, stalling for time.

"First you buy me a drink."

Wendell turned to signal the bartender, but he was already standing there, drink in hand.

"How much did that run me?"

"What are you, some cheapskate?"

"I'm just curious."

"Eight bucks. If you wanna get sexy, we can go in the back room or upstairs."

"What's the difference?"

"It all depends on what you want, hon."

"Why don't we just wait a minute."

"Yeah, sure, I can do that. You wanna hear me talk dirty first."

"I'd just like to ask you a few questions."

"Oh, you're one of those. You gotta ask *the question*."

"What's that?"

"'What's a girl like you doing in a place like this?' That question."

"Tell me."

"I've been promoted." She gave him a lopsided smile that exposed lipstick stains on her front teeth. "Now, go ahead, feel sorry for me, tell me how you'd like to help me out and be my sugar daddy—*then* ask me to go upstairs. You johns is all the same."

"Why do you do this then?"

"Because I'm good at it, that's why. Satisfied?"

"Look, I'm sorry to be wasting your time," Wendell said, searching for an exit line. "The truth is I'm a detective and I'm looking for someone."

"A detective!" she announced for all the room to hear. "Well la-de-da and ring-a-ding-ding. Big deal. So if you don't wanna buy it, get outta my face! Go play with your beef jerky!"

"Hey, no hard feelings," Wendell proffered. "Let me buy you a drink."

"I've already got one, hon, and I don't know nothin'. You know what I mean?"

"I get it."

"I thought you would," she said sardonically. "See you around, stud."

After she walked away the bartender came over to commiserate. "You should have taken her up on that, Rita fucks like it's going out of fashion."

""I'm a friend of Caprice," Wendell said, in a casual tone. "Is she here?"

The bartender gave Wendell another inspection, trying to determine whether he was a narc, a detective, or some other suspect creature.

"Right up those, buddy," he said, waving in the direction of a fancy balustraded stairway and balcony. "But don't expect much, she's on the rag today."

Wendell rather doubted if Caprice was still a working girl, so he assumed the bartender was commenting on her sour mood. He climbed the stairs and walked down a hallway that smelled of moldy leaves. In a large room on his left a woman sat on a loveseat by a bay window. She was wrapped in a peacock-blue peignoir and her hair was hidden by a lavender silk scarf.

"Mrs. Speciale, my name is Wendell Clay," he announced. "I'm a friend of Conor Maguire. He said you'd be willing to talk to me."

She gazed at him with frank curiosity for a moment and then patted the cushion to indicate where Wendell should sit.

"How is he?" she inquired with animation. "I haven't seen him in years. For a dip, he's a real gent. Is he still gassing about how the past had a rosier ass?"

"Conor's fine." They exchanged enough small talk to verify Wendell's credentials and establish rapport before he began to ask questions. "How are *you* doing these days?"

"Take a look. You tell me."

She had world-weary, hazel eyes deep-rimmed in sorrow, but a warm, disarming smile that Wendell found appealing.

"I'm sorry about your husband," he said. "Do you have any idea who killed him?"

"What can I tell you. I found him sprawled in the bathroom with blood all over the floor. You don't ever forget a thing like that. I don't know why. There could be a million reasons. He was too big. He got in someone's hair. He didn't take orders. What does it matter, now that he's dead?" She looked at Wendell with woeful eyes and hugged herself as if she had caught a chill.

"Did he talk much about his work?"

"No, thank God. He told me what he wanted me to know. I never asked the wrong questions. But I wasn't born yesterday, I knew the score."

"Where did you two meet?"

"At the Glenn Rendezvous. 'Hatcheck girl weds mob heavy.' That story. Do you want me to start at the beginning?"

"If you like." Wendell sensed that the best way to learn what he needed to know was to let her talk about her life first.

"I was a hardscrabble country girl with corn shucks in my hair. My daddy was a four-square-gospel Baptist who believed in begetting. Every night I'd hear that bed board banging against the wall and my maw crying like a calf with a cut throat. Daddy loved to chastise us kids. My ass better be firm; he sure polished it enough with his razor strop. By the time I was thirteen I had the body of a woman and I began having conversations with men's lowered eyelids. I thought I was one tough cookie. Barbara Stanwick was my idol. She learned to walk by watching panthers in the zoo. I did the same. When I was a girl I could wag my tail with the best of them. I loved to flirt and talk sassy with the boys, but *I* decided who got a taste.

"The choice was between a life spent pinned under the steering wheel at the drive-in and giving it away for free, or turning tricks on a big brass bed and having something to show for my efforts. I decided to get out of that hayseed town; I didn't want some Clem Clodhopper adding me to his herd. And look where I ended up— Newport. God, what a hellhole!"

"When did you come here?"

"During the war—every guy in uniform wanted to get laid before he was shipped overseas and got killed. I met this dealer at one of the clubs, Swanky Franky Giordano he called himself. What can I say? I'm a woman. I fell for him—hook, line, and sinker. He was a petty hood who started out as a kid stealing fruit from sidewalk stands. Then he decided he was a card shark, a slight-of-hand man. He was strictly small time; he ran a penny-ante game at one of the grind joints on York Street. Also, he boosted stuff on the side and stored the swag in his garage until he could fence it. When he got drafted he begged me to marry him. How could I refuse? For him the war was one long poker game interrupted by occasional gun fire. For me it was learning how to keep my mouth shut and when to put it where the money was. We didn't last long as an Ozzie and Harriet act. He wasn't the lover boy he thought he was either, all hot dog and no mustard. He wasn't much good to me. I knew our romance was on the skids. 'We need to talk,' I said; he said, 'You need to talk, go see a priest.'"

That's what Laura had said, Wendell remembered with remorse, *we have to talk.*

"At the settlement I got the house and car; he got to pay my lawyer. All I wanted was my name back, the bastard. Then I changed it anyway. I needed a stage name. Caprice Speciale—the boom boom lassie with the oomphy chassis—that's what they called me. Do you like it?"

"Very much." Wendell could only regret he'd missed her act.

"I was an exotic dancer for a while. The Desert Inn in Vegas, the Mounds Club near Cleveland, the Montmartre in Cuba—I did them all. That was when I met Conor and Sally—now there was a gal who could make the gentlemen drool! She was even hotter than Tequila Mockingbird. I didn't start dancing until after I met Chucky. It was his idea. He arranged it. He drove me to all the posh night clubs and he'd sit up front and watch me perform."

"I thought you said you were a hatcheck girl."

"I was! Can you believe it? After the divorce I suffered a temporary attack of virtue, so I quit the life for a job at the Glenn Hotel. The hatcheck stand was next to the elevator to the gaming rooms, and one day Charles "Chucky Surprise" Cisternero himself came in and handed me his pearl-gray fedora. He was a fancy dresser and I knew him by reputation, so I gave him my come-hither smile and he said, 'A girl like you ought to be dressed in diamonds and mink.' 'A girl like me often is,' I lied, and he laughed and asked me out. I'm not a gal who plays games or keeps a man guessing. If I like a fella, I tell him so. But if you think we hopped right into bed you're wrong. He had a romantic streak—long-stemmed roses, Beluga caviar, chilled Dom Perignon, expensive furs—you should see my closet. He'd take me to the finest restaurants, and the treatment we received! We always got the best table and ate the finest foods—lobster diablo, that was his favorite. The waiters walked on egg shells in his presence. They knew that a word from Chucky meant they were out the door."

"Or worse," Wendell interjected; he didn't want to offend her, but he was finding her tale of mobster romance more than a little cloying.

"Yes, that too," she admitted. "He's dead now so I might as well tell the whole story. He had men killed. He killed some himself. The truth is, that's how he got his name—from the surprised look on his victim's face. That's what he told me." She delivered this information as calmly as someone mentioning that her former husband had a wart on his back.

"Believe me, I'm not investigating any homicides. Not even your husband's," Wendell hastened to add, without intending the ambiguity. "If I learn anything, though, I'll tell you. If you want to know."

"Of course I want to know. But what good will it do? He's dead and nothing can bring him back. Just what *are* you investigating, Mr. Clay?"

Her formal tone told him she had been put on guard, so he proceeded cautiously to tell her about Devil Dancer, Brad Davis's Las Vegas debt, and why he had come to Newport.

"When Bull Fuller was a cop in Newport he had his hand out just like all the rest," Caprice responded. "Once when I missed a payoff, he and his pals put me in a cell. 'For what I've already paid,' I told them, 'you should've put me in a penthouse.' He loves to hit people, especially women. After he got kicked off the force he was a bouncer here for a while, but I let him go. There's something vile about him. I hear he works for CREEP—you know, the Committee to Re-elect the President—he punches out anti-war protestors for pocket change."

"So he's just a free-lance thug."

"Exactly."

"What about Scarbono and Zentko? Are they working for somebody?"

"Why do you want to know?"

"Because I don't know."

"What are you after?"

"I'm not sure."

"Then why the questions?"

"It's my job, that's what I do."

"But what's the point?"

"I don't know yet, first I need more information. I need your help."

"Vinnie and Jack are Ohio guys—Youngstown, I believe. Chucky was from Steubenville—Dean Martin, Nick the Greek were his playmates. He used to say the Jewish Boys in Cleveland got the money and the Italians did the dirty work. For a while I was a carrier pigeon between the Newport casinos and the Cleveland mob. I carried the cash in my hat box. A lot of the dough made here went there and then to Vegas before it came back again as skim."

"Sounds confusing."

"It's meant to be."

"Who did you deliver the money to in Cleveland?"

"Even that's confusing. Usually I gave it to Maishe Rockman, who's Jewish; but he grew up with John Scalish, the boss of the Cleveland mob, and married Jack White's sister."

"Who's Jack White?"

"That's James Licavoli. They call him Jack White on account of he's so dark."

"In what sense?" Licavoli, Wendell recalled, ran the Youngstown rackets.

"His skin; he's Sicilian. He made his bones in the old Purple Gang."

"Do you think Fuller and Scarbono are working for Zentko?"

"Probably. Fuller is just a mob wannabe, a dumb goon. Chucky said Scarbono was a stone killer, a slugger. A very scary guy. Once he started to tell me how Vinnie got his nickname, "The Vice," but I stopped him. 'Spare me the gory details,' I said."

"I hope I never have to meet him."

"You're not looking for trouble, are you?"

"No."

"Then you're in the wrong place. Newport can be dangerous, you know. Did Davis make you come here?"

"No."

"Who then?"

"My conscience, I suppose. Devil Dancer was a great horse; he didn't deserve to die. I've got a job to do and I'm trying to do it well, and the trail led here—to Newport, to the mob, to you. What do you know about Zentko?"

"He's a dapper Dan who thinks he's George Raft, who thought he was Bugsy Siegel. That's why he wants to be known as John Lane. It fits his image of himself. Like all those Youngstown guys, he gets a cut of the bug and the barbut action."

From his truck-driving days, Wendell knew that she was referring to the numbers racket and a Greek dice game the steelworkers loved to bet on.

"What about the Teamsters?"

"That too. He's the man who tells a bar owner what vending machines he needs, or else his joint is a fire hazard. But I think he's in on more than that. Youngstown is between Cleveland and Pittsburgh, and both mob families want it for their own. That's why there's been so much violence there. Chucky had a hunch that Zentko was playing both sides against the middle by working as a hit man—for one of the families or maybe even for the Jewish Boys."

"Why did he think that?"

"I really don't know. But Chucky was convinced that Zentko clipped Mike Farah, the guy who fronted for Moe Dalitz at the Jungle Inn. He got shot while he was practicing his putting in his front yard. Chucky figured that Zentko was involved in some of the Youngstown car bombings: Christ Sofocleous, Vince DeNiro, Cadillac Charlie Cavallaro. That last one was awful—it killed both Charlie and his young son Tommy, crippled the other. Terrible!"

"Do you know which boss would want these particular people dead?" Wendell was troubled by this new information. If what Caprice suggested were true, then John "Jack the Ripper" Zentko could murder people more ways than one.

"Who knows? If there's a pattern, I don't see it. It's like a feud: you kill one of mine so I'm gonna kill two of yours. Maybe Zentko is a rogue playing a double game."

"Does he have any interest in horses?"

"Chucky used to take me to River Downs a lot. That man loved to bet. He'd wager on raindrops sliding down a windowpane. He placed his bets with Gil Beckley here in Newport. I love horses but I hate the races. What's the fun of watching guys the size of Santa's little helpers whip Dancer or Prancer down the home stretch? We *would* see Zentko at the track on occasion."

"Has he been around Newport earlier this summer?"

"Why do you ask?" Caprice gave him a probing look. "I thought you wanted to know where he is now, not then."

Wendell hadn't forgotten what Conor had told him about Zentko's signature style of killing. Did he kill Caprice's husband? Should he confront her with that question? If he asked her about that case, would she be less willing to help him with his?

"How do you think Zentko got his nickname?"

"I've always heard he was handy with a knife," she said. "He even wore yellow gloves and carried a cane, with a stiletto inside, because he heard that Jack White had one."

"Did he and your husband get along?"

"There was a rivalry, I'm sure. Chucky had a lot of things that Zentko wanted to have."

"Here in Newport? The place looks dead to me."

"You're telling me, mister. When Ratterman got elected, most of the wheelers and dealers moved to Vegas. But all the stations of the cross are still here—if you know where to look. Chucky was one of the few who stayed behind. I bought this place; Chucky took over what was left of Gil's layoff betting operation, this and that."

"Didn't he ever get caught?"

"One time. But even in the pen he was treated like a prince; a deputy used to chauffeur him home on weekends."

"That must have cost a pretty penny."

"It was all small change to Chucky. He was a beautiful man—very virile. I would have hocked my diamonds to have him home. He made me feel complete." Her voice became more tender as she spoke, and she paused a moment to rub her eyes, but when she resumed it was in a sardonic vein. "He wasn't like these johns we get in here; most of them fuck like they're double-parked. In this business you see them all: even the occasional do-gooder who wants to save your soul. 'Listen,' I tell them, 'when I'm on my knees it's not to pray.'"

"Do you think your husband was killed because somebody wanted to take over his operation?" Wendell decided the time had come to be more direct about the murder.

"Could be," she responded warily.

"Do you think Zentko might have killed him?"

Caprice looked startled by this scenario. "His name didn't come up in the investigation."

"Whose did?"

"Screw Andrews is back in town. The rumor is that he wanted to control the numbers again; years ago he killed a black guy, Melvin Clark, to get control in the first place. There's talk that Newport might stage a comeback. They've even re-opened the Beverly Hills; it's a supper club now, no gambling, but times change. They've certainly got the look and the space."

"Who runs that?"

"Shilling is his name. He also owns The Lookout House, Gameboy Miller's old place."

"Do you think he's a mob front?"

"It's possible."

A moment later a maid walked in with a vase of flowers and placed them on a circular, marble-topped stand beside the loveseat.

"Yellow roses," Caprice said. "I love freshly cut flowers. They make me feel so clean." She fixed Wendell with a perplexed look and added, "I hope I've been of help."

"Thank you," Wendell said. "You've given me something to go on."

"Well, don't go on it too far. You could regret it."

"That's a chance I'll have to take."

"I hope not," Caprice said, holding out her hand in parting. "Newport is not a town to take chances in."

5

After he left the Kitty Kat Klub, Wendell took a last, desultory loop around what remained of Newport and decided to have dinner at the recently reopened Beverly Hills before heading back to Lexington. On the way out of town he pondered what he had learned from Caprice and what he still needed to know. That the men sporting sinister nicknames who had come calling on Brad Davis were dangerous characters was clear, yet Wendell still wasn't sure who they worked for. Zentko might indeed be a rogue trying to make an opportunistic move, or he could be following orders. Perhaps he was part of a Mafia effort to take over Newport again. Maybe shooting Devil Dancer to grab Sycamore Springs was part of the plan. Whatever the plot, apparently it originated in Ohio, where the relationships among the Jewish Boys, the mob, and the Teamsters—all with interests in Vegas—were so tangled that Wendell wondered if he would ever find out the truth. The closer he looked and the harder he searched, the more confusing everything became. Just thinking about all the complications made him dizzy.

Wendell drove up the steep, winding road to the Beverly Hills, which reigned over its surroundings like a medieval castle. The building was flat-roofed, low-slung—no turrets or towers—spread in a rectangular shape. The bland cement-block walls had been gussied up with the Las Vegas Look. Fountains and statuary, inspired by Caesar's Palace, lined the driveway to the porte-cochere entrance, and the new facade featured lancet arches suggestive of a Gothic monastery. But while Caesar's Palace had gone the whole hog, with fiberglass centurions guarding the door and a replica of Michelangelo's David in the foyer, this was a relatively low-budget attempt to out-kitsch kitsch. The three statues in front, Wendell noted, were triplicates from the same mold: a quasi-classical shepherdess, her musing face slightly canted to the right, draped in a flowing toga and sprouting wings. The patron saint of sheep to be sheared, he thought, but then remembered that the Beverly Hills was a supper club and no longer a casino.

A crew-cut attendant parked Wendell's car in the spacious lot that wrapped half-way around this popular local eatery that proclaimed itself "The Showplace of the Nation." Upon entering, Wendell was offered a dinner-and-entertainment deal for one price, but he was in a hurry and settled for a la carte. The circular Frontenac Room, located to the left of an enormous curved bar, was designed to create the ambience of some north-woodsy outpost of empire. Huge fake rosewood beams crisscrossed a ceiling that was centered by a wagon-wheel chandelier; candles in silver sconces along the walls highlighted murals of hunting scenes. A massive stone fireplace with a golden oak mantle dominated one side of the room.

The pseudo-gourmet menu consisted of standard American fare with a few fancy items mixed in—"Breast of Capon with Beverly Sauce," and so on. Wendell decided that "Roast Prime Rib of Beef, Au Jus" and a glass of burgundy was the best bet. The service was fast, he had to admit, and the food wasn't bad. Wendell finished his desert and coffee within an hour.

Before departing he decided to look around, strolling down the Hall of Mirrors past the Empire and Cabaret Rooms where a poster said "live big-name entertainers" performed every weekend. He peeked in the Viennese Room, now reserved for banquets, but in former times the location of the gaming tables. Wendell imagined he could still hear the click of chips, the whirl and clatter of the roulette wheel, the croupier calling "Place your bets," the simmering patter of ghostly players. The hall ended at an elaborate staircase, a photo-opportunity setting, that spiraled up around a small rock garden with a miniature waterfall. A bulbous two-tiered chandelier hung in the stairwell. Half-lost in a reverie about days gone by, Wendell found a men's room around the corner. As he stepped up to a urinal, next to a mural of a naked boy lifting a large fish by the tail, he became eerily aware of someone standing behind him.

"What is it you wished to ask me, Mr. Clay?"

The voice was mellow, the kind broadcasters crave, but the instant he heard it Wendell's legs felt unstrung. He zipped up and turned around and found himself looking at a tall man with an angular face, one drooping eyelid, black brilliantined hair streaked with silver, and a lupine smile that exposed tobacco-stained teeth. He wore tinted aviator glasses and a shiny gray sports jacket over a wide-collared opened-necked silk shirt. A gold medallion on a golden chain nestled in his chest hair. Beside him hulked an even larger man with a wide, fleshy face, a large Roman nose, a baleful gaze beneath bushy eyebrows. His monogrammed golf shirt, stretched tightly across his pectorals did nothing to conceal the yardbird tats on his biceps: one of a dagger skewing a skull, the other a coiled cobra with dripping fangs.

"Who are you?" Wendell asked, although he was certain he was in the presence of none other than John "Jack the Ripper" Zentko and Vinnie "The Vice" Scarbono.

"I'm a businessman."

"What kind of business?"

"My business. If I make a buck, that's good business. Anybody that gets in the way of my making a buck has got a problem. *You're* butting into my business, Mr. Clay."

Wendell felt the color drain from his face. He glanced at the other man warily.

"Whatchulookinat?" he rasped.

"Nothing."

"Are you callin' me nothin'?"

"You look uncomfortable," the tall man observed. "Is there some-place you'd rather be?"

"Why are you threatening me?" Wendell demanded.

"I don't do that." His voice was oil on troubled waters. "I discuss things. Does my friend here frighten you?"

"Yes."

"He should. He's like that."

"I think he's gonna shit himself," the larger man said.

"That's normal."

"If he's got the shits, he should do it here."

"Have you, Mr. Clay? We can wait."

Wendell assured them in a shaky voice that he was fine. "You've made a mistake," he ventured. "I only came here to have dinner."

"Bad news travels fast. We know all about you. You think you're a detective, right? That's why you went to see Caprice today. You shouldn't have done that. You were sticking your nose where it doesn't belong. This is a local matter. It doesn't concern you."

"I did talk to her," Wendell conceded, "but it wasn't about any-thing important. I was just saying hello for an old friend. Now, if you'll excuse me, I'd like to go home."

"You're coming with us."

"For what reason?"

"Your health," the tall man said, still in his mellow tone. "If you don't, Vinnie here is going to hurt you."

"He looks capable enough."

"That's what people say."

"Where do you want me to go?"

"Not far. There's a person here who would like to meet you."

"Who's that?"

"You'll see. Don't look so worried, Mr. Clay. What happens, happens."

"Do it," Vinnie said, giving Wendell a shove in the back, "or your ass gets mangled."

The two men, fore-and-aft, escorted Wendell out of the men's room and pulled aside a curtain that concealed the door to an L-shaped storage area beneath the spiral staircase. Wheeled racks of folding chairs lined a corridor to the back half of the room, where a fat man sat in the shadows chomping on a dead cigar stub. As Wendell stepped closer he saw a thick-lipped mouth and the hooded, wrinkled eyes of an old snapping turtle. He was wearing baggy trousers over shiny black loafers with white tassels. The man appeared to be in his sixties, with a beer belly so big it looked like he'd swallowed the keg, yet the impression was not of flabbiness but strength.

Wendell introduced himself and held out his hand. Under the circumstances, his only defense was defenselessness and his best hope was to keep the conversation civil.

"You don't need to know my name," the fat man said gruffly. "We ain't friends. You didn't invite me to your wedding, and I'm not sticking around for your funeral—which could be today, if you don't cooperate. My associate here thinks you shouldn't leave this room alive. I ain't decided yet. You might, if you take me very serious and listen to what I got to say."

"Clip the guy and be done with it," Vinnie said. "Whack him."

"Shut up, Vinnie," the fat man said; then he added, "Vinnie here was a boxer."

"When I was a kid."

"How many fights did you win?"

"You know." Vinnie's mouth bent slightly in resentment.

"Tell me again."

"All but ten."

"All but ten. That's good. You still think we should kill him right now, Vinnie?"

"I say hit him," he insisted, smiling like a sadist about to enjoy himself. "Get rid of him."

"Whadda you think, John?"

"Too much heat. What about the body?"

"I got a chainsaw in the trunk," Vinnie volunteered.

"Too much noise," the fat man said, "too much splatter."

"Disposing of a body is not easy," Zentko said with airy irony. "Try it sometime."

"You saw Caprice today," the fat man said accusingly. "How do you know her?"

"A friend of a friend."

"That broad has had it," Vinnie said.

"Yeah, from me," the fat man boasted.

"Don't you wish," Zentko said.

Wendell looked for a reaction, but the fat man didn't even blink.

"That ain't what I meant," Vinnie said. "She's beat."

"Who can blame her?" Zentko spoke with an empathy that surprised Wendell.

"Caprice wasn't a bad biff in her time," the fat man said. "They didn't call her the tops in pops for nothing. She was a class act around here. That broad broke hearts."

"She breaks mine just thinking about her," Zentko said.

"Did you ever get any?" Vinnie asked with obvious envy.

"Naw, me and Chucky were too close for that."

"Did you try?" he persisted.

"I don't chase women," Zentko announced. "They come to me."

"That one you've got now is a real barracuda."

"She's teaching me things I never knew before," Zentko remarked, deadpan.

"What was Cisternero like?" Wendell asked on impulse. The three men stared at him a moment, startled by the interruption, as if they had brought him to this room for the sole purpose of vicariously partaking of their banter.

"Chucky wasn't a bad guy," the fat man said. "He had a soft heart. He used to stand on the corner and give away quarters to kids that done good in school. Stuff like that."

"He shoulda tried social work," Vinnie said. "He mighta lived longer."

"Why was he killed?"

"That's one question too many, Mr. Clay," Zentko said. "Who can say why anybody gets clipped before his time?"

"He ended up dead," Vinnie said. "A lotta guys do. What's to know?"

"I heard a rumor that 'The Rat' did it."

Wendell wondered if Zentko was offering this particular information to mislead him.

"No way," the fat man said.

"Where is Ray now, then?" Zentko insisted. "He's missing."

"He's down in Georgia."

"Doing what?"

"Working for his uncle."

"What kind of work?"

"Road work."

"What's he looking at?"

"Five to ten."

"Five to ten is a stretch. I wonder what that's like."

"You ain't never done time?" The fat man looked at Zentko incredulously.

"Not me, not in the pen—only overnights for questioning. What were you in for?"

"Aw, I was a bad boy," the fat man muttered in a throaty voice. "Your typical guy in the joint," he continued, "lifts weights to toughen up and protect his ass, then he studies the law; after all his appeals are denied, he reads the Bible; but the parole board ain't buying he's born again, so he finds himself a sissy and settles down to dream about pulling off one big score and retiring to Florida. That's life in the can. Am I right?"

"Yeah, that's it," Vinnie agreed. "But it ain't no life."

The fat man extracted the noxious stub from his mouth and eyed it with displeasure. Zentko offered him another from a slim pack.

"Gimme a real cigar," the fat man insisted, "not one of them guinea stinkers."

Zentko produced from his jacket pocket a lengthy La Palma cigar in its own aluminum container. The fat man took it out and held it up for inspection in his stubby fingers. Then he rolled it around in his mouth, moving his jaw slowly with bovine satisfaction, before he accepted a light. The three other men stood and watched while the cigar fumed and sputtered between his thick lips like a fuse; then he nodded toward Wendell and said, "Talk to him, John."

Zentko fixed Wendell with a wintry gaze and began speaking: "Like I said before, I'm a businessman. We're all businessmen here. You might say we're in the cash-and-carry business. If a man owes friends of mine money, I get involved. I negotiate. Now I can be nice, a pleasant man to deal with, but I also have another side you don't want to see."

"Show it to him," Vinnie urged. "That's my favorite part."

"Hey, Italian, shut up, let me handle this."

"I'm proud of my inbreeding," Vinnie quipped, pleased with himself.

"If your guy had a voice like Sinatra's," Zentko said, "maybe we'd tear up his marker, but that isn't the case here. Davis is a degenerate gambler. We don't need to break his legs, we just shut off his credit at the casinos. He won't be able to play marbles."

"He's working on it," Wendell said. "I'm sure he'll pay you as soon as he can."

"Yeah, that's what we thought too. But then there's you. Where do you fit in?" Zentko asked. "If he's gonna pay up, how come he hired you? We just want to live and let live, none of this tricky stuff. We figure maybe he's trying to get cute."

"Tell your friend," the fat man added, "that if he wants to fuck with me, he's gotta kiss me first. That's how it's done, see? No kissy, no fucky."

"He didn't hire me to deal with his gambling debts."

"Then let me ax you this," the fat man said. "What the fuck do you think you're doin' here?"

Wendell felt the back of his neck tingle as he hesitated to answer.

"Who do you think you are?" Zentko demanded. "Talk, or we'll fuck you up good."

"Let me work on him a little," Vinnie pleaded. "Break a few ribs, bust his face, so he knows next time it can only get worse." He eyed Wendell as if he were debating the relative merits of a rabbit punch to the kidneys or a short jab to the solar plexus.

"I'm working on another case," Wendell said. He tried to make his face go lax to hide his fear, but a muscle in his cheek kept twitching.

"Yeah, what's that about?" Zentko asked.

"The shooting of Devil Dancer."

"What does that have to do with us?"

"I get it," the fat man said. "Pallie here has been watching too many movies. He thinks that horse was a Mafia hit. La Cosa Nostra, what's that? The Our Thing. Hey Vinnie, you ever joined The Our Thing?"

"Naw. Not me. No way."

"I never fool with horses, too risky," the fat man said. "How about you, Vinnie?"

"Only if I'm sure it's a sure thing."

"You're no racetrack tout," Zentko said sardonically. "You can't even pick your nose."

"Fuck you."

"Whatsamatter, can't you take a joke?"

"Show it to me," Vinnie insisted. "If I can see it, I'll take it, but I don't see it."

"Let me tell you something," the fat man said, returning to the death of Devil Dancer. "We didn't do it. But now that you mention it, I like it. This works in our favor."

"Let's whack Davis," Vinnie said, "teach him a lesson."

"I've got other plans for him."

"We should send roses to Davis's home," Zentko suggested. "He'll get the message."

Wendell's heart surged and subsided as he faced the realization that his investigation was only making the situation worse. Davis was now more involved than he could ever imagine; if he didn't render unto Caesar all that he owed soon, he was chum.

"I promise you," Wendell said. "Davis will pay. You have my word."

"Don't promise me no promises or tell me any tales," Zentko said. "I've talked to you like a gentleman. None of your blood is on the floor. Understand? If your guy doesn't come through, we're gonna harm him. That's simply how this business operates. If he doesn't know that, he's got no business in this business."

"What about this piece of shit?" Vinnie demanded. "Do I rough him up or what?"

"We know where you live," Zentko said. "Some cubbyhole out at Idle Hour apartments, right? You better always park under a streetlight, because if you mess with us again, the next time you start your car could be your last."

"A Youngstown tune-up," Vinne chortled. "I love it."

"If you don't want Vinnie knocking on your door," the fat man added, "this meet didn't happened."

"I was never here," Wendell said solemnly.

"This is Davis's last chance to pay up and shut up," the fat man said. "We don't want no squawker on our hands. He's either gonna do what we tell him or he's goin' down. That's his choice. You tell him. Some guys won't take a cigar, if you know what I mean."

"You're gonna let this scumbag walk?" Vinnie was incredulous. He reached out with one of his large hands and squeezed Wendell's collarbone with a grip like a garbage compactor. "What if he turns canary?"

"He won't sing," the fat man said, rising to his feet and poking Wendell once in the sternum with a blunt finger then patting him lightly on the cheek. "He knows what happens to rats. Now get him outta here. He's been told."

6

Wendell, a man reprieved, walked on unsteady legs out of the Beverly Hills and waited for the parking attendant to bring his car. His brain was buzzing like a tree full of locusts. He swiped at the cold sweat on his face and touched his chest to muffle the drum beating there. The August twilight was laden with intimations of autumn. He heard a low rumble of distant thunder and caught a scent of rain in the breeze through the trees. With a little luck, he'd be in Lexington before it began to pour.

As he drove, Wendell brooded over what his trip to Newport had revealed. He had a queasy feeling that he had taken one step forward and two steps back—or did he have one foot in the grave, the other on a banana peel? Or was the secret that there was no secret, only the giddy sensation of peering into the void and sensing that nothing but nothingness was peering back.

He had glimpsed into the mob netherworld of Newport and seen only a murky confluence of shadows. Either Zentko and his friends were not involved in the shooting of Devil Dancer, or they had staged a dumb show exclusively for his benefit. What he had learned was grim enough. The Mafia knew that the way to get rich gambling was not to make bets but to take them; unless Brad Davis paid up promptly, he could come to harm. Even if they didn't do it, Wendell worried that they now might add the death of Devil Dancer to their calculations. What would that mean? Those three men were capable of anything. Zentko was a mob lothario with manicured fingers and blood on his hands; Vinnie, batting cleanup for the Cleveland mob, probably considered murder a misdemeanor; and the fat man with the thick lips was obviously an underworld lord of dark corners who could order a man clipped as easily as he snuffed out a cigar.

For decades, Newport had been sewn up tight by the Mafia. The cops were on the pad and the mayor was in their pocket. Wendell wondered if the man who owned the Beverly Hills was just a sucker who had put up the cash. If the place prospered, the mob would rake in the profits; if the joint failed, then he was left holding the bag. That was how they operated: take the money up front and run with it. Was it possible they were planning a comeback in Newport? If so, wasn't Wendell's life in danger, even if they didn't shoot Devil Dancer, because of what he knew? They had given him the classic Mafia warning—you don't know us, but we know all we need to know about you. Should he get a remote control to start his car? Would he ever again feel secure? He felt woozy for a moment, as if the earth had just shifted under his feet. On the other hand, if they had meant to kill him, wouldn't they have done it when they had the chance? At least he would return to Lexington alive, there was that to be thankful for. At the moment he was driving his car, not sinking in the mud on the bottom of the Ohio River anchored by a Newport Nightgown of poured cement.

What should he do next? That was the question. He had learned that Zentko was acting on orders from the fat man, but both had seemed genuinely surprised when Wendell brought up the shooting of Devil Dancer. Did that mean that Grady was still his best suspect? If so, he'd better increase his efforts to find him. Or were there a set of possibilities he hadn't even thought of yet? Perhaps he should be looking for a crazy man with a mind as twisted as Charles Manson's. As his father used to say, "It's a smart fox that knows which rabbit trail to follow."

It was dark by the time Wendell reached Lexington. When he got home he'd call Davis to warn him that paying his gambling debts was more urgent than he thought. But first he decided to stick his head in the Mecca Bar to get Conor's advice about what had happened and see if Grady had turned up. Out front a drunk was making a determined effort to run into himself. The place was crowded. A group of men were gathered around watching Ed Fuller play pool. Wendell stood in the doorway, letting his eyes adjust to the smoke while he tried to scan the men's faces. He saw Conor signaling urgently from the bar and started to push his way toward him, nudging the end of the big man's pool cue as he brushed by.

"Watch yourself, sweetheart," Ed snarled, spinning around and giving Wendell both barrels with his eyes.

The man had no neck. The solid block of his face was sunk up to the ears between his bulging shoulders. He stepped closer, keeping one big-knuckled fist wrapped around the cue stick, waiting for Wendell to give him an excuse to slap it down on his head. He kept staring, working the muscles in his blue-black jaw.

"Sorry," Wendell said.

"Talk it up, buddy," Ed snapped. I don't read lips."

"I said excuse me. I didn't mean to bump you."

"Next time watch your ass. I'm playing pool here."

He glowered at Wendell and turned his back on him.

Wendell was about to respond, but Conor intervened, pulling him over to the bar.

"Don't argue with fools, young man," he counseled. "Spectators get confused."

"Is he as bad as he looks?"

"Worse," Conor replied.

"Maybe he's just been misunderstood." Wendell's hands shook. He had already had enough dire confrontations for one day.

"Grady's here," Conor stated as soon as they ordered their beers.

"Where?" Wendell looked around wildly. He could feel his heart flutter and roll.

"He's in the crapper. Drink your beer and calm yourself. He'll be out in a minute."

"How long has he been here?"

"Not long."

"Have you talked to him?"

"Some." Conor nodded. "He came in with the fair-haired fellow over there in the booth."

Wendell looked across the room and saw a slim pink-faced man with hair so blond it was almost white. His blue and red jacket was draped like a cape over the headrest of the seat. He watched him take a few sips from what appeared to be a Bloody Mary.

The blond guy sidled over to the pool table. Fuller set his cigarette flat on the table's edge and chalked his cue. He racked up the balls in a tight bright triangle and broke them with a sharp splat, sending the glossy stripes and solids skitter-scattering over the green baize. Nothing dropped. He circled the table like a stalking cat, found his spot, and crouched, squinting for the kill. A flick of his stick and the six ball ducked into the corner pocket.

"Nice shot, Ed," the blond man said with a slight lisp.

The big man straightened up as if he had suddenly remembered something long forgotten.

"I recognized your voice, Lee," he said. "I thought you were dead." He gave the blond man a fierce look. "No. Let me correct that. I *hoped* you were dead."

"Now, Ed," the blond man urged, "don't get nasty."

He looked at Ed with tender eyes, like a man who has just taken off his reading glasses.

"Why should I get nasty?" Ed asked scornfully, moving around the table as he spoke.

"Don't take that attitude," the blond man said, his face tense.

"What attitude?"

"You know how you get." Lee took a jerky step backward. "Give me a break."

"I wouldn't give you the sweat off my balls," Ed sneered, fronting the cowering man.

"Can't we be friends?"

"Life is too goddamn long to be your friend."

"I don't see why you're so upset."

"You know goddamn well why." Ed spat out the words as if they burned his tongue. "We've got serious trouble. You made a fuckin' pansy outa me."

"I didn't mean it, Ed." There was real terror in his voice now.

"You leaned on me, you fuckin' faggot."

"Now, Ed, stop it," Lee pleaded. "I've got to go home."

"You're fuckin' hard on, Lee. The only way you're goin' home is in a hearse. Cause I'm gonna kill you, your brother's gonna bury you, and your cousin'll be walkin' slow behind."

Anger radiated from the big man like heat from an open-hearth furnace.

Lee, white-faced, lips trembling, was sick with fear. If Ed had chosen to hit him, he would have been crushed as easily as bird bones in a cat's jaws, but instead he pulled out a long knife and snapped it open. It looked sharp on both sides. He flashed it in front of Lee's face so that the blond man had no choice but to stare at it.

"Any way I cut you, motherfucker, you're gonna have a new asshole."

Lee was panting like a trapped rabbit, too frozen with fear to think of trying to escape. All the while Conor and Wendell were at the bar, as paralyzed by the situation as everybody else. The pool table stood between them and Fuller, so the possibility of hitting him from behind with a beer bottle or a chair was out of the question.

Besides, he probably wouldn't have felt it. When the trouble started Wendell had noticed Joe's crutches under a chair by the bar. He stooped down and grabbed one of them in case he needed it.

"I'm going to talk to him," he whispered.

"In what language?" Conor replied, shaking his head.

Then Fuller, still holding the knife in one hand, placed the tapered end of the cue stick between his legs and pointed the handle at Lee's mouth.

"Eat my meat, you popeyed cunt," Fuller commanded.

"You have no right to say that!" Lee cried out.

"Leave him alone," Wendell shouted on impulse. "Why pick on him?"

At that moment Grady came out of the john scratching his crotch.

Fuller turned to face Wendell.

"You're cute, askin' questions. I warned you already about crowdin' me, wise guy."

When Ed turned, Lee pulled a small knife of his own, and before anyone could respond, stuck it high up in the bulging muscles of Ed's right shoulder, close to the neck. Ed roared, spinning around so quickly the knife slipped out and fell to the floor, while Lee ran panic-stricken past Wendell. At the same time Grady rushed toward Ed on his blind side and smashed a beer bottle against his head.

The big man staggered a few steps before he recovered. Then his knife shot out in a glitter of speed and caught Grady in the gut, sliding in as easily as a wing cuts through air. A rib popped from the impact of the hilt. Grady said "O" and put both hands over the wound, trying to hold himself in. Everyone was locked in place from the shock for a split second longer; then the whole room broke into motion. Wendell started toward Grady, but before he took two steps, Ed slammed into his chest. Wendell crashed back against the bar, smacking his hip with terrific force, but somehow he didn't lose his feet. He still stood between Ed and Lee. Fuller's eyes were intent on Wendell now, and the double-edged blade was lowered in his direction.

"Don't fuck with me." His brow seemed to darken as he spoke. He lowered his head and moved in with slow, arrogant challenge.

Wendell looked for a place to take a stand, gripping Joe's crutch in self-defense. The two men circled in a narrow space, watching each other like wrestlers on the alert for a sudden opening. When Ed moved close to the bar, Conor tried to chop him down with a chair. The blow sent him crashing across the room like loose cargo on a rolling ship, but he didn't fall.

Instead he turned and charged at Wendell, who tried to shove him away with the crutch while he spun in the opposite direction. But Ed swiped out with his knife as he barged past, and Wendell felt a razor-sharp edge slide across the side of his throat as lightly as a leaf. He didn't realize he was cut until he saw the blood on his shirt.

"Watch out!" Conor shouted.

Wendell looked up to see those cruel eyes bearing down on him again. One side of Ed's face was swollen with a big bruise the color of rain clouds, but he was still as formidable as a stone wall, filling the room with his size. Wendell felt tired and strangely detached. Even though he was loggy-legged and winded, he had to avoid that knife. Ed put his feet together and came at Wendell in what seemed like slow motion, yet he was on top of him in a second. Wendell struck out with the crutch and gave him a glancing hit on the side of the head, trying at the same time to pivot away and elude the hooking sweep on his blade. But Ed swerved in the direction of his turn and slammed into him with pile-driving force, lifting him by the thrust of his neck and shoulders. Wendell dangled for a moment in the air with his head down Ed's back, smelling blood and sweat. Then Ed shifted his weight and tossed Wendell in what seemed like a long, slow, dreamlike glide onto the pool table.

The rest was darkness.

When Wendell came to the first thing he saw was the ashen face of Grady Shifflet, who sat on the floor in a daze while Conor pressed a blood-soaked towel to the seeping fountain in his side. Grady kept blinking his small eyes like a lizard in the sun. His face seemed to be all slack jaw up to the level of his eyes. He looked as if he were trying to chew and swallow his pain, the entire lower part of his face moving up and down, closing and collapsing.

"Grady," Wendell said in a strained voice, "I wanted to talk to you."

He squinted at Grady's face as though it were a keyhole.

"So?" Grady said, sounding like a man sucking pebbles.

He gave Wendell a wry, paperclip grin, revealing an odd assortment of rotted teeth; then he coughed up a frothy gout of blood and his eyes faded.

"There's another old horse gone back to the barn," Conor said, easing Grady's head down to the floor. Somebody found a blue and red jacket to spread over his face.

Wendell looked up and saw the urgent twirl of a cruiser's flashing blue lights coming through the front window of the Mecca Bar.

7

Conor brought a chair and Wendell sat down, averting his eyes from Grady's body.

"What happened after I got clobbered?"

"While Ed was teaching you how to pinwheel, the blond guy snuck out," Conor explained. "When Ed saw that he was gone, he took off after him."

"And the cops?"

"They just got here."

One of the policemen lifted the jacket off Grady's face. They could hear the other one outside calling on the radio for more cars.

"I thought you'd gone to your eternal reward," Conor said, shaking his head.

"I would have been a dead man if you hadn't hit Ed with that chair."

"I was drunk," Conor explained. "It seemed like a good idea."

Barney came over, dangling his Lugar in his hand, and looked at Wendell with alarm.

"This shit ain't had to happen," he said.

"Why didn't you drop the net?" Conor demanded.

Barney lifted his eyes to where it was spread across the ceiling. "Oh fuck, I forgot."

"It wouldn't have held him anyway," Wendell said, letting Barney off the hook.

"That guy," Barney said, "I never wanted him in my place, but how could I tell him?"

The side of Wendell's neck felt chilly, as if he were sitting in a draft. He reached up to feel it, and his fingers came away wet. Conor looked concerned.

"Turn your head, boyo," he said. "Let me see what you've got there."

He leaned closer, putting one hand on Wendell's jaw and the other on his shoulder to steady himself.

"Looks like big Ed did a half-ass job of slitting your throat." Conor was trying to joke, but Wendell could feel his hands shaking. "My nerves are shot," Conor added, distractedly patting Wendell on the back. "Let's get you to a hospital."

With Conor holding one arm, Wendell walked unsteadily toward the door. Grady's body lay beside the wall with only Joe, still stranded on a chair by the bar, looking down at it. The two policemen were taking statements from witnesses. Just then the first ambulance arrived. The intern glanced at Wendell's neck, told him not to take another step, and eased him onto the gurney. Conor wanted to come along, but the police made him stay for questioning.

"I'll talk to you later," Conor said, giving Wendell the high sign as the ambulance left.

The intern cleaned the cut and placed a thick gauze pad on Wendell's neck.

"They get some tough customers in that bar," he commented.

"I noticed."

"We had a call there a few years back," he continued. "A guy got killed in a fight over whether or not there was an afterlife."

"How bad is the cut?" Wendell didn't like the expressions he saw on people's faces when they looked at his neck.

"Can't say for sure; it's not bleeding," the intern said casually. "Missed the jugular."

"That's nice to know."

"I'll say. You'd be back there on the floor beside that other guy."

When they arrived at the hospital the intern walked Wendell into the waiting room and told him to sit down, while he whispered for a moment with the nurses at the admitting window. He must have told a good story, because all of them turned with shocked curiosity. A nurse came over to ask Wendell to fill out some papers. They were about as clear as an average tax return, and he couldn't find his Blue Cross card. Lucky for him the cut wasn't deep, or by the time he had finished proving his solvency he would have bled to death.

Wendell sat very still, trying not to jiggle his neck. He was too stunned to think clearly. All he could do was look and listen.

It was a weekday evening and the Emergency Room wasn't crowded. A leaning tower of plastic chairs was stacked in a corner, and five wheelchairs waited by the door. Several people were ahead of Wendell waiting their turn.

A friendly-faced black man in a bus driver's uniform, holding the hand of a big-eyed child in pigtails and a party dress, cast admiring glances at a red-headed woman sitting nearby.

"Just look, don't touch," she said, bantering with him. "Married woman, you know."

"I'm just lookin', I ain't touchin'," he said, smiling. "You see me, I'm just lookin'."

A ratty-faced man across the way gave the two a hate stare and spat a dark gob of tobacco juice into the flip-top beer can he was holding in his hand.

"That's a cute little girl," the woman said.

"You ain't bad yourself."

"You're pretty good-lookin', too."

"Oh yeah!" the black man said, chuckling deeply. "Now you're talkin'."

After that they began an animated conversation about food prices and television shows.

At last Wendell was called to the consulting room where a prim-faced nurse took the gauze pad off his neck and cleaned the cut again.

"Does it hurt?"

"Not really," he answered truthfully.

She winced. If it didn't hurt him, it certainly hurt her simply to look.

"Doctor will be with you in a minute," she said as she left.

Wendell sat on the examining table listening to someone trying to cough up his lungs in the next room. Outside the door a woman shouted, "Do something. You're a doctor, aren't you?"

One day they'd wheel the oxygen tent in for him, drawing the screen around the bed so as not to disturb the other paying customers, and ease him out of life with medicines. He was lost in self-pity when the doctor came in.

She was a svelte, intelligent-looking woman with a finely lined lived-in face that appeared to be accustomed to disappointments. A face that realized life wasn't turning out as expected and the point was to make the best of things.

"Smile," she said seriously.

"I thought I was."

"Try harder."

"How's that?"

"Not bad."

She studied closely a clipboard the nurse had left for her; then she turned her grave eyes back to Wendell with a no-nonsense smile.

"Now then, Mr. Clay, let's have a look."

She swung a lamp over and touched his neck with cool fingers, using a small stick with a cotton tip to probe the wound gently. She nodded and compressed her lips in sympathy.

"You don't seem to be the type to be involved in a barroom brawl, Mr. Clay."

"That was my first."

"A little old to be starting, aren't you?"

She had a soft, remarkably soothing voice.

"I guess so."

"You're very lucky to be alive."

"That close, huh?"

"Closer. How do you feel?"

"Not too bad."

"You feel OK?"

"No."

"Does your neck hurt?"

"It's not my neck," he said, gagging on the words.

Suddenly he felt a hot clamp tightening in his chest, and he had an overwhelming need to cry. It came upon him so quickly he didn't have time to resist. A harrowing gasp wrenched his throat and his whole body trembled.

"Let it out," she said, resting her hand on his shoulder.

He was crying for Grady, for himself, for the futility of everything.

"You've had a great shock." When she frowned deep wrinkles bracketed her mouth.

"It was all my fault," he sobbed.

"Was he a friend of yours? The man who died?"

"I hardly knew him. I only wanted to talk to him."

"And the man who killed him?"

"He got away."

"I see. I'm sorry for what happened."

She looked at him with sad eyes and then brought him some water in a paper cup.

"Here. Rinse your mouth."

She steadied his hand with hers while he drank.

"I cried today, too," she said. "I delivered a blue baby. Poor thing got turned in the womb and strangled on the umbilical cord. We all knew it was dead before the operation. When I saw the images I went into my office and cried; then I went in and performed the delivery. We have too many days like that."

There was an awkward pause in which their eyes avoided each other. Then Wendell looked at her and asked, "What's the verdict on my neck?"

"You have an extensive cut that, lucky for you, is superficial. Had it been any deeper, you'd be Chester Hager's problem, not mine. It's only a long scratch, really. But that's all you could afford at that particular spot. I'm going to stitch you up, and then you should be free to go home. Later it will probably hurt more than it does now, but I don't think it will give you any problems. You might have a lovely scar."

"I don't mind about that."

The nurse came back to assist. The doctor scrubbed up, pulled on a greenish-yellow operating gown, and proceeded to stitch his neck. She screwed up her face, as if she wanted all her features to migrate to the tip of her narrow freckled nose, and worked away with deliberate speed. Wendell stopped counting the stitches when she reached eleven. He had a strangely close-up view of her face as she worked, noticing an eyelash that had fallen out and caught on the ledge of her cheekbone, smelling the unguent odor of freshly washed skin, hearing her curse under her breath when she made a slight slip. It didn't take very long. When it was over she looked at Wendell more closely than before; he gazed back into her dark-circled sea-green eyes, watching the fine-veined eyelids flicker.

"How's the heart?" she asked.

"Still ticking."

"Good. You've had a tremendous shock, and you've lost some blood. The wound is cleaned and closed now; if you're careful you shouldn't have any further problems with it. Come back in a week or so, and I will take out the stitches. I'll write a prescription for some pain pills if it should start to hurt. But I want you to take it very easy. Go home, go to bed, and try not to think about what's happened. I'm sure you did your best."

She gave him her card, which said "Doctor Leah Wiltiham," and told him to call if he had any problems. When he thanked her she was still frowning. It was the kindest frown he had ever seen.

Conor was waiting for him when he walked out of the hospital.

"How is it?" he asked, scrutinizing his neck.

"Just a scratch," Wendell replied, trying to sound nonchalant.

"Hell of a lot of stitches for a scratch."

"Thanks for coming."

"Grady told me something before you got to the bar that maybe you're not gonna thank me for," Conor said. "He saw something."

"What?" Wendell asked in alarm.

"A man throwing a rifle in a pond."

"Where?"

"You tell me."

"Sycamore Springs Farm." He said the words before he even had time to think.

Conor nodded.

"Who?"

"He wasn't sure."

"Did he think the man saw him?"

"He wasn't sure of that either."

"Is that why he's been hiding?"

Conor nodded again. "I suppose so."

"I've got to go out there."

"Young man, you're not fit to go anywhere. Whatever's in that pond will stay there."

Wendell had to admit that Conor was right; he shouldn't do any more investigating that evening. The case would keep until the morning. Then he could talk to Brad face to face.

"Did Grady give you any kind of description?"

"He didn't have time. I talked to him briefly before he went to the john. You know what happened when he came out."

Wendell's mind raced with possibilities. He tried to picture the location of the ponds. If the killer had fired from behind the fence on the edge of Devil Dancer's paddock, why would he have entered the farm to dispose of the rifle?

"Don't torment yourself," Conor said, patting Wendell on the arm. "You look as woebegone as Jerusalem Slim before he took the fall. Don't worry about a thing. Go home and get some rest. You need it."

8

A policeman at the hospital took Wendell's statement about what happened at the Mecca Bar, then drove him to where his car was parked. As Wendell settled behind the steering wheel, he became aware of a sharp pain in his hip where he had crashed into the bar and of the excruciating ache in his chest from Ed's impact. Comparatively, his neck hardly hurt at all.

On the way home he stopped at the Winn-Dixie for groceries. He would probably be sore for a few days, so he decided to stock up. In a somnambulistic daze accompanied by Muzak to buy by, he maneuvered a screaky-wheeled pushcart through the aisles, being bumped by little old ladies in their spritely rush to get at the cottage cheese, Jell-O, and Geritol.

Wendell shifted from foot to foot, trying to find a stance to ease his hip, while he waited in line to pay. He didn't have many items: some frozen vegetables, a small sack of potatoes, two six-packs, a bottle of Advil, and a round slab of sirloin rubbed to a succulent redness with sodium sulfate. He gave the girl a ten; she poked the register in the nose and its mouth shot open, ringing bells. Wendell picked up his bag and hobbled out. Conor was right, maybe he should get some rest and try not to worry too much about the case.

As soon as he pulled in the driveway at Idle Hour, he started to think about Anna. He had made a conscious effort to keep her out of his mind during the day, but after the events of the past few hours, he wanted to see her. It was crazy, he knew, but he couldn't resist the impulse. Maybe he should give her a call. If she regretted what had been said and done last night as much as he did, perhaps she might give him another chance. From where he was parked, he saw the ghostly blue flicker of television sets in several windows. Anna's apartment was completely dark. He sat paralyzed, resolved to go home, yet seeking, at the same time, a position in the bucket seat that relieved the ache in his chest and hip. Once comfortable, he didn't want to move. He took a can of beer from the shopping bag and took a sip. It was just like a stakeout.

Sitting in his car listening to the silences interspersed with the whir of tires on the highway, Wendell felt as forlorn as a foghorn. A silken breeze caressed his face, reminding him of Florida: how the gusty gulf wind rattled the coconuts and tossed the sea gulls around in circles, while the pelicans sat unperturbed on their pilings, heads tucked down among the feathers of their breasts, and slept with one eye open. Maybe he would go back there, rent a mobile home between the pink flamingos and the shell shops, and play shuffleboard. Then he thought about Grady and the mute, humiliated look the dead have—as if they were so indignant about something that they refused to speak. Brooding on Grady, he contemplated his own mortality. Lying there on the floor of the Mecca Bar, had Grady known he was about to die?

No wonder he was feeling morbid! When he reviewed the submerged lives he had explored, waves of despair washed over him. He had learned a lot of things about a lot of people he never thought he wanted to know. Once, on a whim, Wendell had turned up the underside of his tongue and was perturbed by how strange it looked in the mirror: a primeval slug-like creature lurked in his mouth! He had a similar sensation when he considered his experience in Newport, a place where it was hard to tell where the upper world ended and the underworld began. He had been exposed to enough male-female crossfire recently to qualify for combat pay in the war between the sexes; only last night he himself had grabbed Anna by the throat. And a few hours ago he had come within a fraction of an inch of having his own throat slit. As if he were a condemned man granted a pardon, he experienced a moment of relief. But then he remembered Betty meekly waiting to inherit her plot of earth. He had seen how a gambling debt and a gun shot could fracture even Brad Davis's privileged world, and he thought of the sorrow in Lily's eyes and Charlene's shield of sophistication. Now he knew what Conor meant about being *still* alive and not finding what you were looking for.

What he trusted (or did he?) was his own eyes; as far as he could see, nothing turns out as expected. Nothing lasts, nothing stays the same, nothing is as it appears to be. As usual, he wasn't sure what he would do next. There didn't seem to be any valid way to choose. Maybe none of it had to happen, or nothing could have been prevented. Perhaps it all could have been different. Was life merely a random roll of the dice? He didn't know. Who was it that said he never found two realities the same? The only thing Wendell knew for certain was that tomorrow he would talk to Brad and stop at the morgue to make sure that Grady received a decent burial. He ought to tell the police about what Grady had seen, but something told him to wait. He wanted to take one more look for himself first. After all, it was his case.

Through the windshield he had been watching the moon, yellow-orange and twice as big as it had any right to be. The face had the familiar pocked cheeks, lopsided grin, tilted nose, dark cavernous eyes, and round inadequate brow. Heat lightning scribbled on the horizon, and the leaves began to shiver, but the sky was still clear. The rain was still north of the city. He stuck his head out the window and, lost in reverie, watched the vast star-swirl wheeling overhead.

A few minutes later a long white car pulled in front of him and stopped. The driver simply sat there for a while, with his head leaning back against the headrest. Wendell wondered what he was waiting for. Then Anna's face appeared beside him. When Wendell saw her, his heart jolted. When they passed under the streetlight, he got a dim glimpse of the man—it was Brad Davis. He walked with a slight limp, as though his shoes were too tight. Then, waving a brown bag in his hand, he started to sing some kind of ditty. Anna, leaning against him, guided him up the steps and in the door.

His hot heart pounding, Wendell sat in his car and tried to calm himself. A knife of grief cut to his guts as he thought of her body supple as water. His mouth tasted of salt and ashes. Still, he felt the pull of her strange attraction, compelling him like a solar singularity, drawing him toward her like a dark star. How he wanted her, knowing she was with him! He felt overwhelmed by envious rage. Had Davis played him for a sucker from the start? He retrieved his Beretta from the glove compartment, stepped out of the car in a trance, and walked behind Anna's building. In the alleyway a tomcat with tattered ears leaped and landed lightly on a trash can beside him, watching a long-haired tail-swishing white cat spooked in the wind-blown grass. The courtyard in back, enclosed by the dark silhouettes of the surrounding apartments, was suffused with a lambent moonlight glow. He could hear the wind whickering around the corners of the buildings. He stood and studied Anna's balcony.

Breathing in deep troubled droughts he stared at her windows. The curtains were open, but from that angle he couldn't see what was happening. He looked around and spotted a bicycle leaning against a nearby building. He propped it beside one of the square wooden pillars supporting Anna's balcony. Using the bike as a ladder, he climbed until he had one foot on the seat and the other on the handle bars. From there he could get high enough to grip the railing and pull himself up onto the balcony. He had a clear view through the sliding screen doors that led into the living room.

Davis was still singing as he squirted Anna in the face with what Wendell now realized was a bottle of champagne. Her shrieks of delight pierced him like a spear. With a thief's thudding heart he watched her take off her blouse and reach behind to unfasten her bra. Her fingers fumbled at the snap before it gave; she shrugged the black cups aside and her breasts swung free. Her bra fell to the floor, and she bent forward to pull off her pants and panties. Wendell felt a wing-beat of longing when he saw her. Then she turned to Davis and unbuttoned his shirt. Through the screen door he could hear their voices.

"God, I've missed you, baby," Davis purred. "You should never have left me!"

"Let's not go through all that," Anna said, stepping back from him.

"You made me feel like a man again," Davis persisted, "and then you told me it was over. Do you know what that did to me?"

"I told you not to count on anything."

"Yeah, but look what's happened!" Davis implored, reaching out to hold Anna by the shoulders. "Look what you made me do!"

"I didn't make you do anything. It's not *my* fault if you freak out when you're drunk and pull some crazy stunt."

"You're in my blood like a drug. I couldn't stand to be without you."

"I *don't* want to hear this." Anna waved an arm in a gesture of futility and turned away.

"You've got to listen to me. I was tense and restless that night, no matter how much I drank I couldn't sleep; so I grabbed my rifle—maybe I wanted to kill myself— and I went for a walk. Then I saw Devil Dancer in the moonlight. Do you know what he was doing? He was masturbating! He wouldn't perform in the breeding shed, but here he was mocking me, just for spite. He knew I was watching him. He was laughing at me. I could see it in his eyes."

Wendell could hear the anguish in Brad's voice.

"You're really something else, you crazy man! What did that horse have to do with me?"

"Don't you see, I thought I had lost you, and now I've lost everything."

"What's done is done. Who knows why things happen. Come here, you haven't lost everything."

Wendell felt a prickling in his scalp and a rush of nausea. The world began to blur as Brad moved behind Anna, and she got down on the floor, elevating her ass like a cat in heat. As if he were a deaf man watching dancers, Wendell saw Davis's dark face come forward over her back, the hair flopping over his forehead, and her mouth begin to move. Wendell considered the gun in his pocket. A vivid image of Brad Davis propping a rifle on a fence to shoot his own horse suffused his sight. Wendell felt a strange affinity with him. Hadn't he experienced similar agonies? Nevertheless, he had a burning urge to kill him. He hated to be played for a fool. What a sap he had been! Suddenly an intense pain shot up and down his left arm, sending a stinging sensation to his fingertips. He felt a searing heat in his chest, like a red hot branding iron, and an appalling ache under his rib cage, as if he were being crushed. He had an impulse to cry out for help, but immediately he pictured Anna and Davis coming to his aid, and his voice was trapped in his throat. Then a fiery pain fanged his heart, and he dropped to the balcony floor like a stone. -

9

Wendell woke up flat on his back in a strange room. He stared for a moment at the fluorescent lights in the ceiling before his mind would focus. His throat was raw. Small plastic tubes piped oxygen into his nostrils and the latest elixirs dripped from an IV baggie into his arm. A set of electrodes attached to wires studded his chest to monitor his heart rate. He glanced groggily over at the beeping screen and watched the jagged peaks and precipitous gorges of his cardiogram. His world had shrunk to one pound of busted pump.

He closed his eyes again and when he opened them Leah Wiltiham was gazing at him with mournful perplexity. Anticipating his thirst she fed him one at a time some slivers of cracked ice. She smiled a sustaining smile and placed a cool hand on his forehead.

"You have some fever," she remarked. "That's normal."

"Normal for what?"

"You've had a heart attack, don't you remember? Your friends brought you in last night."

Wendell had vague memories of faces floating above him asking, "Is he dead?" Then what happened? Was he carried to a car? He thought so, but he wasn't sure.

"How do you feel?"

"I could use a cigarette and a blindfold." Wendell was proud of himself—gallant deathbed quips were de rigueur in these circumstances.

"This is no time for metaphor," Leah said, with only a twinkle in her eye to indicate she enjoyed his wit. "What about your left arm, how does that feel?"

Her question revived the memory of the shooting pain in his arm that had preceded his attack. It was all coming back to him now—the shame of it, the humiliation, the blazing rage.

"My arm feels OK now, just a little tingling."

"You must try to relax. The worst is already over. You've had more than enough excitement for one day. You've got a wound to your heart that will take time to heal."

"How bad is it?"

"I'm not a specialist, Doctor Eisenstein will have to tell you that, but I'm sure you're going to be fine. I don't know why you disobeyed my advice last night, but whatever your reason or whatever you were trying to do, you've got to let it go now. It's no longer your concern. Focus all your energy on getting well. I know it's hard, life isn't always fair, but you must make the best of things and not take what happened to you too much to heart."

"Yes, thank you, I'll try," Wendell said.

Taking things too much to heart, he thought, maybe that had been his problem. Maybe life was better lived skating on surfaces and never letting anything get under your skin. Curious how often the word "heart" came up in discussions of how to live a life. You could take things too much to heart, but on the other hand if you didn't care you were heartless; you could have a heart of gold, or of stone; your heart could be light with joy or heavy with sorrow; you could receive heartening or heart-breaking news. You could have a change of heart. How many heartbeats did he have left, at what second would the clock stop ticking? The problem was that the human heart was like a cat, smooth-moving and silent, impervious to another's will power. It did no man's bidding, would not come when called, and kept its own counsel.

Wendell was determined to live, he *couldn't* die now, not yet, not before he knew the end of the story! After all, he was a detective and he still had a job to do.

A few hours later Dr. Eisenstein, a bearded man with thick glasses, came by and gave him a crash course in cardiovascular disease. Wendell hung on his every word.

"You've had a myocardial infarction," the doctor said, restating the obvious in medical terms that sounded vaguely obscene. "We don't believe the necrosis was massive."

"What does that mean?"

"We think the death of cell tissue was not severe. We're still assessing the muscle damage. You've lost some heart."

"How much?"

"The electrocardiogram was equivocal. We'll have a much better idea tomorrow when your enzyme count stabilizes."

"What will that tell you?"

"Let's give it a day or two, then I'll know for sure and we can talk. You should be stable in twenty-four hours or so."

When Wendell heard the words "stable" and "stabilize" he could only think of the brass nameplate on Devil Dancer's stall. The thought of Brad Davis shooting his own horse made his heart race with indignation. That bastard, he fumed, he's the one that deserves to die.

The doctor noticed the change in Wendell's expression and took alarm.

"Whatever is bothering you, drop it," the doctor said. "Nothing can do more damage at this time than bottled up anger. That only taxes the heart, and you can't afford it. The worst thing you can do right now is nurse a grievance. Just do what I tell you and you'll be fine."

"As good as new?"

"None of us is new any more, Mr. Clay. But I believe you have a future."

Wendell realized that he stood a better chance of recovery if he placed full trust in his doctors and stopped worrying. If only he could relax—stop brooding about the melodrama being staged in his chest, to say nothing of the Devil Dancer case—he'd come out of this OK.

Wendell dozed off, slipping into a twilight zone punctuated only by nurses with needles and pills. The words "hotpants" and "bad news" reoccurred in his fitful dreams. Around midnight he woke with a start because of an inept intern who jabbed and jabbed again.

"Stop that," the night nurse commanded, stepping forward and taking charge. She tapped Wendell's wrist until a good vein popped up and then slipped the needle snugly in. She was an Irish lass of the old school, who showed Wendell pictures of her grandchildren and surreptitiously prepared for him an eggnog laced with a wee bit of cognac that she swore by as a curative. She crossed herself for his benefit every time she visited his bedside, and muttered Galway sayings about the ever-changing medications of doctors and God's ever-lasting mercy.

She even wheeled him once around the corridors on the belief that it was good to be sociable. There were only men in Wendell's wing, cardiac cases all. Each bed positioned on the brink of each man's private abyss. Some of the patients summoned images of the concentration camps—pavement-gray, phantasmagoric faces that betrayed the skull beneath the skin. Other men, pink-fleshed and chipper, looked like aging boys shuffling around in their pajamas.

Night in the hospital belonged to the nurses. Wendell had a hunch that his guided tour of the coronary-care unit was not what the doctor would have ordered. Carrie Shannon's methods might not have been orthodox, yet Wendell had faith that her intentions were good. Back in his room, she hooked him up again to the cardiogram and there was his dogged heart still scribbling "Killroy was here" across the screen.

Leah Wiltiham came by in the early morning to wish him well.

"Thank you for saving my life, again," Wendell said.

"I did the best I could for you," Leah replied, "but it wasn't me that saved you the second time. It was your friend, Anna. She was the one who came to your rescue and administered artificial respiration. She also knew enough to push on your chest to resuscitate your heart."

"A jump start." Wendell laughed, picturing Anna walking toward him with jumper cables in her uplifted hands.

"It wasn't that funny, you had a very close call."

"I know, it's a private joke."

"She's very attractive, this Anna, but what were you doing... I have no right to ask."

"It's a long story," Wendell said softly. "I don't want to keep you."

"I see," Leah said, noting his reluctance. "Well, lucky for you she was there."

"Yeah, lucky for me. Thanks for coming by. Will I see you tomorrow?"

"Of course." Leah smiled and patted him gently on the shoulder.

Doctor Eisenstein arrived later, announcing that Wendell's heart attack was mild and his condition had been upgraded to satisfactory. "Your collateral circulation is good," he said.

Wendell remembered Julian railing about words like "collateral damage" in Vietnam—was his condition as good as the doctor suggested? "Does that mean I'm in the clear?"

"Not exactly. You might not have another, but..." The doctor picked up his stethoscope and placed the chilly disc on Wendell's breast. "Your left ventricle is missing an occasional beat. I hear murmuring. I think we're probably going to have to go in there and look around."

Open heart surgery! The doctor made it sound like a walk in the park.

"You mean you're going to cut?"

"I'll know for sure in a few more days."

"I thought you said my attack was mild?"

"This is standard procedure. I do them every day. I'll have you fixed up in no time."

Doctor Eisenstein, Wendell realized, was a cold fish who wasn't about to elaborate or show concern. This was no Aztec priest with a chipped-flint blade, he was a highly trained surgeon who could draw his scalpel across human skin as lightly as a caress. In that hushed hospital world violent acts were being performed all the time, and, if the perpetrator were skilled enough, usually the victim lived. Probably the man with ice in his veins made the most precise incisions. Wendell would simply have to hope that he was putting his heart in gifted hands.

Before he left the doctor told him that he could receive visitors. There were some people waiting to see him, but he must keep the visits brief and not let anything upset him.

Conor came in with a smile across his face designed to bring good cheer.

"Doc tells me you got a bum motor, boyo. That happens. Time to take the old jalopy in to the repair shop, get a lube, a valve job, replace a piston, no problem."

"Easy for you to say."

"Don't be too sure, young man, look at this." Conor unbuttoned his shirt and showed Wendell a beaut of a scar running across his chest. "See, I've already got what you're gonna get, only more so. I had a fucked-up pump. Triple bypass, that's me. They took some clean pipe out of my leg there and replaced the gummed-up stuff.

Some plumbing! The clutch still works, that's what counts. That was five years ago. Don't fight it, fella, you're gonna come out of this better than you was before."

Wendell did feel cheered by Conor's presence; if that geezer could pull through so could he. Maybe he'd live on to be an old timer too.

"If you need any cash," Conor offered, "I could help you out a little."

Wendell eyed him with suspicion. "You sure you have some to spare?"

"Thanks to you, young man." Conor grinned and flashed a thick roll of bills. "There's nothing like a crowd at the scene of a crime."

"I thought you'd given that up."

"Once a dip, always a dip," Conor admitted. "As long as marks wear pants, I'll pinch their pokes. They may think they've got it nailed down, but it's mine."

"Thanks for the offer," Wendell said with a smile. "Luckily, my premiums are paid."

After a few minutes they were interrupted by a shapely starched swan of a nurse.

"There's a woman named Anna Crane to see you," she announced. "Do you want her?"

Wendell said that he did.

"Did you get a load of that babe?" Conor asked with a lascivious leer. "You know why God made women with nice tits and ass, don't you? So they can tickle a man's pecker both coming and going." Conor cackled at his own joke, tapped Wendell lightly on the chest before he left, and told him to take it easy.

Anna stood in the doorway. Brad Davis was with her.

Be still, my heart, Wendell thought. How did that song go: "I am a rock, I am an island," that's what he would be—hard, remote, unfeeling. He had scores to settle, but he must control his emotions.

Revenge was a dish best served cold. But when Anna walked into the room Wendell began to lose his resolve. She still had the power to move him.

There was an uncomfortable silence and an exchange of anxious glances.

"I understand you saved my life," Wendell said.

"I heard you fall," Anna said. "When I saw you on the balcony, I knew what to do. Brad carried you to the car and we got you to the hospital on time."

His face working, Davis stared at Wendell and could not speak.

"I saw, I heard," Wendell said, answering the unasked question.

"All this was my fault, I suppose," Anna said. "I should have told you from the start about me and Brad."

"You should have told me from the start about Devil Dancer." Wendell could feel his control over his anger slipping. "You knew all along."

"No, I didn't. Brad told me last night."

"I didn't want you to get involved in this," Davis said. "But when you showed up at the farm, I figured why not."

"You figured I wouldn't solve the case, didn't you? You used me as your patsy."

"Wendell, I wasn't in my right mind." Brad spoke in the same pleading voice Wendell had overheard from the balcony. "When Anna left me I went on a toot that you wouldn't believe. Shooting Devil Dancer was a lousy thing to do, I loved that horse, but I swear to you I couldn't help myself. I lost all control. It was like someone else pulled that trigger. I was sorry the second I did it, but it was too late."

"If you loved Devil Dancer so much, why were you over-breeding him?" Wendell insisted. "One way or another, you were determined to destroy him."

Davis flinched; he was at a loss for words when confronted with the depth of his own ambivalence toward Devil Dancer. "I can't defend myself," he finally mumbled, "my life has been going to hell for a long time now." Davis paused, regretting his show of vulnerability; before he spoke again he tried to muster his old authority. "Look, Wendell, don't forget you're working for me. What you know is strictly between us, right? When Anna and I found you, we also found your gun, and we didn't say a word."

"You've lied to me from the start," Wendell spoke slowly and deliberately. "Any business arrangement we have is off. Keep the gun. If you want your money back, you can have that too. You're going to need all the money you can get together to pay off your gambling debts. If you don't, believe me, your life will be in danger. I'll make my own decision about what to do with what I know. You must have found out for yourself about Charlene's life, and you calculated if I couldn't solve that case I couldn't solve this one either. You figured me for a fool. That's how you repaid our friendship. You put me on a case that was no case, and all I got out of it was a bunch of sad stories, including my own."

"Well, what are you going to do then?" Davis demanded with a baffled look.

"You'll do what you feel is the right thing, Wendell," Anna said in a voice between ironic and sincere. "You've got a good heart."

"That's not what my doctor says," Wendell said. "Now leave me alone and let me be."

After they left Wendell spent a long time pondering the situation. They had played him for an easy mark and made him taste the dregs. That was hard to forgive. Brad had shot a great horse that deserved to spend the rest of his days covering mares and munching on bluegrass. An unspeakable act. Beneath contempt. After his three-day ordeal Wendell's own heart had become a landmine buried in his chest. From now on, because of this case and his own shortcomings, his days were numbered. How many of them would depend on a man with a scalpel. At that moment he wished with all his heart that he would enjoy a long life. Who was it that said, "Longevity has its place"? Was it Martin, Bobby, or John? They were all bushwhacked, too, just like Devil Dancer. Everything, it seemed, came down to dust and disappointment.

Anna was a fantasy he would have to relinquish. Like so many men, he'd been thinking with his dick. Looking at him in his hospital bed she had tried to show her concern, but her eyes would never shine with Leah Wiltiham's beam of compassion. Brad Davis now struck Wendell as pathetic, feckless. There would be other horses, other women, he had too much to ever lose it all. Once he realized the true seriousness of his situation, he would make a few calls, move some money, and the mob would be off his back. Wendell and Brad may have been friends, but that was over now. They still shared more affinities than it was comfortable to acknowledge. Hadn't his own turbulent emotions mirrored Brad's? After Laura left, hadn't he felt murderous urges? And what about his out-of-control antics when it came to Anna? Wendell thought ruefully about Charlene and all she seemed to promise, yet what was her life behind all its glitter? He thought about how Lily had already seen the hollowness of her parents' lives. What would she have thought had she seen *him* on Anna's balcony! There was more than enough pathos to go around, more than enough heartbreaks and humiliation. This wasn't about justice—Wendell felt his own complicity—he was in no position to pass final judgment. Nor was it about forgiveness; too much had been done that was unforgivable. Nothing Wendell could do now would change the way the world was or spare his own human heart. He would get no satisfaction from revenge. Somehow he had to put the case behind him, for his own good. The important thing was to protect himself. Let the rifle rust in the pond. Let Devil Dancer's bones molder in the earth. That was some horse.

Afterword: to the Happy Few

Hope, ye unhappy ones; ye happy ones, fear.
—Robert Burton, *Anatomy of Melancholy*

I began *Devil Dancer* in the summer of 1980 in Maro, a small, cliff-side pueblo whose whitewashed houses were surrounded on three sides by green fields instead of the high-rise eyesores that dominated the Costa del Sol. At the tip of the town stood the Casa Grande, upon whose patio Raquel Welch once parachuted in *Fathom,* a shallow movie memorable for her contours and some shots of the spectacular coast. Maro's unspoiled state was due to a feudal anomaly: the aristocratic family that owned the place had banned any development. My upstairs apartment on Calle Maravillas (Street of Marvels) overlooked the Mediterranean. Every day the water was a different blue.

In the mornings I awoke to a perturbed rooster and the bleating of goats being led out to graze, their low-slung udders tolling from side to side and each with a long rope trailing from one foreleg. A relentless sun beat down and everyone who could remained inside, but invariably I would see one woman, and only one, whitewashing her house. Apparently the single bucket and brush in town had to be kept in constant use. In the fields a bare-chested man shoveled manure from large mat baskets drooping from his weary horse, while a few women in black swept the streets with straw brooms. For lunch my favorite bar was El Guapo, whose handsome owner asked if I had noticed that all the residents had similar faces. "Todo el mundo son parientes," he explained, we're all related. Since I always ordered red wine, his apt name for me was Señor Tinto.

At the time I saw *Devil Dancer* as part one of a trilogy entitled *Forbidden Voices.* The other volumes, *Lily's Song* and *Tom's Lament,* would be based on Lexington's most notorious unsolved murder, the Betty Gail Brown case, involving a Transylvania coed found strangled with her bra in her car parked in front of Old Morrison, the centerpiece of the campus and tomb of Rafinesque, a professor who had left his curse upon the college. But that's another story. The immediate challenge was to create a novel about a middle-aged detective who, while investigating the shooting of a thoroughbred, wandered into a labyrinth. My recipe for the novel: pour heartache through a typewriter repeatedly until it comes out poetry. Or, as one old pro put it: Writing is easy, you simply stare at the blank page until blood drops form on your forehead. Above all, I wanted my words to evoke a world that I remembered—Lexington, circa 1972—which, protected by no edict against development, was rapidly disappearing. I would type a page, proof it, then walk the room, a rolled *Newsweek* in hand, swatting flies and an occasional wasp.

In the afternoon I might put on my swimming trunks and walk down to the beach. The narrow path began at the ruins of a 16th century sugar works and descended along ledges lined with cactus-like plants. Quick green lizards scooted past my feet, rattling the dry leaves and setting my heart aflutter. The beach, edged with bamboo shoots, might as well have been in Tahiti. I saw two topless German girls jumping waves and a masked man rise from the surf with an octopus on a spear, but mostly I had the sand to myself. It was so secluded a movie crew had shot a scene there, leaving a tangled snake's nest of film behind. One day, a copy of *The Portable Joyce* in my pocket, I followed goat trails to a Moorish watchtower on a nearby cliff. The slippery slope of sharp, loose stones and nasty shrubs cut hieroglyphics in my arms and legs. The view was magnificent. I dreamed of constructing a house there, with my own Martello tower as writer's studio. Another time I hiked up the mountainside behind town to visit a cave, discovered by five boys in 1959, where Neolithic people had left ochre hand prints on the walls.

In the evenings I took a bus to Nerja for dinner then watched the tourists stroll up and down the famed Balcony of Europe that extended over the water. Some nights the four kilometer uphill hike back to Maro was utterly beautiful. A half-moon, brushed by dark-grey clouds, cast just enough light to reflect off the water in the Águila Adqueduct and design the sea in intricate patterns of pale moon shine and purple shade. A light breeze rustled the sugarcane stalks by the road, my feet kicked up chalky puffs of dust, and my only guide in the dark was the bright new streetlights of my summer home.

After sundown, Maro came alive. Following a meal at about ten, the women placed chairs outside their doorways and in loud, throaty voices kept up a constant commentary across the streets to each other. The men whittled sticks or gathered in bars and debated crops and politics. On hot nights the children played in the street past midnight, while young girls linked arms to sashay by the boys and laugh at their remarks. The nightly clamor was so intense I surmised that the windows of the houses lacked panes because the shrieks of the children would have shattered the glass. One little girl with a horn proudly walked the streets tooting it intermittently to the delight of all—with the single exception of an American who wanted to sleep.

I had assumed that I was the only foreigner in Maro, but one afternoon shortly before I had to depart, I was summoned to a house on another street where a drunken Dansker had passed out naked on his patio. The pitiless sun had seared his skin the color of broiled lobster and his ravaged bedroom made mine look clean in comparison. Since he spoke no English, my services were not needed. I left when the doctor arrived and never learned what happened to him. The diagnosis could not have been good. His plight, Señor Tinto decided, was a cautionary tale worth heeding.

My first teaching job had been at Kenyon, a college noted for producing writers. I lived on the second floor of the old John Crowe Ransom house, where Randall Jarrell and Robert Lowell once had bedrooms. At Ransom's eightieth birthday party I met a dozen famous authors, not to mention those who stopped by *The Kenyon Review* office. Encouraged by visiting poets Toby Olson and Paul Blackburn, I dropped the idea of being a literary critic and began writing and publishing poems. This, I learned to my grief, was an unlikely way to get tenure. After two years at Kenyon, and five each at Transylvania and Vassar, I was fortunate enough to receive a Fulbright to teach American literature at the University of Seville.

I had come alone to Spain in despair over my failed relationships and diminishing prospects. The shelf life of a vagabond professor with shoulder-length hair who had published only poems and book reviews was limited. After my summer in Maro, I returned to the heart of the old city, Barrio de Santa Cruz, on a dead end alley named Consuelo (consolation), where I had rented a room from a taxi driver named Santos and his California wife Barbara. The theater had died in Seville, my friend Rafael told me, because the drama was in the streets. April was a continual Fiesta: processions of candle-lit floats featuring Jesus and Mary during Semana Santa, followed by Feria, a week-long party of riding in horse-drawn carriages and dancing *sevillanas*, capped by Rocío, a holiday blending religious ceremonies with festive celebrations. As enthralling as these spectacles were, I found the happenings outside my door more fascinating. In truth, the rain in Spain does not fall mainly on the plain but in the mountains, while the country's pain, seen daily in the streets, made a mockery of my own troubles. I was an American, and the first time a gypsy woman held out her hand to me I shook it. Watch your wallet, I learned, never look a beggar in the eye. I recall seeing a small boy, in an effort to generate more coins, show his sister how to expose one bare foot from beneath a shawl full of holes and then slap her to make her cry. In the evenings when I went tappa-hopping along Sierpes, the serpentine street through the old city, the crippled woman who sold lottery tickets on the baby Jesus would cry out "Niño! Niño!" while the silent blind man beside her tapped his stick and an old soldier propped his crutches against the wall to take a piss. Once I saw a man dressed in white playing a fiddle, a bagpipe under his arm, a drum on his back, who waggled his foot in a way that made a puppet dance beside him and play a fiddle too. When I tossed pesetas in the fiddle case, the puppet smiled.

The university occupied an eighteenth-century tobacco factory, where once upon a time a Navarrese soldier met a tempestuous gypsy named Carmen with a penchant for matadors. The fortress-like structure took up an entire block and was protected by a brick wall, moat, drawbridge, and sentry boxes. On my way to class one day I had no choice but to join a protest march that packed the street. We were brought to an abrupt halt in front of the university by a formation of Spanish troops, who fired teargas. A strong wind carried several high-arching canisters onto the grounds of the five-star Alfonso XIII hotel. I clung to the wall to avoid the retreating protestors, whose cause I never learned. My colleagues yelled from a window to get inside, which I did when I could. It was the Sixties all over again. My job was to expose English majors to my Ohio accent while leading discussions of American authors. The light teaching load enabled me to sustain the concentration essential to compose a novel. As a result, on December 14, 1980, I finished a 286-page draft of *Devil Dancer.* I knew I still faced revision after revision. Little did I realize what a long, arduous a process that would be.

On February 23, 1981, I went to teach my evening class and found the huge university building completely dark and all the doors locked. Baffled, I stopped at my local bar, where the owner shrugged and said, "Adiós, democracia." Patriotic music blared from every radio. Barbara and Santos turned on the television for the nine o'clock news. Instead a Bob Hope pirate movie came on, which, under the circumstances, was deeply disconcerting. What was happening? Later we learned that there had been a coup. A small band of soldiers led by a Colonel Tejero had taken over las Cortes and held the legislators hostage. When King Juan Carlos I adamantly opposed the coup, however, key generals had second thoughts and did not deploy their troops in the major cities. By morning the democracy that had replaced Franco's dictatorship at his death was safe. The next day I returned to my bar and was offered a *Tejerito*, a newly concocted drink from a bottle with a cork carved like the face of the disgraced colonel. Unbeknownst to the conspirators, las Cortes had cameras. We watched replays for a week. Everyone agreed that Colonel Tejero and his duped crew had behaved very badly and that if you were going to conduct a coup this was not the proper way to do it.

During two years in Spain my personal life took a turn for the better—much more than I could have imagined. "As the need is sorest," Lotte Lenya sang in *The Threepenny Opera*, "so the answer comes soonest." In December of 1979, I met Roser (pronounced rosé like the wine) at a conference in Santiago de Compostela, the end of the road for many a pilgrim. She taught English literature at the University of Barcelona. We began corresponding and I went to see her several times. "You are big boys, really, you American men," she once said, but then one day added, "I love you just a lot." Before my summer in Maro, we had spent two weeks at Saffron Walden, a picturesque English village where a few stone cottages had steeply pitched roofs of thatch, the village green sported a maze, and we walked arm in arm through the streets of the town in love with architecture. One evening a drunk grabbed my jacket, fixed me with a bleary eye, and talked about how Harry Truman in the Great War was a man tough enough to do whatever was necessary. "But now you've got a softie, 'aven't you?" he asserted smugly, referring to President Carter and the hostage crisis in Iran. I pushed him aside but not before he stroked, in parting, Roser's bare arm. London had changed since last I saw it. Men in bowler hats with umbrellas under their arms had been superseded by young punks in black boots, tie-dyed jeans, and Mohawks of purple hair, who leaned out the windows of the speeding train and spat at each other. Thankfully that ugly episode was followed by a high tea of scones with clotted cream at Stratford on Avon.

The summer after Maro, I stayed with Roser and her parents at Vilanova i la Geltrú, a coastal town thirty miles south of Barcelona. We were married that July, honeymooned in Granada, and began our new life in Frederick, Maryland. About this time *The New Yorker* came out with a cartoon of a happy couple in bed clicking flutes of champagne and the caption read: "To Senator Fulbright!" I had found a job at Mount Saint Mary's University, where I would teach American literature and retire as a professor emeritus. Roser still teaches Spanish at Hood College in Frederick and publishes novels in her native Catalan. I continued to revise my manuscript and sought the advice of authors I respected at Bread Loaf, a mountain-top retreat for people in love with words. "Every time this guy opens his mouth," Stanley Elkin said of my old pickpocket Conor, "he signs his name." John Gardner generously offered to read *Devil Dancer* but died in a motorcycle crash shortly after the conference.

In the fall of 1985, Ruth Cantor agreed to represent *Devil Dancer*. In my naiveté I assumed that if a novel had an agent publication was assured, a movie version to follow. I should have looked more closely at her savvy words, which I quote in her memory: "Lots of interior action, lots of brutal insights into the human condition.... It's awfully good despite a very poor market outlook and I'd be willing to try it. There may be some market somewhere still for high literary quality, but after thirty plus years in the business, I'm inclined to be wholly cynical about that." To her credit, she found several editors who praised the book's sense of place, gritty realism, poetic language, unorthodox play on the genre: "It's the story of a goodhearted but slightly ineffectual detective," one said, "who learns more about himself as the book goes on than the case he's trying to solve." I was a talented writer, editors agreed, but they all rejected *Devil Dancer*: "Despite the resonance of the prose, I think _____ would still have a tough time publishing this as successfully as either you or we might wish."

Having a first novel rejected is a common fate. Like many a writer I buried my manuscript in a drawer. A pile of rejection slips did not enhance my dossier, however, while publishing essays on classic American authors did, and I was awarded tenure. Afterwards, I spent ten years working on a novel about the civil rights movement in Mississippi, *The Children Bob Moses Led* (Milkweed Editions 1995). Then something strange happened: three non-fiction books appeared that revived my interest in *Devil Dancer* and made my novel seem prophetic. Sally Denton's true crime account of drug-running in the 1980s by the scion of a prominent thoroughbred family, *The Bluegrass Conspiracy*, featured a few of the people I had drawn on for my characters. One, for example, lived with a cocaine dealer, turned FBI informant, and disappeared into the witness protection program. Lush horse farms and seedy dives described in my novel reappeared as settings for Denton's exposé of Kentucky corruption. *Wild Ride*, by Ann Auerbach, explained how the suspicious death of Alydar in 1990 brought down the famed Calumet Farm. Finally, Ken Englade's *Hot Blood* detailed a plot by a few financially strapped owners to hire an assassin called the Sandman to make the murder of their race horses look accidental so that they could collect the insurance. These books goaded me to re-work *Devil Dancer*, adding chapters on the money involved in stud fees (my novel takes place shortly before Secretariat sent prices through the roof) and a possible extortion racket. To gather more information, I made excursions to Lexington and Newport, Kentucky, and returned to my birthplace, Youngstown, Ohio, a mobbed-up city when I was a boy notorious for its gangland bombings, to research the Mafia.

Long story short: Simon Lipskar at The Writer's House submitted the improved version of *Devil Dancer*. Literary editors said it was a crime novel, crime fiction editors said it was too literary. Their consensus: he certainly can write, thanks but no thanks, manuscript is being returned under separate cover. One revived my dreams of a film: "Thoroughly researched, very textured, very authentic.... Novel has great cinematic potential, just calls out to be turned into a screen play."

For the next decade I focused all my energies on writing a novel grounded in the authentic history of the Ohio Valley frontier, 1770-1812: *Blacksnake's Path: The True Adventures of William Wells* (Heritage Books, 2008). Since I had already done the research, my agent Michele Rubin said that I ought to write the biography. I was reluctant to repeat myself, but I took her advice and completed *William Wells and the Struggle for the Old Northwest*. Michele also suggested that I revise *Devil Dancer*, bringing the murdered race horse alive so we care about his death, enhancing Wendell's motivation to solve the crime, and showing how his genuine sympathy encouraged people to confide in him. In addition I made countless changes to tighten the prose and sharpen the focus. As the surgeon said: when in doubt, cut it out. Call me Mack the Knife. I have always seen *Devil Dancer* as a noir novel in the Raymond Chandler tradition. I'm no fan of crime fiction in general, but I admire such works as George V. Higgins' *The Friends of Eddie Coyle*, for its expertise on how criminals talk and operate, and John Berendt's *Midnight in the Garden of Good and Evil*, in which Savannah is the true subject of the book and "who done it" of secondary importance. While Michele was submitting *Devil Dancer,* Jaimy Gordon's *Lord of Misrule,* a novel that evokes the same sleazy side of the horse racing world as mine, won the National Book Award.

I have put much of what I learned during the five years I lived in Lexington into *Devil Dancer.* The book is comprised of stories within the story and is distinguished, I think, by a series of distinctive voices that evoke personal worlds: Conor's pickpockets, Brad Davis's big-time horse racing, Julian's Vietnam veterans, Betty's poor Kentucky coal miners, Grady's small-time crooks and homeless men, Caprice's Newport and the Mafia, are all authentic. I even once knew an old alcoholic whose throat was slit, not fatally, in the Mecca Bar. While he was telling me the tale he peed his pants.

Devil Dancer owes a direct debt to three Kentucky authors: Ed McClanahan's inspired essay in *Famous People I Have Known* brought me to Boots Bar to see Little Enis perform. David Maurer's *The Whiz Mob* provided the argot of pickpockets and Hank Messick's *Razzle-Dazzle* related how Newport was once Kentucky's Las Vegas. Finally, my debt to Roser, as I trust this memoir has made clear, is beyond words.

Over the decades, as I persistently revised *Devil Dancer,* I drew strength from the example of Thoreau, who, after *Walden* was initially rejected, worked on the manuscript for years, until each sentence sang. My novel was now a far better book than the draft I completed in Spain, but in the meantime conglomerates had bought up the New York publishing houses and the bottom line trumped all poetic ones. Serious mid-list authors were shunted aside as the plot-driven blockbuster express sped by carrying nothing that mattered to no place of importance. As for me, I preferred the local stops. In a final ironic twist, after *Devil Dancer* was at last accepted, the publisher suddenly decided that it contained "too much bitterness" and asked me to brighten up its dark vision of life. I refused and returned the contract unsigned. Fortunately ("as the need is sorest...""), Hope Maxwell-Snyder and Somondoco Press came to the rescue. For this relief, much thanks. Since its inception I have believed steadfastly that *Devil Dancer* deserved to be in print. If you have stuck around for this account of the book's prolonged genesis, then I hope that you liked it as well. Welcome, as Stendhal hailed his dedicated band of readers, to the happy few.

A graduate of Hiram College, with a Ph.D. in American Studies from Case Western Reserve University, William Heath has taught at Kenyon, Transylvania, Vassar, and the University of Seville, where he was a Fulbright. In 2006 he retired as professor emeritus of English at Mount Saint Mary's University and now teaches in the Hood College honors and humanities programs. He has published a book of poems, *The Walking Man*, an award-winning novel about the civil rights movement in Mississippi, *The Children Bob Moses Led*, a work of historical fiction, *Blacksnake's Path: The True Adventures of William Wells*, and a dozen critical essays on Hawthorne, Melville, Twain, William Styron, and Thomas Berger, among others. His most recent work of scholarship is a biography: *William Wells and the Struggle for the Old Northwest*. He and his wife Roser Caminals, a highly regarded Catalan novelist from Barcelona and a professor of Spanish literature at Hood, have lived in Frederick, Maryland, since 1981.

To contact the author: heath@msmary.edu.

SOMONDOCO PRESS

ROB CARNEY
Weather Report
Story Problems

FLOYD COLLINS
What Harvest

WILLIAM HATHAWAY
The Right No

AMY HOLMAN
Wrens Fly Through Broken Windows

HOPE MAXWELL SNYDER
Houdini Chronicles

PETER STITT
Hard Roads Home

ED ZAHNIZER
Mall Hopping with the Great I Am

P.O. Box 3602 | Shepherdstown, WV 25443